Investing for Good

OTHER BOOKS BY THE AUTHORS:

Peter D. Kinder, Steven D. Lydenberg, and Amy L. Domini
The Social Investment Almanac

Peter D. Kinder (and Lawrence S. Clark)
Law and Business

Steven D. Lydenberg (and Alice Tepper Marlin, Sean O'Brien Strub,
and the Council on Economic Priorities)
Rating America's Corporate Conscience

Amy L. Domini (with Dennis L. Pearne and Sharon Rich)
The Challenges of Wealth

Amy L. Domini and Peter Kinder
Ethical Investing

Investing for Good

Making Money
While Being Socially Responsible

Peter D. Kinder, Steven D. Lydenberg,
and Amy L. Domini

HarperBusiness
A Division of HarperCollinsPublishers

Since this page cannot legibly accommodate all permission copy, pages 317–318 constitute an extension of this copyright page.

This publication is designed to provide accurate and authoritative information in regard to the subject matter covered. It is sold with the understanding that the publisher is not engaged in rendering legal, accounting, or other professional service. If legal advice or other expert assistance is required, the services of a competent professional person should be sought. *From a Declaration of Principles jointly adopted by a Committee of the American Bar Association and a Committee of Publishers.*

Portions of this book first appeared in a different form in *Business Ethics, Banker & Tradesman, NGO Finance,* and *Pension World.*

FIRST EDITION

Designed by Alma Hochhauser Orenstein

Library of Congress Cataloging-in-Publication Data
Kinder, Peter D.
 Investing for good: making money while being socially responsible/by Peter D. Kinder, Steven D. Lydenberg, Amy L. Domini.—1st ed.
  p. cm.
 Includes bibliographical references and indexes.
 ISBN 0-88730-565-2 (cloth)
 1. Investments—United States. 2. Stocks—United States. 3. Social responsibility of business—United States. I. Lydenberg, Steven D. II. Domini, Amy L. III. Title.
HG4910.K53 1993
332.6'0973—dc20   91-58507

93 94 95 96 97 CC/RRD 10 9 8 7 6 5 4 3 2 1

Contents

Tables

Boxes

Acknowledgments

IT IS IMPOSSIBLE TO IMAGINE writing a book on socially responsible investing without the assistance and advice of the Interfaith Center on Corporate Responsibility (ICCR) and its executive director, Tim Smith. We owe special thanks to Diane Bratcher, ICCR's able communications director, for her rapid and always thoughtful responses to our queries.

Our good friend at the Social Investment Forum, acting executive director Joan Kanavich, supplied us with charts and information we would have spent hours developing ourselves. The Forum's quarterly meetings provided the opportunities to explore the ideas described here with the people who were putting them into practice.

Investing for Good is the second book on which we have worked with Dick Luecke. His abilities as an editor, writer, and critic are well known. His unfailing cheerfulness in the face of unreasonable—if not irrational—demands should be.

With world securities markets moving ever closer together, it is comforting to know that social-investment professionals are organized and spreading the word in Canada and the United Kingdom. But socially responsible investment has different emphases and screens in those countries. We have had the benefit of two excellent guides: Mark de Sousa-Shields, executive director of the Social Investment Organization in Toronto, and Alan Miller, president of the U.K. Social Investment Forum and principal of Financial Platforms in Croydon. Alan has an uncanny knack for putting his hands on just what we need and faxing it immediately.

Jon Dreben of Cambridge, Massachusetts, volunteered to critique the entire manuscript. We could not have asked for a more sensitive, thorough review.

Donald Korn of DHK Associates in Los Altos, California, took a hard look at drafts of two chapters. Both benefited from his encyclopedic knowledge of investment and accountability issues. Veronica Froelich worked for us while she completed Harvard Divinity School. Her exhaustive research on the religious origins of social investing in the United States was of immense value. Alan Harman of Scotia McLeod in Toronto provided useful data on Canadian mutual funds. Our friends—and clients—at the Vermont National Bank Socially Responsible Banking Fund, David Berge and Nevada Bromley, helped us with data on their program and offered sound editorial criticisms.

Mindy Lubber, president of Green Century Funds, offered her observations on environmental investing. Laurie McClain of Progressive Securities in Eugene described her experiences with us. David Nitkin, founder and president of EthicScan Canada, read parts of an early draft and offered the same kinds of thought-provoking criticisms that make his *Corporate Ethics Monitor* a must-read. John Horton of Horton Ahern & Bousquet in Providence, Rhode Island, shared with us his experiences in transmitting financial information to lay audiences. Danna Osterweil of the American Association of Fund-Raising Counsel, Inc., in New York, supplied us with fascinating statistics on giving.

The trustees and staff of the Loring, Wolcott, Coolidge Office in Boston once again rendered help well beyond what we could have asked for. And we owe special thanks for the able assistance and encouragement of all the people at Kinder, Lydenberg, Domini & Company, Inc.: Libby Edgerley, Beverly Gendon, Holly Grano, Jill Grano, Tony Rousmanierre, and Jerri Udelson. In particular, Lloyd Kurtz made many valuable contributions to this book.

Last but definitely not least, Wendy Wolf and the staff at HarperCollins made many helpful suggestions and criticisms.

All of these people and others we have unforgivably forgotten to mention deserve credit for this book's strengths. The authors alone bear responsibility for its failings.

Introduction

Think globally, act locally.

—Environmental slogan (ca. 1985)

All politics is local.

—Thomas P. (Tip) O'Neill, Jr. (attrib.)

FOR ALL ITS NATURAL BEAUTY AND QUAINTNESS, Vermont is a hard place to live. The Yankee virtues of frugality and making-do grew out of necessity. Even a successful bank, like Vermont National, will recycle an old auto dealership into its operations center. For those not safely in the middle class, affordable housing and blue-collar jobs are in short supply. And as everywhere, very small loans for very small businesses—micro-enterprise loans—are hard to find.

In the mid-1980s, a group of Brattleboro residents decided to start a bank to meet the capital needs of Vermont's less-than-wealthy. They planned to solicit deposits from socially concerned individuals and to make loans that advanced the agendas of these depositors, but they became daunted by the regulatory and capital requirements. So instead of starting their own venture, they approached Rick Hashagen, president of Vermont National Bank. Vermont National is a relatively small bank with thirty-one offices statewide and total assets of $894 million.[1] They presented Hashagen with the idea of a bank fund that would accomplish the same goals.

Hashagen found the idea exciting. Vermont National had some experience with social investors through its trust department. He recognized that the bank's customers were increasingly concerned about where their money went. More importantly, such a fund would meet a critical need across the state. As Hashagen and his staff—working with a community advisory board—went to work to implement the concept, they decided the fund would make depositors three simple promises:

- Deposits would only support loans for affordable housing, environmental and conservation projects, agriculture, education, and small-business development.
- Deposits, which could go into any type of account Vermont National offered, would receive the same interest rate and federal insurance as all other deposits.
- Deposits would be kept separate from other bank deposits and, until the money was loaned out, it would be managed using social screens consistent with the depositors' expectations.

On January 1, 1989, the Vermont National Bank's Socially Responsible Banking Fund (SRB Fund) began taking deposits. Three and a half years later, 4,140 depositors from forty-three states had put in $57 million, and the SRB Fund had 801 current loans totaling over $38 million.[2]

The loans are the real story here, for they show how you can make a real difference by choosing where to put your money. They also show how a bank can use creativity and flexibility to make large and small loans to advance important community projects. In recent years the Lake Champlain Housing Development Corporation received a $925,000 loan to construct twenty-eight units of affordable, cooperative housing. Two organic vegetable farms received small loans for greenhouses. A storyteller received a $2,500 loan so that she could produce tapes of her stories to sell at her appearances.

The SRB Fund has also committed a loan to Vermont Energy Recovery, a firm that burns methane from a landfill to produce electricity. (Methane is an ozone-depleting gas, so the project has the added advantage of preventing the gas's release into the atmosphere.) Small community land trusts—nonprofits that provide affordable housing, limited-equity housing cooperatives, and farmland conservation trusts—have also benefited from SRB Fund loans. The SRB Fund has also extended a line of credit to Working Capital, in Manchester, New Hampshire, a unique loan fund for very small borrowers. Working Capital's Vermont borrowers have used their loans for a secondhand clothing store, a taxi service, and an animal-training business, among other ventures.

These types of loans require considerable servicing. And it takes time and effort to train lending officers to make them. Why was Vermont National Bank keen to set up such an unusual operation?

David Berge, the SRB Fund's director, sees the fund as a part of the bank's effort to cultivate customers. He believes the SRB Fund strengthens three types of relationships. First, it gives depositors a more direct connection to their money and its use. The depositors have chosen to put their money to work in a targeted way.

Second, the SRB Fund builds a link between depositors and important community projects. Their deposits do not disappear into anonymous pools of money. Rather, they can learn about the projects their deposits support in Vermont newspapers, from their neighbors, and in the SRB Fund's quarterly updates, which describe some of the borrowers. These depositors can take pride in what their money is doing.

Third, the SRB Fund strengthens the relationship between bank employees (from tellers to commercial-loan officers to the bank's president himself) and the people involved in community activities and businesses that need support.[3] Jack Davidson, the head of Vermont National's trust department, is a volunteer for the Brattleboro Area Habitat for Humanity. When Habitat finished building a duplex for two local families, Jack knew that the SRB Fund would support Habitat with a $30,000 loan. Tim Kononay, a branch manager in Fairhaven, volunteers as a board member for Rutland West Neighborhood Housing Services, an affordable-housing provider and an SRB Fund borrower.

So the SRB Fund represents the bank's commitment to its communities—funding creditworthy projects and businesses that would not qualify under a conventional program—and practical business development—expanding the bank's customer base. The bank's trust department, which is not part of the SRB Fund, has developed expertise in managing securities portfolios that are consistent with the social values of their clients. These symbiotic relationships have benefited the bank's trust clients and its depositors, *and* the bank's bottom line. That is what socially responsible investing is about: making a difference while making money.

Notice two other things about the SRB Fund loans. First, their objectives are long-term: building small businesses, creating affordable housing, supporting innovative agricultural projects, and setting aside environmentally sensitive land. The socially responsible investor's objective is positive social change. Negative change can occur overnight as it did at Bhopal in India when a Union Carbide plant spewed poisonous gas over a sleeping village. Permanent, positive change takes years of work.

Second, the SRB Fund's loans deliberately relate to movements for social change. Socially responsible investing is one of a range of tactics people can use to make a positive difference in the world in which they live. Make no mistake about it: Socially responsible investing is political; it is intended to achieve social and political ends. And it is succeeding.

* * *

Investing for Good describes social investing in the context of the political movements it serves. We want to help you answer the questions "How can I implement my political objectives in my investment decision making?" and "How can I participate in the redirection of capital for the greater good?" The challenge here is to express these objectives in ways that can be incorporated into investment decisions. For that reason, we emphasize bellwether issues—ones that indicate how a company performs in a particular area of investor concern. But to say that we approach these issues from the investor's perspective is not to say that socially responsible investors are all the same or that they have common objectives. There are many types, and one profile will not fit all. We have tried to identify a middle ground by focusing on the most widely shared concerns.

The authors are social-investment advocates. By vocation, we are social researchers and advisers who help investors implement their objectives. There are experts in each area of concern to socially responsible investors who know more about their subjects than we do. As researchers, we rely on their work and guidance.

Whatever their profiles, most socially responsible investors examine companies and report on them using a set of predefined, uniform lenses. It is the focusing of these lenses—social screens—that allows investors to make their own decisions. These decisions may not always be perfect. Applying social criteria in the investment decision-making process is not historical or sociological research, any more than security analysis is academic economics. In both instances, the orientation is practical and applied. One of *Investing for Good*'s main goals is to guide you toward realistic, implementable standards.

Social investing in the United States historically has had three distinct facets: guideline portfolio investing, shareholder activism, and community investing. The first two primarily relate to publicly traded corporations—our larger companies. The third focuses on smaller, local projects that have economic, social, or environmental benefits for their communities.

Most treatments of socially responsible investing have looked at each of these three facets independently. *Investing for Good* examines each of social investing's issue areas and shows how the three interact toward a common goal. In the first four chapters, we define social investing and its political context. We look at how socially responsible investors, using research, incorporate their social objectives in the investment decision-making process. Since most investment vehicles (excluding government issues) are issued by corporations, understanding the political and social context requires a firm notion of what corporations are and where they came from. We discuss in detail the nature of screening, showing how socially responsible investors evaluate the nonfinancial aspects of an investment opportunity.* But you should never forget that socially responsible investors are, first and foremost, investors.

What are the specific social issues that lead people to invest, or not to invest, in certain companies? The next seven chapters describe the seven most common themes:

South Africa
Alcohol, tobacco, and gambling
Military weapons and services
Effects on the environment, including nuclear power
Company relations with the community
Company relations with employees
Treatment of women and minorities
Product quality and attitude toward consumers

As we have said, we write on these issues from the perspective of the investor, not the lobbyist, policymaker, voter, or consumer. We will describe the effects that socially responsible investors and the movements they support have had on corporations.

One of the challenges of socially responsible investing is that many of its screens are multifaceted and encompass different levels. Some investors will not include *any* weapons makers in their portfolios; others eliminate only nuclear weapons makers. To illustrate the effects of the aspects of the most common screens, chapters 5 through 12 list representative companies that pass or fail particular tests. We derived these lists from the KLD Social Investment Database^sm, a universe of 825 publicly traded companies.

The final chapters discuss two larger issues that socially responsible investors must confront in the next ten years: the institutional control of the equity markets and the growing internationalization of investment portfolios. How these two issues play out will have much to say about the impact of social investing in coming years.

In their work, social researchers rely on a host of publications and books. Many of these are relatively unknown to the general public but are available at a reasonable cost. We have highlighted some of these in a series of boxes entitled "Indispensable Resources." In this small way, we

---

*At some level, responsible corporate behavior makes a healthier company. Many social-investment professionals, therefore, argue that every investor should take into account a corporation's social performance.

also acknowledge our debt to them. We encourage you to inform yourself through your mailbox, bookstore, or library.

What distinguishes resources, such as *In These Times* and *The Corporate Ethics Monitor,* is the commitment of their publishers to a cause. Such commitments also characterize socially responsible investors. Institutional investors—such as TIAA-CREF, the Calvert Group, and Working Assets—have used their great influence to put the cause of corporate accountability into the mainstream. Shareholder activists, especially the religious groups comprising the Interfaith Center on Corporate Responsibility (ICCR) in New York, connect the theory of corporate accountability with the everyday reality of, say, the *maquiladora* plants along the Mexican border.

Important as the contributions of institutions and shareholder activists are, they would have little effect without the growing support of individual investors. Socially responsible investing's strength comes from its capacity to translate an individual's goals into collective actions. Our ability to persuade depends not on grand gestures but on everyday examples. What do we tell others about our investments? What investments directly affect individuals in a community? Local efforts—such as the Vermont National Bank SRB Fund, South Shore Bank in Chicago, and the growing numbers of community-development loan funds—touch real people and change their lives.

Investing for good: That is our means to good ends.

1

Socially Responsible Investing: Doing Good While Doing Well

> Like it or not, the days when portfolio decisions could be made in a complete moral and social vacuum are numbered.
>
> —*FINANCIAL TIMES* EDITORIAL (1990)[1]

CONVENTIONAL WISDOM HOLDS that you can't mix money and ethics. Conventional wisdom is wrong. Socially responsible investors have proven it so.

Socially responsible investors (also called social investors) are investors who factor ethical and moral considerations into the investment decision-making process.* For a few investors, the motivation is pure avoidance. They do not want to profit from something that repels them: from nuclear weapons or tobacco products, say. For most, however, the motivation is political. They want their money to move society toward positive objectives: a cleaner environment or a fair employment system, for instance. Thus, most socially responsible investors view their investment policies as another means to work toward a just society. For them, social investing is not an end in itself.

It is worth the time to pick apart word-by-word this mouthful— socially responsible investors—starting with *investors*. They may be

---

*Not all investors who apply social constraints can be called socially responsible investors. In particular, institutions that by law or ordinance must not invest in companies doing business in South Africa are not socially responsible investors unless they have chosen to go beyond what they are required to do.

individuals, revolving loan funds, religious orders, corporations, pension funds, banks—anyone at all. Socially responsible investors put their money where their heads and hearts are. Socially responsible investors are usually conservative investors seeking appreciation, not meteoric growth. These investors expect that they will make at least a market rate of return* on their conventional portfolios of securities and bank instruments. They are not interested in giving their money away to the market. Many do tend to give large sums to charities. But they expect their investments to generate income and appreciation to fund those gifts.

The second word, *responsible,* refers to investors' ethical obligations. They cannot be passive whether in managing money, deciding to invest, or ensuring that businesses in which they put money act responsibly. People who do not master their money are slaves to it and to the people who manage it for them. Socially responsible investing empowers investors and, as we will see, some recipients of their investments.

Socially refers to the investor's responsibility to society at large. To some ears, however, it connotes "socialist" and leads them to infer a narrow, left-wing agenda. In the United Kingdom (U.K.) and Canada, socially responsible investors are known as "ethical investors." In many ways, this term is more apt. The investor's goals may be to improve our collective well-being. But foremost, this philosophy of investing is rooted in the individual's ethical—not social—concerns.

In another sense, "socially responsible" describes American investors far better than "ethical," because this type of investing is a natural outgrowth of their religious or political beliefs. For example, in 1970 Methodist clergy deeply concerned about the Vietnam War launched the Pax World Fund, one of socially responsible investing's oldest funds. The movement for corporate accountability to society owes its existence to forces for economic and social change, as do community-based economic-development programs. Thus, socially responsible investing (SRI) is a part of a strategy for achieving change rather than an end in itself. Table 1-1 lists common goals of social investors.

TYPES OF SOCIALLY RESPONSIBLE INVESTORS

But how do socially responsible investors work? What's in social investing for them—and you? Although these investors do not fall into neat

---

*"Market rate of return" refers to what similar investments are earning. For stocks, the "market" is usually the New York Stock Exchange, but it is not the "market" for bonds or certificates of deposit. In chapter 2 we will look at how investment returns are evaluated.

TABLE 1-1. SOCIALLY RESPONSIBLE INVESTORS' AREAS OF CONCERN

South Africa	Alcohol
Gambling	Tobacco
Nuclear power	Military weapons
The environment	Corporations' relations with communities
Corporations' relations with employees	Product quality and consumer relations
Affordable housing	Protection of environmentally sensitive
Organic/sustainable agriculture	land
Oppressive regimes	Cooperative working arrangements
Equal opportunity in hiring and	Animal testing
promotion	

This representative list suggests the areas of concern for socially responsible investors. They frame their goals in terms of these areas. Few investors focus on only one area; most concern themselves with several.

categories, the easiest way to look at social investors is to divide them into three main types:

- guideline portfolio investors
- shareholder activists
- community-development investors

Most social investors fit into at least two of these categories. A look at their objectives will help you understand how the social-investment dynamic works.

GUIDELINE PORTFOLIO INVESTORS

Guideline portfolio investors manage their holdings of publicly traded securities—stocks, bonds, and mutual funds and the like—within social or ethical guidelines or screens. Screens can be wholly exclusive, as one that eliminates all tobacco companies. Or a screen can mix positive and negative elements, as one that eliminates companies with bad labor-relations histories while identifying companies with good records.*

Standing alone, guideline portfolio investing expresses personal integrity by conforming a portfolio to social objectives. Done quietly and individually, this type of investing has no effect whatsoever on publicly traded corporations. If you tell your broker that you will not consider gambling stocks, you will not affect even slightly Hilton (which has

*Screening processes are described in chapter 3. The chapters that follow it describe the most commonly applied screens. It bears reiteration that passing social screens is only a step in the investment decision-making process. The company must also pass the investor's financial screens.

casinos) or Control Data (which designs hardware and software systems for lotteries).

Impact.   The power in guideline investing comes from linking a private act with public acts. It comes from people talking about what they are doing, or hiring a portfolio manager or buying a mutual fund that the companies know represents socially responsible investors. These representatives and those who do research for them can press corporations to respond to social concerns—through their discussions with corporations and through voting their shares, because millions and sometimes billions of dollars back them up. And the companies respond. We will look at dozens of examples in the chapters that follow.

For years, however, it has suited both corporations and their critics to picture big business as monolithic, all-powerful, and unchanging. We know now that is not true. Books like *Corporate Cultures*[2] have shown that corporations respond as much, perhaps more, to outside pressures as they do to internal ones. Take Disney's speedy withdrawal of its 1991 proposal for a nationwide lottery show. The idea of Mickey Mouse promoting gambling was a bit much for most Disney constituents. Or look at the tuna processors' response to the outcry about the deaths of dolphins in fishing-boat nets. Consumers, environmentalists, and shareholders convinced H.J. Heinz that the slaughter had to end, and the industry followed.

Social investors and the corporate-accountability movement as a whole have had a major impact. Today the effect is most evident on environmental matters. Socially responsible investors—together with many others from environmental groups to regulators—have convinced many companies of the need to work on environmental problems in a context much broader than just obeying the law and fixing problems. In large part their success has come from forcing corporations to disclose what they are doing. People who are accountable not just to regulators but also to an informed public tend to behave quite differently from those who are not.

For instance, pressure from a coalition of environmentalists and social investors has led Du Pont, Dow, and Monsanto, among others, to produce corporate environmental policies and implementation guidelines and to publish accounts of their environmental initiatives. Similar coalitions have won other battles. They have convinced retailers to reduce packaging, increase the percentage of recycled materials in packaging, and incorporate recycling into their daily operations. The companies report these moves to the public, and when the battles are forgotten, they get full credit for their efforts.

Such breakthroughs do not mark the beginning of an "ecotopia." In the fall of 1991, Monsanto announced that its controversial Roundup pesticide now came in boxes made of recycled cardboard.[3]

Financial Returns.   But can you make money investing consistently with your conscience? Until recently, social investors had to rely on anecdotal evidence to support a "yes" to that question. Now data suggest that at least for common-stock portfolios social screening does not necessarily lead to underperformance.

To say that you *can* make a market rate of return on your common stock investments is not to say that you *should* on your entire portfolio. You may have good reasons for investing in vehicles you know will not generate a market rate of return. In the next chapter we will explore the issues relating to the return on investment of a social portfolio.

SHAREHOLDER ACTIVISTS

Shareholder activists comprise the second type of socially responsible investors. Shareholder activists apply direct pressure to corporations to improve performance in specific areas.

Who Are They?   Shareholder activists range from individuals, like Jamie Gamble, who filed a resolution with Procter & Gamble on purchasing coffee from El Salvador, to the largest pension funds in the United States, the California Public Employees Retirement System (CalPERS) and the Teachers Insurance and Annuity Association-College Retirement Equity Fund (TIAA-CREF), which file resolutions on corporate-governance issues, among others. But since the early 1970s, Roman Catholic orders and the mainline Protestant churches have been the leaders on social issues. For the 1991 cycle of annual meetings, religious groups filed 280 resolutions in twelve issue areas with 175 companies; in 1992, 228 resolutions with 154 companies.[4]

Shareholder activists are in numbers the smallest group within the U.S. social-investment community. But they are by no means the least important. Their achievements regarding South Africa—increased public awareness, changed behavior among companies doing business there, and divestment of in-country holdings—have provided both the impetus and the model for U.S. social investing. Because many religious groups are also deeply involved in community investing, they link the portfolio investment side to the community investment side. It is this central, unifying function that SRI movements in other countries lack.*

---

*More and more shareholder resolutions are being filed in the E.C. However, they relate primarily to governance issues. *See* M. G. Star, "Shareholder Activism Picks Up in Europe,"

Shareholder activists define and refine ethical issues in public and private forums in which they confront intelligent, well-financed opponents—representatives of corporations, not-for-profits, government agencies, and others. They do not merely preach to the converted. Religious groups, led by the Interfaith Center on Corporate Responsibility (ICCR), have proven uniquely effective in the shareholder arena. They take long-term views of issues and address core values. The future motivates shareholder activists. Immediate results are few. The potential for long-range progress—as with South Africa—is infinite.

An outstanding shareholder activist is a Medical Mission Sister, Sister Regina Rowan. Her order serves where the need is greatest, in places like Bangladesh. Sister Regina's job is to make sure that pharmaceutical companies respond to the needs of developing countries. She has helped change corporate policies on issues ranging from infant formula distribution to dumping drugs banned here in the Third World. Her approach is always one of love. "How can *we* make our company better?" she asks.

Historically, leadership on shareholder issues has come from Roman Catholic orders and the mainline Protestant churches. These groups recognized the power of the social-issue shareholder resolution when consumer and civil rights advocates first used it on General Motors in 1970. (Project GM is discussed later in this chapter.) With ICCR as coordinator and facilitator, religious shareholders have developed a sophisticated approach to the process of "lobbying the corporation." This phrase, probably coined by Berkeley professor David Vogel,[5] describes exactly what shareholder activists are about. They have applied to corporations the techniques citizens groups have used to influence governments.*

In recent years the business press has increasingly used "shareholder activists" to refer to large pension funds that use the tactics of shareholder activism. The interests of the two groups of shareholder activists overlap sometimes. TIAA-CREF has sponsored shareholder resolutions on South Africa; the New York City Employees Retirement System (NYCERS) has led the fight to convince corporations to adopt the CERES Principles on the environment. However, the pension funds and their allies tend to be most concerned with corporate governance—the relationship between the owners (shareholders) of a corporation and the board of directors and managers who run it. Chapter 11 looks at these

---

Pensions & Investments, June 8, 1992, p. 43. Social-issue resolutions have almost always failed to get on the proxy because of extremely difficult legal requirements. The lack of an effective shareholder-activist movement has stunted the growth of social investing outside the United States.

*Whether corporations are, at least in origin, quasigovernmental units is a matter of considerable debate. Professor Vogel argues no. For our view, see chapter 11.

new shareholder activists who have the potential to redefine the relation-ship between corporations and society.

The Shareholder Resolution.   The most visible tools of shareholder activists are resolutions to be voted on by shareholders at the annual meeting—proxy resolutions. Box 1-1 contains a sample resolution.

Box 1-1. A Proxy Resolution

In 1992, St. Peter's Lutheran Church of Manhattan and the Evangelical Lutheran Church in America submitted the following resolution to Humana, the nation's largest health care chain.

WHEREAS, cigarettes are the leading cause of death and disease in the U.S., claiming an estimated 400,000 lives annually, and costing $52 billion in health costs and low wages;
WHEREAS, cigarette smoking in the U.S. kills more people than heroin, cocaine, alcohol, AIDS, fires, homicide, suicide, and automobile accidents combined;
WHEREAS, cigarette smoking is an air pollutant more cancer-causing than many widely banned toxic chemicals;
WHEREAS, in the U.S. alone, Environmental Tobacco Smoke (ETS) has become the third leading cause of preventable death;
WHEREAS, companies have been held liable for failing to provide a safe workplace and for inadequate protection of the health of non-smokers in the workplace in various states;
WHEREAS, the Surgeon General of the U.S. has found that the simple separation of smokers from nonsmokers reduces risks but does not eliminate them;
WHEREAS, our company's identity is linked with proper approaches to health;
RESOLVED, that shareholders request management, by September 1, 1992:

1. To have all our facilities, including headquarters, be smoke free throughout, to the greatest extent possible;
2. To be free of all cigarette vending machines and to prohibit sales on the premises, for any entity connected with our company.

Source: Interfaith Center on Corporate Responsibility, *Church Proxy Resolutions* (New York: ICCR, 1992), p. 12.

The issues shareholder activists develop often become screens applied to portfolios. Equally importantly, activists influence public opinion. Their tactics are dialogue and public persuasion. When they ask a corporation to provide better reporting on its environmental impact, they are not solely interested in the details of a company's current actions. They hope to affect its future.

Shareholder activists have used this strategy with the CERES Principles,* a voluntary environmental code of conduct for U.S. corporations. They begin by talking to the corporation. If they do not achieve their goals, they file a resolution asking a company for a report on environmental performance in each of the Principles' substantive areas. In later years, they ask for reports on progress toward each of the goals. Finally, they ask the company to adopt the Principles.

Proxy resolutions open the door to corporate management—private-sector opinion makers whom social activists could not otherwise reach. And the resolutions are surprisingly effective. This tactic is somewhat like the method generations of hillbilly humorists said Ozark farmers used to get a mule's attention: They hit him between the ears with a two-by-four. Tim Smith, ICCR's first and only executive director, uses a different metaphor. He emphasizes that "shareholder resolutions on their own do not accomplish change. They're just one flower in a bouquet."[6]

The proponents' goal is not so much the resolution's passage—they rarely win—as the start of a dialogue with the company. Shareholder activists often accomplish through talk what they cannot through the ballot process.

To file a resolution, a shareholder must own one thousand dollars of stock for one year. These requirements may seem minimal, but one share bought the day before the filing deadline did the trick until the Securities and Exchange Commission (SEC) decided to stem the tide of resolutions with stiffer requirements. At this writing, the SEC was considering still more stringent filing requirements aimed at limiting the number and scope of social resolutions.

Once a resolution is filed (assuming it meets various formal requirements), the corporation must include it in the proxy statement. The proxy statement is a small pamphlet supplied to all shareholders that is supposed to contain all the information a shareholder will require to vote intelligently on the issues presented at the annual meeting. The proxy statement always includes information on the candidates for board seats

*From their inception in 1990 until 1992, the CERES Principles were referred to as "The Valdez Principles." They are discussed in chapter 6.

and on the carryover members. It describes the compensation board members and senior executives receive. And it contains the full text of each resolution shareholders will vote on.

With the proxy statement, the shareholder receives a small sheet of paper that looks like a ballot. Actually, it is a power of attorney—a proxy—that authorizes a stated representative to vote the shares as the shareholder specifies. Few shareholders choose to attend annual meetings. They prefer to vote by proxy, so the resolutions are called "proxy resolutions."

Socially oriented proxy resolutions ask a company to do something: leave South Africa, sign the MacBride Principles on operations in Northern Ireland, report on minority representation among its employees, and the like. The resolutions must not relate to the corporation's "ordinary business," a catch-all for matters on which management has discretion. The SEC has shown some inclination to expand this category. In 1992, it ruled that shareholders could not ask Wal-Mart for a report on its employment of women and minorities and its steps to increase their numbers among management.[7] The resolution's proponents have argued that if shareholders cannot question management's compliance with laws whose violation can cost millions in fines and civil damages, it is hard to see what would *not* be "ordinary business."

Some might argue that shareholders do not need proxy resolutions to influence corporate policy. A leading specialist in proxy solicitations, Georgeson & Company, disagrees.

> The effectiveness of [the institutional investor's] direct negotiations with management hinges on the power it can ultimately assert through proxy voting. In fact, it is largely through the use of the proxy process that shareholders have succeeded in capturing the attention of the corporation.[8]

Were social investors to lose this lever—which the SEC is now threatening—the result would be disastrous.

COMMUNITY INVESTORS

> [The] architecture of the 60's was destroying our communities. The tragedy is that in the 60's there was all kinds of money for urban renewal, but architects and planners didn't know what to do. Now the profession knows what to do, but has no money.
>
> —VINCENT SCULLY (1992)[9]

In September 1992 a black-tie affair marked the thirtieth anniversary of the completion of Boston's West End Urban Renewal Project. The developers celebrated the erection of a complex of "luxury" apartment towers displacing neighborhoods where Jews, Italians, and Irish entered American life. A few elderly souls picketed the party to remind the guests of the human cost of the project. The pulsing life along the winding seventeenth century streets disappeared and the people dispersed. The straight twentieth century streets resemble nothing so much as the corridors of the adjacent Massachusetts General Hospital—impersonal by day, empty by night.

Even allowing for memory's softening effect on the reality of mean streets, something very fragile—a community—was destroyed. And a new community did not replace the old. The hideous effects of "renewals" like the West End project, and better understandings of the environment and the social fabric, have led to a new focus among investors on what a community is.

From colonial times to the present, many Americans have tried to found utopian communities. All failed. In recent years we have become more conscious of the need for preserving the ways in which humans actually live best, rather than imposing a new system—building low-rise low-income housing instead of towers, for instance. Starved for funds, government no longer responds effectively in this area.* The third aspect of social investing, community investment, addresses that need.

Community investments—which are sometimes called "direct" or "targeted" or "high social-impact" investments—usually take the form of loans or deposits in financial institutions often at below-market rates of return. The vehicles—the means by which people invest—tend to be small lenders, such as community loan funds and credit unions. For instance, you can make a deposit—in effect, a loan—with the Community Invested Banking Fund of the Sunshine Bank of Wheeling, West Virginia. Sunshine Bank will use the deposits to make loans to small businesses in the perennially economically depressed upper Ohio Valley. Community investors address the absence of economic building blocks required to cope with our society's critical needs for food, capital for the disadvantaged, and preservation of environmentally sensitive areas. However, they focus mainly on housing and jobs.

Housing.   A favorite example of community investment is South Shore Bank in Chicago. South Shore solicits Development Deposits[sm]

---

*Whether government can ever respond effectively in the area of community economic development is a very different question from whether it *should* respond to these needs. Yet contemporary conservatives who raise these questions never explain why their laissez faire ancestors, who built—with substantial government assistance and subsidization—railroads, bridges, and trolleys, would have answered both questions affirmatively.

from investors outside its service area and uses them to fund loans within it—thus reversing the traditional pattern of removing savings from poor communities for investment elsewhere. The bank serves an area that was in the early 1970s headed toward disaster. Landlords were abandoning apartment buildings. Other banks would not make mortgage loans in the area. South Shore did, and new landlords rehabbed apartment buildings—creating jobs as well as housing. Today the borders of South Shore's lending area are clearly defined. Well-maintained brick apartment buildings line one side of a street; blasted-out ruins are on the other.

South Shore's housing loans have gone mainly to conventional projects. But many community-investment projects are nontraditional. These may include limited-equity coops, housing projects whose owners agree to limit the asking price for their units so that the housing remains affordable. While South Shore is best known for its work in housing, it also makes small-business loans.[10]

Job-Creation Programs.   Community investors also fund job-creation efforts. These might include loans to organizations, such as the ICA Revolving Loan Fund in Somerville, Massachusetts, that offer financing to worker-owned businesses. Accion International, based in Cambridge, Massachusetts, makes microenterprise loans rarely exceeding five hundred dollars to people in Central and South America who want to start their own businesses. You can participate in these microenterprise programs by making a loan to them. You can also participate indirectly in community economic development. Some social investors make a point of including in their portfolios companies that make targeted investments. Several of the big insurers, such as Ætna Life & Casualty, make these investments. Amoco and BP America are among other significant investors.

LOOKING INTO THE FUTURE

Portfolio investment, shareholder activism, and community investment are distinct emphases within social investing. Each has its own political agenda and tactics. What they share is a commitment to positive social change.

The futures of portfolio investment and community investment look bright. Investment advisers of all types and levels offer to screen equity investments. The consolidation of the banking industry has made obvious the need for local control of economic decision-making.

As we have noted, shareholder activism is under attack. Corporations have always found social-issue resolutions nettlesome. With the rise of governance activists with millions of shares behind them, they now feel threatened. We will look at this battle in chapter 11. Should the Securities and Exchange Commission restrict shareholder resolutions, the entire corporate-accountability movement will suffer. There will be less information made public. But more importantly, there will be less opportunity to engage corporate managers in dialogue about the principles that should govern our society.

History rarely repeats itself. But a brief look at where social investing has come from does reveal how much is at stake today.

THE HISTORICAL ROOTS

Social investing really started with the Quakers in the seventeenth century. These great merchants refused to profit from war or slave-running —major industries then. The Quakers stood for social change of the most profound sort. They even named the city they founded Philadelphia, "The City of Brotherly Love." Their contemporaries, recognizing the threat of this philosophy, persecuted the Quakers.

One hundred and fifty years after the death of George Fox, the founder of the Quakers, the greatest of Britain's nineteenth-century historians still felt compelled to vilify him. Fox, Lord Macaulay said, had "an intellect in the most unhappy of all states, that is to say, too much disordered for liberty and not sufficiently disordered for Bedlam."[11] Until perhaps 1987, that is how many regarded social investors.

The Age of Reform and Prohibition

Contemporary social investing in the U.S. has its roots during the period from 1890 to 1917, which has come to be called the "age of reform."[12] The need for reform was best described by the embodiment of that age, Theodore Roosevelt. Since the Civil War's end in 1865, there had been, according to Roosevelt:

> A riot of individualistic materialism, under which complete freedom for the individual . . . turned out in practice to mean perfect freedom for the strong to wrong the weak. . . . The power of the mighty industrial overlords . . . had increased with giant strides, while the methods of controlling them, . . . through the Government, remained archaic and therefore practically impotent.[13]

The assertion that collective action—through government, labor unions, the Legion of Decency, and the like—could remedy social ills characterized the Age of Reform. And for a quarter century ending just after the country entered World War I in 1917, social change—whether one favored it or not—defined the political agenda. A contemporary observer noted,

> The first fifteen years of the twentieth century may sometime be remembered in America as the Age of Crusades. There were a super-abundance of zeal, a sufficiency of good causes, unusual moral idealism, excessive confidence in mass movements, and leaders with rare gifts of popular appeal.[14]

The items on the agendas of these mass movements can be grouped into three very broad categories:

- Personal reform—the attainment of higher standards of private conduct, such as not consuming alcohol, tobacco, or certain drugs;
- Social welfare—the protection of groups and classes who lack the power to act for themselves, such as the poor, women, children, and industrial workers; and
- Institutional change—the redefinition of government's relationship to the governed and the definition of the modern business corporation's relationship to society.

This agenda reflects the political goals of social investors today.

Personal Reform.   As the Quakers illustrate, social investing springs from the urge for personal integrity—the wish to make one's investments consistent with one's ethics. The first socially screened mutual fund, the aptly named Pioneer Fund,* served evangelical Protestants in the United States who opposed consumption of alcohol and tobacco and would not own the stock of companies that made liquor, cigarettes, or cigars.

The impulse for personal reform by banning vices found expressions well beyond the personal or parish level. Prohibition, of course, is its most widely recognized legislative success, but there were others. Horse racing, "gambling dens," and lotteries were regulated, in some cases out of existence. Over-the-counter opiates, such as laudanum and heroin, were banned, along with marijuana and cocaine.

We are still living with the consequences of this mixture of personal improvement and prohibition. Social investors have tended to emphasize their personal unwillingness to support alcohol, tobacco, and gambling through their investments. Some shareholder activists have veered uncomfortably toward prohibition, particularly with regard to tobacco.

---

*The Pioneer Fund is one of a family of mutual funds offered by the Pioneer Group in Boston. It added a partial South Africa screen in the 1970s.

Social Welfare.   On December 4, 1908, the Federal Council of Churches adopted "The Social Creed of the Churches." This remarkable document still expresses the core of social investors' beliefs about the goals of a just society.

The Federal Council of the Churches of Christ in America stands:

- For equal rights and complete justice for all men in all stations of life.
- For the abolition of child labor.
- For such regulation of the conditions of toil for women as shall safeguard the physical and moral health of the community.
- For the suppression of the "Sweating System."
- For the gradual and reasonable reduction of the hours of labor to the lowest practicable point, and for that degree of leisure for all, which is the condition of the highest human life.
- For a release from employment one day in seven.
- For the right of all men to the opportunity for self-maintenance, a right ever to be wisely and strongly safeguarded against encroachments of every kind.
- For the right of workers to some protection against the hardships often resulting from the swift crises of industrial change.
- For a living wage as a minimum in every industry, and for the highest wage that each industry can afford.
- For the protection of the worker from dangerous machinery, occupational disease, injuries, and mortality.
- For the principle of conciliation and arbitration in industrial dissensions.
- For the abatement of poverty.
- For the most equitable division of the products of industry that can ultimately be devised.[15]

Add to this creed environmental concerns and fiddle with its archaisms, and you will have a fair statement of the standards social investors apply to corporations today and of the objectives of community-investment programs. Socially responsible investment emphasizes the individual's responsibility for his or her wealth. It means putting money to work where it will create both wealth and a more humane society. The appeal of community investing lies in its promise of rebuilding and reknitting communities through the creation of jobs and affordable housing.

Institutional Change.   In 1906 the corporation counsel for the City of Chicago called AT&T a "ruthless, grinding, oppressive monopoly," a view business historian John Train regards as "clearly a reflection of the popular opinion of the day."[16] Eighty-five years later AT&T's chief executive officer tried to build a business coalition to support passage of the 1991 Civil Rights Act in the face of President Bush's opposition. That AT&T could develop a social conscience would have seemed impossible during the age of reform. Yet it was just such transformations that the reformers dreamed of.

In the late twentieth century, people do not appreciate how new this challenge was. Big Business has not always been with us. Indeed, the modern corporation dates to no earlier than 1850, and it didn't take its present form until the 1880s and 1890s.[17] Apart from armies, no one had ever put together human organizations the size of, say, U.S. Steel (now USX) which was created in 1901. Nor had anyone ever tried to concentrate so many functions—so many human relationships, both internal and external—in a single structure.

The enormity of the challenge to society posed by these new economic forces compelled governments at every level to reorganize themselves. Regulatory agencies such as the Food and Drug Administration, unknown until the 1870s, began to proliferate. Most states revamped their constitutions and municipalities their charters to make government at once more responsive to people and less vulnerable to business's corrosive influences.* America redefined its social and political relationships because of the rise of the corporations. We are still working out these relationships.

REBIRTH

From its modest origins in the Age of Reform until 1967, social investing progressed little. Some churches and individuals excluded sin stocks from their portfolios. Otherwise, little happened.

The civil rights movement provided the catalyst for change. The need for direct investment in poor communities was clear. In 1968 the United Presbyterian Church voted to channel 30 percent of its unrestricted funds into community-investment projects.[18] However, as Jack Mendelsohn, a Unitarian minister, wrote at that time, "There are no maps. On the question of investment policy with its staggering stakes, there is no carefully worked-out rationale, let alone fiduciary law support, for novel social approaches."[19]

---

*Even Richard Hofstadter in his classic *The Age of Reform* understates the transformation of governments at every level between 1890 and 1917. In no small part, the great social reforms of the New Deal and the Kennedy-Johnson-Nixon eras succeeded because structures were in place to institutionalize them.

Box 1-2. Indispensable Resource:
Corporate Ethics Monitor

Corporate Ethics Monitor is a bimonthly (six issues per year) publication that reports on the social and environmental performance of Canadian business. More important for U.S. readers are its extraordinarily insightful articles on issues directly relevant to the screening process.

Each issue highlights the performance of fifteen companies within two different industry sectors. Corporate practices in such areas as community relations, charitable giving, progressive staff policies, labor relations, environmental management and performance, international operations, and military contracts are highlighted in chart and essay format. Readers are able to compare the performance of prominent Canadian firms within their respective industry groups.

Corporate Ethics Monitor also contains feature articles on current ethical and social management issues. Regular contributors include David Nitkin, the president of EthicScan Canada, whose column highlights leading-edge management trends. Nitkin offers practical advice on how to manage more ethically and effectively, based on the experiences of other professionals who have faced similar challenges in the workplace. David Olive, editor of *Report on Business Magazine,* brings his unique style to the *Monitor* when accenting and analyzing current trends in the business press. Edward Waitzer, a securities lawyer, gives a legal perspective on issues as diverse as whistle-blowing, shareholder rights, and executive compensation. Guest contributors review books and articles of use to investors interested in corporate social responsibility.

Now in its fourth year of publication, the *Corporate Ethics Monitor* offers a unique view of corporate accountability tailored to the social investor's needs.

Corporate Ethics Monitor, EthicScan Canada, Lawrence Plaza Postal Outlet, P.O. Box 54034, Toronto, Ontario M6A 3B7, Canada; (416) 783-6776, fax (416) 783-7386. C$399 per year.

Starting in the mid-1950s, some efforts were made to push corporations into the fray, but these took the form of boycotts and letter-writing campaigns.[20] Eastman Kodak became a target in 1965 after riots in the black ghetto of its headquarters city, Rochester, New York. Church groups hired the legendary Saul Alinsky to mobilize Rochester's black community. He formed a coalition—Freedom-Integration-God-Honor-Today (FIGHT)—whose aims were to improve living conditions and job opportunities for blacks. Recognizing the dominance of Kodak in the local economy, FIGHT demanded this model corporate citizen commit itself to hire six hundred unemployed people.

In 1966 a lower-echelon manager delegated to negotiate agreed to FIGHT's demands. The next day Kodak's executive committee repudiated the agreement. In response Alinsky decided to confront management at the company's 1967 annual meeting and to convince shareholders to withhold their proxies from management. Protests at annual meetings were not new, but withholding proxies when control of the corporation was not at issue was. The votes of forty thousand shares—representing a very small percentage of shares outstanding—were withheld.

Nonetheless, Alinsky's strategy worked. FIGHT and Kodak reached an agreement, and the precedent was set.[21]

CAMPAIGN GM

In the United States, we can date the start of modern social investing quite precisely: the tumultuous year 1969.

The Vietnam War raged on despite the departure of President Johnson. Few trusted his replacement, Richard Nixon. The turmoil over civil rights and the assassination of Dr. Martin Luther King made economic support of South Africa's apartheid system inconceivable. Divestiture began to be argued in university councils. Congress enacted the National Environmental Policy Act (NEPA), which permanently changed how Americans look at their relationship to the environment. The nascent environmental movement was planning the celebration of the first Earth Day in 1970. But most importantly, Ralph Nader was well on his way to creating a small army of consumer activists.

Nader lit the fuse that set off social investing. Or rather, General Motors did. In 1966, Nader's book, *Unsafe at Any Speed,* had been published, exposing the safety hazards of the Chevrolet Corvair. GM responded with a clumsy vendetta, complete with private detectives and a smear campaign. Nader struck back with Campaign GM, which proposed to put before GM's 1970 annual meeting nine resolutions dealing with issues as diverse as minority hiring and representation on GM's board and consumer rights. The SEC allowed two to appear on the ballot. No one had ever put social-responsibility issues on a proxy ballot before.

U.S. churches and religious orders grasped the importance of what Nader had done. In 1971 they formed the Interfaith Center on Corporate

Responsibility (ICCR),* which has filed a torrent of shareholder resolutions ever since. It led the battles on withdrawal of U.S. businesses from South Africa. Today it is becoming increasingly involved in the environmental movement through the CERES Principles.

ICCR has also involved itself with community investing. Many of its members are deeply committed to affordable-housing projects and microeconomic loan programs. In retrospect, it was fitting that a major result of Campaign GM was the appointment in 1970 of the Reverend Leon Sullivan to GM's board. A black minister from Philadelphia, Sullivan had made his reputation as an advocate of community-based development. As a member of GM's board, Sullivan became famous for his efforts to end corporate involvement in South Africa. For ten years his Sullivan Principles† were the centerpiece of shareholder resolutions and divestment campaigns. By 1992 in the U.S. alone there was at least $550 billion in portfolios screened on South Africa.

An acquaintance who is no friend of social investing has compared the events of 1969 to 1971 to the lightning bolt that gave life to Dr. Frankenstein's monster. No other social-investment movement has had a start like ours.

SOCIAL INVESTMENT TODAY

To be viable, an investment philosophy must offer sufficient products to meet client demand for diversification. Social investing has reached that point.

Mutual Funds.   In 1992 more than sixty U.S. mutual funds screened at least on South Africa and at least thirty screened on more than one issue. When we refer to social mutual funds in this book, we exclude entities that screen only on South Africa. Every U.S., U.K., or Canadian fund we mention has a South Africa screen, but it is not the fund's main screen.

The first modern social fund, the Pax World Fund, appeared in 1971. Nineteen years later, it reached $100 million. Because of stellar performance in 1990 and 1991, it reached $250 million in early 1992. As its name implies, Pax's principal screen is military, but it also screens on South Africa and other issues. The largest socially screened fund family is the Calvert Social Investment Fund. It broke $1 billion in 1992. Its screens are as comprehensive as any fund's.

---

*ICCR calculates its birth from that of the two groups that merged in 1973 to form it.
†In 1987, Sullivan disavowed the Principles out of frustration at the lack of progress in South Africa. As we will see in chapter 5, the Principles lived on as "The Statement of Principles."

As you will see from Table 2-1, social investors have diverse concerns, and the multiscreened mutual funds reflect the varying emphases of these investors. The Green Century Funds reflect the environmental and social concerns of the Nader-created Public Interest Research Groups (PIRGs) that sponsor them. New Alternatives in Great Neck, New York, emphasizes environmentally compatible energy producers. An important sign of social investing's maturity is the range of investment philosophies represented by the multiscreened funds. Equity funds now range from an index fund (the Domini Social Index Trust) to a contrarian growth fund (Parnassus). We will have more to say about the range of funds in the next chapter.

Word about Pax spread across the Atlantic. Charles Jacob—the father of British ethical investing—was managing Methodist church funds when in 1973 he proposed the Stewardship Trust. The regulators turned it down. He later revived the idea and with the help of one of Britain's leading insurers pushed it through the regulatory obstacles in 1984. The insurer now manages the fund—the first U.K. ethical fund—which bears the euphonious name "The Friends Provident Stewardship Trust."

In the United Kingdom today there are about thirty ethical funds and perhaps another five that do not claim to be ethical funds but that do apply screens—sometimes quite elaborate ones. In this latter category would appear the TSB Environmental Fund, Britain's largest. According to Alan Miller, principal of Financial Platforms in Croydon and president of the U.K. Social Investment Forum, giant institutions such as Citibank and Skandia Life have entered the field, and other large institutions have launched social products. In mid-1992, £320 million was invested in ethical funds, up from £144 million in 1989.[22]

In Canada, the first socially responsible mutual fund, the Ethical Growth Fund, appeared in 1986. Today there are six funds that screen primarily on the environment. At the end of 1991, the funds held approximately C$150 million.

Money Managers and Financial Planners.   For many years money managers have accommodated clients with social screens for alcohol and tobacco, and even South Africa.

Financial services professionals specializing in socially responsible investing did not appear until the mid-1970s. Among the first was Robert J. Schwartz, now a senior vice president at Smith, Barney. Schwartz worked at several large brokerage firms, which as a class have not been hospitable to SRI professionals. In spite of this, he built a thriving business and helped launch an industry.

In 1982 Joan Bavaria and Don Falvey founded Franklin Research &

Box 1-3. The Social Investment Forum

The Social Investment Forum is the national clearinghouse for information and the advocate for socially responsible investing.

The Forum connects its international membership with the key people involved in social investing—the investors, financial institutions, advisers, and planners—the entire array of people behind this growing $625 billion industry. The Forum's membership also includes and serves many of the nation's pioneers of commitment to social change through community investment.

Through its educational foundation, the Social Investment Forum Foundation, the Forum offers an opportunity to direct charitable contributions toward educational efforts. The Foundation supports the outreach program of the Forum through a quarterly series of public meetings held at various locations throughout the country. These meetings are designed to inform and educate attendees about the principles and practices of combining social and financial analyses in investing.

Members receive a comprehensive membership directory, *Social Investment Services: A Guide to Forum Members*. This indispensable guide lists hundreds of mutual funds; venture capital fund managers; individual and institutional investors; research providers, foundations, educators, and publishers; community development banks and loan

Development Corporation of Boston, the first money-management firm devoted exclusively to SRI. Had that been their only contribution to socially responsible investing, it would have been a great one. But Joan and Don also cofounded, housed, and bankrolled the Social Investment Forum (see Box 1-3), the industry trade group, for its first five years. From meetings comfortably accommodated in small conference rooms, the Forum's quarterly meetings now can attract over 300 people. By 1992 the Forum's professional members numbered over 1,000.[23]

CONCLUSION

From modest beginnings among people who just did not want to own tobacco or liquor stocks, social investing has grown into a vibrant, funds; and brokers, advisers, and planners. The guide is available at reasonable cost without Forum membership.

The Forum quarterly newsletter (included with Forum membership) regularly covers developments in the field, profiles members in depth, summarizes quarterly national meetings, tracks performance of the socially responsible mutual funds, and keeps readers informed of events. The newsletter is available without membership to interested parties.

The Forum is the vehicle through which one can:

- track the performance of socially invested assets;
- access the latest information on socially responsible investing;
- learn about nationwide Forum meetings, which include presentations and panels on social investing;
- provide the general public with knowledge about the concept of social investing;
- support the nationwide advocacy for socially responsible investing.

In short, Forum membership benefits the member, the Forum, and the development of socially responsible investing.

The Social Investment Forum, 430 First Avenue North, Minneapolis, MN 55401; (612) 333–8338.

broad-based movement. Was its growth a miracle or an accident? No question, a miracle or two along the way certainly helped.

But social investing grew because some financial professionals realized that by putting their money where their hearts were, they would make money and advance their causes. They spread the word, and investors began to come to them. U.S. social investing is only a little more than twenty years old, and it is growing.

2

The Performance Question:
Getting Your Money's Worth

MONEY MANAGERS OFTEN ARGUE against screening conventional portfolios. "Why don't you just make as much money as you can and then give it away?" Sometimes they point to the good works Alfred Nobel funded from the proceeds of his munitions business. *The Economist* recently responded to a variation on this argument.

> James I of England [1566–1625] was a virulent anti-smoker. . . . So strong were James' feelings on the subject that he penned a "Counterblast to Tobacco," noting, half-presciently, that smoking was "harmful to the brain and dangerous to the lungs." He also beheaded the man who first imported tobacco into Europe, Walter Raleigh. Nonetheless, it was the same James who first derived serious revenue from an import duty on the weed. Four centuries later, Eurocrats are busy banning domestic advertising of tobacco products while subsidising European growers to sell their cancer-dealing goods to the third world. There are nastier smells than stale tobacco smoke after all.[1]

Many managers who argue against screening do not find avoiding hypocrisy a valid argument for screening. They prefer a "practical, dollars-and-cents" approach to investing. Screening, they say, eliminates opportunities for profits and increases the risk of losses by limiting the range of investments from which they can choose.

Framed as a choice between hypocrisy and money, any right-thinking person would choose the honorable path, right? Wrong. It is not that simple. As a socially responsible *investor,* you should understand why the choice is not simple. As an advocate of social investing, you must know how to respond to those struggling with this choice.

In both instances, understanding the choice demands some knowledge of the concept of performance—the change in the value of a portfolio over time—and how performance is measured. Knowing what performance means empowers you to defend your investment decisions. This is not as trivial as it might seem. Many social investors find it humiliating to talk finances with Uncle Bud, the family Neanderthal, who always seems to make 30 percent on his investments. How can you explain to him why you only made 13 percent and were happy about it? "Well, Uncle B.," you should be able to say, "the half of my money in a conventional portfolio was up 22.3 percent this year. That's a couple of points above the S&P. What brought my overall performance down was a bridge loan to ACCION International. It was only paying 5 percent. So overall, I'm up 13.65 percent. Not bad when inflation's only running 4.5 percent!" You don't have to hem and haw about what you decided. You made an intelligent choice, and you chose to *make* a little less. You didn't *lose* anything.

Another reason you should understand performance has to do with "fiduciary duties," the legal responsibilities of anyone entrusted with property—including money or investments—for another's benefit toward the property in his or her care. The courts take fiduciary duties *very* seriously. Therefore, fiduciaries—persons with fiduciary duties such as trustees—pay close attention to them. The most common type of fiduciaries is trustees.

Trustees of pension funds oversee $3.3 trillion.[2] Trustees of charities control $138.1 billion.[3] There isn't any reliable estimate of how much money is in private trusts held for individuals. Through their jobs, pensions, religious affiliations, avocations, and the like, individuals have stakes in these pools of money. This capital can be mobilized to do an enormous amount of good. But trustees must be convinced that they can defend socially responsible investing on performance grounds to their lawyers and the courts. Otherwise, those trillions will remain unaffected by social investing.

PERFORMANCE—THE BENCHMARKS

Performance is the change in the value of a portfolio over time. Here's what that means in practice. In a newsletter, you might read, "The value of a share in the Pax World Fund rose 6.67 percent over the quarter ending September 30, 1991. Over 1991's first eleven months, a share of Pax ranged from a low of $13.57 to $16.21. Had you invested $10,000 in Pax on the last day of 1985, it would have been worth $19,780 on the last day of November, 1991."[4] Those figures tell you nothing about how an investment in Pax compared either to a comparable investment or to the market for stocks and bonds generally. And those are the gauges to which most investors look to evaluate performance.

COMPARABLE INVESTMENTS

"You can't compare apples and oranges." How many times have you heard that? But did you ever stop to ask yourself, "Why *can't* I? They're both fruits; they're more or less round; they're more or less juicy; and they're interchangeable in box lunches." In fact, you often compare the two and pick the one that suits your palate.

Investors do the same with mutual funds. The criteria defining the category of mutual funds that they buy are their investment objectives— current income or capital appreciation, for instance. But except for the purpose of deciding which type suits your particular objectives, funds should not be compared across categories. Of course, mutual funds are not the only financial assets you might buy for your portfolio. A good finance guide will discuss your full range of options. We, however, will use the socially screened mutual funds to show how investors evaluate performance by comparisons to other investment opportunities.

Lipper Analytic Services is the most widely cited evaluator of mutual funds. It categorizes the 2,072 funds it tracks* according to thirty-four definitions of mutual fund objectives, that is, generally, what the fund managers say their goals are in the funds' prospectuses. For instance, a prospectus for a technology-sector fund might say that its managers intend to keep at least 65 percent of the portfolio in high-tech stocks. Table 2-1 lists some of the better-known multiscreened social funds. The funds fall into seven Lipper categories.

Lipper categorizes three social funds as growth funds. A growth fund is one that invests in the stocks of companies the fund's manager thinks will grow faster than those of the companies that issued "the stocks in the major market indexes."[5] Growth-fund managers invest for appreciation in their shares' value, not for income paid in dividends. Parnassus, a growth fund, was up 8.67 percent for the third quarter of 1991 and 43.21 percent for the twelve months ending September 30, 1991.

---

*Lipper does not track, among others, money market mutual funds such as Working Assets. These funds invest in short-term cash equivalents, like commercial paper, in order to remain very liquid.

TABLE 2-1. SOME SOCIAL MUTUAL FUNDS
Comparison of Socially Responsible Stock Mutual Funds with Multiple Screens
Open to All Investors

Fund Name	Investment Objective	Load	Annual Fees
Calvert Social Investment Fund Equity Portfolio	Growth	4.8%	1.04%
Calvert Social Investment Fund Managed Growth Portfolio	Growth and Income	4.8%	1.31%
Calvert Social Investment Fund World Values Global Equity	International Growth	4.8%	NA
Calvert Ariel Appreciation Fund	Small-Company Growth	4.8%	1.44%
Covenent Fund	Growth	4.5%	2.02%
Domini Social Index[sm] Trust	Growth	0%	.75%
Dreyfus Third Century Fund	Growth	0%	1.08%
Green Century Balanced Funds	Growth and Income	0%	2.50%
New Alternatives Fund	Growth	5.6%	1.18%
Parnassus Fund Equity Portfolio	Growth	3.5%	1.51%
Parnassus Fund Balanced Portfolio	Growth and Income	3.5%	1.25%
Pax World Fund	Growth and Income	0%	1.20%
Rightime Social Awareness Fund	Growth—Market Timing	4.8%	2.85%
Schield Progressive Environmental	Growth	4.5%	2.50%
Working Assets Citizens Growth	Growth	4.0%	1.65%
Working Assets Citizens Balanced	Growth and Income	4.0%	1.65%

Sources: Social Investment Forum; *Franklin's Investing for a Better World.*

Calvert Ariel Appreciation, which Lipper categorizes as a small-company growth fund, was up only 3.43 percent for the same quarter but rose 45.31 percent for the twelve months.[6] Small companies are considered riskier—meaning the share prices are likely to fluctuate more—than the much larger blue chips, like IBM.

Lipper's categorizations are not 100 percent reliable. Lipper categorizes the Rightime Social Awareness Fund as a specialty fund, one whose "prospectus limits its investments to a specific industry or [which] falls outside of other classifications."[7] Rightime invests in most industries, so that criterion doesn't apply.

What distinguishes Rightime from its competitors is its reliance on market timing, an investment technique that relies on economic factors or technical analysis of the market's outlook for indications as to whether to buy or sell securities. If Rightime's straightforward social screens put it into the specialty-fund category, all of the social funds should be there, too. But as Table 2-1 shows, Lipper puts others into categories consisting mainly of unscreened funds.

Lipper's categories of mutual fund objectives provide one way of looking at types of mutual funds or of investment management. Management style, the technique a manager applies to implement the invest-ment objective, provides another way.

Management style may have more to do with how your investment performs than you might think. Investors buy not only a fund, but a fund manager with distinct ideas on how to make money. As you might expect, the terminology used to describe investment objectives and man-agement styles overlaps considerably. The most common styles are: growth, value, balanced, and contrarian.

Growth managers look for companies with a history of reliable earn-ings growth and good prospects for continued growth. Indicators of continued earnings growth include: high-quality management initiatives, new-product development, and expansion of markets. A growth manager would approve of the solid record of expansion that Wal-Mart provides. Dreyfus Third Century Fund is managed with a growth style.

Value managers look more at a company's tangible assets than at its earnings stream. They seek companies whose merits might be over-looked by those focusing too closely on past earnings growth. A value manager might be drawn to Sears because of its vast real estate holdings. Real estate may not mean higher earnings, but its sale would generate a lot of money. The Calvert Social Investment Fund Equity Portfolio is managed with value investing in mind.

Both growth and value refer to ways of investing in stocks. Balanced managers invest in both stocks and bonds. After assessing the economy and predicting its course over the next several months, balanced-fund managers decide how much of their portfolios will be in which types of securities. The stock part may then be invested for value, growth, or in any other way. Balanced investment funds tend to be less volatile than stock funds. Including bonds means that the fund will do less well overall in good times and less poorly in bad times. Pax, Calvert, Citizens, and Green Century offer balanced funds.

The contrarian manager looks for sound securities that are out-of-favor, believing that when the market awakens, the fund will realize a gain. If everyone is selling a stock, the contrarian sees a chance to buy cheap. When bonds are unpopular, the contrarian buys them. When banks are failing, the contrarian buys them. The contrarian wins by being right when everyone else is wrong, so it is a high-risk strategy. The Parnassus Fund's objective is growth. Its manager, Jerry Dodson, is a contrarian.

BROAD MARKET BENCHMARKS

In addition to comparing numbers to a specific portfolio or a similar investment, investors look to the performance of "the market." "The market" usually refers to a benchmark, a measurement device like the Dow Jones Industrial Average. Narrow indexes, such as the Dow, are chiefly mood barometers. Broad gauges, such as the Standard & Poor's 500 or the Domini 400 Social Index, tell you how prices in a financial marketplace are moving. See Box 2-1 for a discussion of benchmarks.

The most widely used benchmarks are indexes, indicators of the up or down motion of the stock market, the bond market, or even the economy as a whole. For example, the U.S. Government's Index of Leading Economic Indicators measures the health of the economy in terms of motion. The Index consists of some statistics that have indicated trends in the economy: the cost of borrowing, the cost of fuel and job postings, among many.

A stock index is made up of a portfolio of stocks, just as a mutual fund is. And, like mutual funds that buy different securities, indexes behave differently from one another. Some indexes are more volatile than others, that is, they move up or down more quickly than other indexes. Box 2-2 takes a closer look at volatility.

Indexes that measure entire markets are called broad-market indexes. The best-known broad-market index is the Dow Jones Industrial Average (DJIA). Historically, this collection of thirty very large New York Stock Exchange (NYSE) companies reflected the U.S. stock market's mood pretty well, though it has not since 1991. Sophisticated market watchers argue that a more accurate reflection of the market of publicly traded stocks demands a larger basket (collection) of stocks. The Standard & Poor's 500 Composite Index, popularly called the "S&P 500," probably reflects the market of large capitalization stocks more truly than does the DJIA.

The DJIA and the S&P 500 are neither the only nor the broadest market indexes. The two most important of the very broad market gauges are the Russell 1000 and the Wilshire 5000. The broadest gauges will not work for most investors because they emphasize much smaller companies than those on the S&P 500. They also include a great many banks whose stocks rarely trade. So they are not representative of what investors buy. Most investors stick to companies that are of the S&P 500 class, if not on the S&P itself.

Sophisticated investors can now keep tabs on most market sectors by means of a specialized index. There are theories that you can predict market action by watching the different indexes and how they behave with regard to one another. For instance, the Dow Jones Utility Average (comprised of twenty gas and electric companies) is supposed to lead the DJIA and the S&P 500 by about six weeks. Another theory runs that the strongest markets begin with the DJIA doing better (in terms of percentage gain) than the other indexes.

Box 2-1. Benchmarks

The term *benchmark* originated with surveyors, who would mark a permanent landmark, whose position and altitude they knew, so that they could use it as a reference point. In finance, benchmarks serve similar functions: They mark a known position, and altitude is measured with reference to them.

Like so many terms that are borrowed by disciplines to which they are not native, *benchmark* comes from surveying with some ironies. Not the least of these is that a surveyor's benchmark today is a reference point that is—in terms of human existence—fixed and permanent. Over time, surveyors developed the practice of using rocks or making their own markers. When George Washington surveyed land bordering the Ohio River, many of his markers were trees. Floods, the river's changing course, and human development have limited the usefulness of these referents.

In finance and economics, benchmarks have always been relative and in some cases as ephemeral as trees in a flood plain. The value of currency units—the dollar, the pound, the yen—is always changing in reference to both themselves and one another. With inflation running at 3 percent, comparisons of price year to year must be computed to a common basis to have any meaning. Even when prices are adjusted to a common basis, the longer the comparison period, the less meaningful the comparison.

Success in financial performance is defined by matching the performance of the relevant market. Anything above that is excellent. *Forbes* recently implied that a money manager had done well by his clients whose annual return over five years ending on September 30, 1991, averaged 15.2 percent. The S&P 500 had averaged 14.7 percent per year.[9] Indeed for the first time since 1982, in 1991 a majority of equity mutual funds managers (55 percent) and equity managers generally (53 percent) outperformed the broad market indexes.[10]

THE DOMINI SOCIAL INDEX AND OTHER INDEXES

It had become clear to us in the mid-1980s that social investors needed benchmark indexes tailored to their requirements. Financial professionals needed a generally accepted definition of the universe (market) of

What people use money to buy also changes over time. Imagine trying to calibrate the buying power of a dollar before shoes and clothing began to be mass-produced (ca. 1840) to today's standard. Even over relatively short periods, benchmarks change. In 1970, solar-powered hand-held electronic calculators, car tape players, CD players, and VCRs were unknown. So, too, were some giants of today's financial indexes. See Table 2-4. Wal-Mart's shares were first sold to the public in 1970. In 1969 the government had begun the antitrust suit against AT&T that ended in 1982 in the creation of the Baby Bells (BellSouth, Bell Atlantic, Ameritech, Pacific Telesis, and Southwestern Bell). In 1970 Bill Gates had not yet started at Harvard, which he would leave at nineteen in 1974 to start Microsoft.

Depending on your point of view, *The Economist* may have either come up with the ultimate benchmark for our era or reduced the whole matter to an absurdity. Its "Big Mac Index" uses the price of the double burger to compare real currency exchange rates. As of a certain date, the Index might indicate a Big Mac cost, say, $1.49 in the U.S. and C$1.99 in Canada. Thus, the real exchange rate is what people can buy for their money rather than what they can sell it for at a currency exchange.

The funsters at the Union Bank of Switzerland have gone one step beyond *The Economist* by using the McDonald's staple to compare average weighted earnings around the world. Not long ago they calculated that it took eighteen minutes in Chicago to earn a Big Mac but nearly four hours in Mexico City.[8]

U.S. equities (common stocks) social investors could buy. In March 1988, we set out to address those needs. The result was a benchmark equities index, the Domini Social Index.[11]

Selecting the Screens.   Our first task was to identify the nonfinancial screens socially responsible investors imposed. Then we had to develop a universe that passed them. This process was more difficult than it sounds. Some social investors apply only one or two screens, not the ten we use—which are listed in Table 2-2. Others screen on issues we do not, such as Northern Ireland. And still others apply looser or stricter screens than we do. And, social screens are not static. We constantly reevaluate and revise them as investors redefine them.

We divide our screens into "exclusionary" and "qualitative" screens. Exclusionary screens came first historically and are the first screens we

---

Box 2-2. Risk and Volatility

Volatility in stock-price action or in a basket of stocks (index) is called *beta*. Higher betas (volatility) will be considered a risk by some, and a great deal of effort is put into studying whether the higher risk of certain portfolios is justified by higher total returns.

Keep the definition of financial risk in mind when we look at fiduciary duties later in this chapter.

One popular theory of making money is that an investor should diversify into a lot of companies so as to have a higher beta than the S&P 500. The economy will, over the years, expand. If the economy expands, then companies will grow and so will stock prices. Since a more volatile stock will go up faster than a less volatile one and since over the years the stock market will go up, a diversified portfolio with a higher beta will do better.

It says volumes about investing that risk is defined as volatility, which in turn is defined as variation from a specified benchmark. For instance, it explains the hoary joke about the broker who like all brokers was paid by commissions on his customers' transactions. He took a good customer to his yacht club, where he pointed out yachts owned by Mel at Merrill, Keith at Solly, Tim at Kidder, and so forth. Finally his guest exclaimed, "But, where are the customers' yachts?"

---

apply. They are also negative in that they eliminate companies involved in business or activities most social investors find unacceptable. Qualitative screens track corporate responses to the demands of today's society. And it is in these areas that the future of socially responsible investing lies. They are positive screens. They demand evaluations of what a company is doing to make society better.

Social researchers, like us, draw on a multitude of printed sources in deciding whether a company passes a particular screen. We also talk to the companies directly—and most are eager to talk to us. We draft our

TABLE 2-2. DOMINI SOCIAL INDEX SCREENS

Exclusionary Screens	Qualitative Screens
South Africa	Product Quality and Consumer Relations
Sin (alcohol, tobacco, gambling)	Environmental Performance
Military Weapons	Corporate Citizenship
Nuclear Weapons	Employee Relations

reports and ask the companies to review them. In some instances—as with American Express—we have had an extensive discussion with the company about our evaluation. We then make up our minds. We will discuss the details of the screening process in chapter 3 and the specific screens beginning in chapter 4.

Selecting the Stocks.   With the screens in place, choosing companies for the Domini Social Index (DSI) began. We conducted the selection process in three stages. In the first, we applied our screens to the S&P 500; about 255 companies (51 percent) passed. We then turned to small capitalization companies, like Ben & Jerry's Homemade and Isco whose social stories—and good financial performance—made them essential to a social index. There were about forty-five of these. Finally, we looked at companies not in the S&P 500 that were in the top 1,000 in terms of market capitalization and that were in business sectors in which the Index was underrepresented. (For example, our weapons and South Africa screens eliminated the big auto manufacturers, so we looked for auto-parts companies.) Of these, we kept about 100. It took twenty-six months to look at 1,000 companies, evaluate 800, and choose 400 with which to construct a sufficiently diversified, large capitalization portfolio.* We launched the DSI on May 1, 1990.

The S&P 500 was our starting point because it gauges the market of equities generally available to the largest institutions in the U.S. We wanted the broadest use of our Index, and since institutions own 53 percent of publicly traded stocks, we chose generally the size stocks they buy. Table 2-3 compares the twenty largest companies in the S&P 500 and the Domini 400.

The two indexes share 255 members, almost 64 percent of the DSI's constituents. As Table 2-4 shows, the DSI's financial characteristics closely resemble those of the S&P. The market-weighted average capitalization of the DSI is less than that of the S&P. However, at $12 billion, it is still sizable.

The DSI's returns have closely paralleled the S&P's—something we didn't anticipate in 1988. The variation in how the two behave come from their different industry weightings and the difference in the size of the companies comprising the indexes. See Figure 2-1.

When compared to the S&P 500, the DSI is underweighted in several industry segments (particularly oil companies, tobacco companies, and electric utilities). Several industries are overrepresented. The screens

---

*Those shocked by the attrition here should remember that people hire managers and buy mutual funds in order to limit the universe from which they might buy. Their objectives or philosophies tell the investor how they limit the universe of ten thousand publicly traded equities.

TABLE 2-3. TOP 20 FIRMS BY MARKET CAPITALIZATION
(As of August 31, 1992)

S&P 500	DSI 400
Exxon Corp.	Wal-Mart Stores
Philip Morris	Coca-Cola Co.
Wal-Mart Stores	Merck & Co., Inc.
General Electric Co.	Procter & Gamble Co.
American Telephone & Telegraph Co.	PepsiCo Inc.
Coca-Cola Co.	BellSouth Corp.
Merck & Co. Inc.	Amoco Corp.
Royal Dutch Petroleum Co.	Bell Atlantic Corp.
International Business Machines Corp.	American International Group
Procter & Gamble Co.	Microsoft Corp.
Bristol-Myers Squib Co.	Southwestern Bell Telephone
E.I. du Pont de Nemours & Co.	Ameritech Corp.
GTE Corp.	Atlantic Richfield Co.
Johnson & Johnson	Walt Disney Co.
PepsiCo Inc.	Federal National Mortgage
Amoco Corp.	Pacific Telesis Group
Mobil Corp.	Home Depot
BellSouth Corp.	U S West Inc.
Chevron Corp.	McDonald's Corp.
Pfizer, Inc.	BankAmerica

Companies italicized in the S&P column are also in the DSI.
Source: Kinder, Lydenberg, Domini & Co., Inc., August 31, 1992.

TABLE 2-4. THE DSI AND THE S&P 500: FINANCIAL CHARACTERISTICS
(As of September 30, 1992)

	DSI 400	S&P 500
Average Market Capitalization (000,000)	$ 16,161	$ 21,855
Asset Growth*	12.28%	10.87%
Earnings Growth*	15.04%	13.36%
P/E Ratio	21.47	22.01
Dividend Yield	2.31%	3.02%
Dividend payout*	39.91%	47.46%
Price/Book ratio	2.49	2.23
Return on Equity*	21.78%	19.57%
Beta*	1.07	1.00
% NYSE	89.06%	96.36%
% NASDAQ	9.82%	3.36%
% Other	1.12%	0.28%

*Trailing five-year averages.
Source: Kinder, Lydenberg, Domini & Co., Inc., September 30, 1992.

favored firms whose business franchises depend on public goodwill, such as retail stores, insurers, and telephone companies.

There is a considerable difference in the size of the indexes when calculated in terms of the constituent companies' market capitalization—their market price times the number of shares outstanding. The S&P is over 35 percent larger than the DSI. Nonetheless, like the S&P, the DSI is probably best thought of as a large capitalization index. The S&P 400 Mid-Cap Index is about a third smaller in market capitalization than the DSI.

A recently published study by U.S. Trust Company of Boston comparing screened model portfolios to the S&P 500 produced similar results.

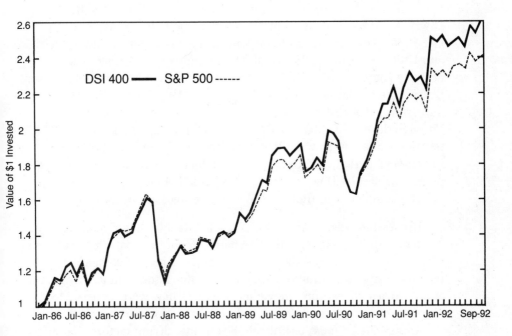

FIGURE 2-1. DSI PERFORMANCE SINCE JANUARY 1, 1986

The data for the period January 1, 1986, to May 1, 1990, represent the results of backtests, the use of computer modeling to analyze how a portfolio might have performed in the past. Backtesting becomes increasingly unreliable the farther into the past you go. Issuers disappear into their parents or return to being private. You may either make assumptions about what would have been in the portfolio and reconstruct it, or you may test the remaining companies without replacement. The dangers of the former are self-evident. Most people choose the latter. We felt 1985 marked the outer limit of reliability. So, the backtested figures for the DSI do not include the early 1980s bear market. Definitive studies on the performance of screened portfolios cannot be done until we have data for a full market cycle—from boom to bust to boom again.

Source: Kinder, Lydenberg, Domini & Co., Inc., September 30, 1992.

They applied five screens—South Africa, weapons, environment, labor relations, and undesirable products—to the S&P 500 from 1979 through 1989. U.S. Trust then reconstituted and reweighed the S&P, drawing new companies that passed the screens from the top one thousand in market capitalization. Over the eleven-year period, the average return of the screened list exceeded the S&P by 0.1 percent.[12]

OTHER SRI BENCHMARKS

The Domini Social Index is not the only SRI equity benchmark. The others represent different approaches from ours.

Good Money Averages.   Good Money in Worcester, Vermont, was the first firm to offer a social-investment index. Professor Ritchie P. Lowry of Boston College constructed the Good Money Averages in the late 1970s. They are meant to be comparable to the Dow Jones Industrial and Utilities Averages. The Good Money Industrial Average is made up of thirty companies. Its Utilities Average consists of fifteen. As Professor Lowry noted in his book, *Good Money,* since 1976 his two averages have outperformed their Dow Jones cognates in both bull and bear markets.[13] Through the end of 1991, the Good Money Utilities Average was up 244.6 percent while the Dow Utilities was up 108.7 percent. For the same fifteen-year period, the Good Money Industrial Average was up 688.9 percent while the Dow Industrial was up 215.4 percent.[14]

The companies in the Good Money Averages are listed in Table 2-5.

The Ex-Indexes.   An ex-index is the S&P 500, the Financial Times Actuaries All-Share Index (the All-Share), or another major market index stripped of an industry—like tobacco—or a category of companies—like military weapons contractors. Ex-indexes came into prominence with the South Africa divestiture movement, when they were constructed to illustrate divestiture's effects on large capitalization portfolios.

An ex-index's most useful role lies in identifying factors that affect the behavior of the base index. By eliminating companies that exhibit certain characteristics and testing the performance of the remaining stocks, you learn how the eliminated companies affected the index's performance. Factor analysis has practical applications, as well. Portfolio managers often use it to determine whether their holdings are, say, overly loaded with companies whose performance depends on interest rates. Managers will adjust their portfolios to reflect their opinions of how interest rate–sensitive stocks will do.

The ex-indexes cannot function as measures of the performance of socially screened portfolios—much less as indications of future perform-

TABLE 2-5. COMPANIES IN THE GOOD MONEY AVERAGES

COMPANIES ON THE GOOD MONEY INDUSTRIAL AVERAGE	COMPANIES ON THE GOOD MONEY UTILITY AVERAGE
Ametek Inc.	CILCORP Inc.
Blockbuster Entertainment	Citizens Utilities Co.
Consolidated Papers	Consolidated Natural Gas Co.
A.T. Cross Co.	Hawaiian Electric Industries, Inc.
Cummins Engine	Idaho Power Co.
Dayton Hudson	LG&E Energy
First Virginia Banks	Magma Power Co.
Flight Safety International	Montana Power Co.
Hartmarx Corp.	NIPSCO Industries
Hershey Foods Corp.	Oklahoma Gas & Electric Co.
Johnson & Johnson	Southwestern Public Service Co.
Maytag	Otter Tail Power Co.
McDonalds Corp.	Southwest Gas Corp.
Melville Corp.	UtiliCorp United Inc.
Merck & Co., Inc.	United Water Resources Inc.
Herman Miller	Minnesota Mining & Manufacturing Co.
Pitney Bowes	
Polaroid Corp.	
Procter & Gamble Co.	
Rouse Co.	
Stride Rite Corp.	
Student Loan Marketing Association (Sallie Mae)	
U S West Inc.	
Volvo	
Washington Post	
Worthington Industries, Inc.	
Zurn Industries	

These companies comprised the two averages on September 25, 1992.
Source: Reprinted by permission of Good Money Publications, Inc.

ance. Their formulators have not added back in stocks of similar quality and market-capitalization. The S&P 500 is a composite of fifty-nine subindexes, each of which is weighted to reflect the sector it represents. The whole is intended to represent the entire market of large capitalization stocks.[15] The validity of S&P 500 ex-indexes as entities on their own is therefore dubious.

PanAgora Asset Management's Boston SAFE Index may be the best-known South Africa–free index.* Started in 1986, the Boston SAFE

---

*Wells Fargo and Brian Rom, a New York investment adviser, also have widely quoted South Africa–free ex-indexes.

Index is an ex-index based on the S&P 500. PanAgora added back S&P companies as they left South Africa. By 1992, the index was coming fairly close to replicating the S&P. It is now a historical artifact. PanAgora stopped publishing it in August 1992.

In 1991 Prudential Securities launched a new set of S&P 500 ex-indexes it calls benchmark portfolios.[16] Of the nine portfolios, which are listed in Table 2-6, the first two are South Africa screened, with the Principles Signers being a significantly less rigorous screen than the South Africa-free screen. (See the discussion of the Sullivan Principles in chapter 1.) The organized-labor screen eliminates S&P 500 companies on the AFL-CIO boycott list. "Sin-Stock-Free" means no alcohol, tobacco, or gaming, so "Cigarette-Stock-Free" is a less rigorous screen. Similarly, the weapons contractor screen is less restrictive than the defense contractors screen because there are fewer of them in the S&P 500. The ex-top 100 defense contractors portfolio itself eliminates only the fifty-five companies on the Defense Department's top 100 list that are in the S&P 500.[17]

The Prudential Ex-Toxic Emitters Portfolio points up another problem with some ex-indexes. Prudential modifies this portfolio each year when the U.S. Environmental Protection Agency issues new data from the Toxic Release Inventory. (The Inventory is described in chapter 6.) In September 1992, for instance, Prudential added ten companies to this portfolio and deleted ten others. Added were companies like Chrysler and Texaco; excluded were companies like Georgia-Pacific and Chevron.[18] Twenty company swings—especially when virtually all the firms affected are giants—make it very difficult to compare this portfolio against itself over time, much less against the S&P 500.

In 1992 Prudential applied the same screens to the S&P Mid-Cap.[19] The Prudential model portfolios, of which there are now eighteen, confirm what instinct might tell you: You can devise more or less strict negative screens using available lists, and sometimes these screens may affect relative performance—if you do not reconstitute and reweight the index to compensate for industry exposures. Since most socially respon-

TABLE 2-6. THE PRUDENTIAL PORTFOLIOS

South Africa–Free	Ex-Top 100 Weapons Contractors
Principles Signers	Organized Labor Screen
"Sin" Stock–Free	Ex-EPA Violators and Nuclear Utilities
Cigarette Stock–Free	Ex-Toxic Emitters
Ex-Top 100 Defense Contractors	

Prudential Securities maintains an ex-index for each of these headings based on the Standard & Poor's Composite Index (S&P 500) and the Standard & Poor's Mid-Cap 400.

sible investors apply at least two screens, single-issue model portfolios do not reveal much about performance of social portfolios generally. Indeed, portfolios are commonly screened in all of Prudential's issue areas at significantly more rigorous levels than these ex-indexes. If reconstituted indexes, such as the DSI, do well despite what the ex-indexes reveal to be tough odds, social investors have a strong incentive to look beyond purely negative screening.

U.K. Indexes.   In 1988 a leading London social-research house, EIRIS, and the U.S. consulting firm BARRA devised eight ex-index portfolios based on the Financial Times Actuaries All-Share Index of the stocks traded on the London Stock Exchange. The portfolios included: three South Africa–screened portfolios; a nuclear weapons–screened portfolio; a tobacco-screened portfolio; a nuclear power–screened portfolio; a banking and insurance screened portfolio; and a South Africa–nuclear weapons–tobacco screened portfolio. The portfolios were backtested. EIRIS's portfolios performed like the All-Share Index from October 1983 through October 1988 even though in some cases up to half the market in terms of market value was excluded.[20]

A 1992 BARRA-EIRIS study using a somewhat different set of model portfolios reached very different results. All of the portfolios save one (ex-political contributors) substantially underperformed the All-Share between January 1988 and October 1991.[21]

Benchmarks SRI Needs.   Despite the growing number of social investing benchmarks, more are needed. No one is systematically screening nonequity issuers and reporting the results. Debt—especially non-U.S. issues—has become important with the internationalization of our financial markets. Also, there is no socially screened international benchmark index because no service applies standardized screens to a significant transnational universe. Social investors need this now.

However, from our perspective as a social researchers, we don't believe we in the U.S. know enough about companies domiciled outside the U.S., Canada, and the U.K. to screen them. And we're not optimistic that sufficient information will either come from the companies or be developed independently any time soon. We will talk more about the problems of international investing in chapter 12.

SCREENS AND YOUR WEALTH

Over the last three years we have looked closely at the Domini Social Index and at other benchmarks and performance studies. Our studies yield no indication that broad social screening leads to underperformance. A manager who chooses stocks from a universe such as ours should look to his or her selections—not the screens—for an explanation of underperformance. The argument against screening presumes the manager's ability to pick winners in off-limits industries, such as nuclear utilities. But increasing the size of a universe of stocks does nothing to increase the manager's skills in picking winners and losers. These skills are in short supply.

We are not alone in drawing this conclusion. For instance, the 1989 Annual Review of the Charity Service of the World Markets Company (WM) reports the results of a study of its accounts with social constraints. World Markets, an international investment performance and consulting firm that measures £3.7 billion of charity funds, concluded:

> Ethical constraints in their own right seem to have little impact on the performance of the Constrained universe other than through the small company/large company effect. The performance of actual funds indicates that other factors, such as stock selection, can more than offset these constraints.
>
> At an extreme level of constraint, where a significant number of large companies are excluded, a very large fund may find difficulties with liquidity, but in practice this is unlikely to arise.
>
> In general the message seems to be that constraints do not damage your wealth.[22]

FIDUCIARY DUTIES AND THE PRUDENT PERSON

Individual investors and the people who manage their money are not the only persons concerned with the performance of screened investments. Indeed for another group, persons entrusted with other people's money—fiduciaries*—performance balanced against safety defines their duties. A full discussion of a fiduciary's duties as they relate to social investment is beyond our scope. However, you should understand the basic framework within which they are defined because much of the debate about socially responsible investing centers on issues of fiduciary responsibility.

A fiduciary acts for *another's* benefit. The "other" is the beneficiary. Suppose a woman establishes a trust to pay her grandchildren's college expenses. The assets transferred to the trust make up the trust's principal. The trustee, who actually has title to the property, is

---

*"Fiduciary" comes from a Latin verb meaning "to trust" and is related to the Latin word for "faith." Hence, a fiduciary is a person you can trust to act in good faith.

a fiduciary. The grandchildren are the beneficiaries. And, the grand-mother is the settlor or grantor. Suppose a college has an endowment. The board of trustees would be responsible for its management. The board members are fiduciaries.

For more than 160 years, a paragraph from a decision of Massachusetts' Supreme Judicial Court has defined a fiduciary's duties:

> All that can be required of a trustee to invest is, that he shall conduct himself faithfully and exercise a sound discretion. He is to observe how men of prudence, discretion and intelligence manage their own affairs, not in regard to speculation, but in regard to the permanent disposition of their funds, considering the probable income, as well as the probable safety of the capital to be invested.[23]

While fiduciaries may phrase their questions about socially responsible investing in the elaborate terms used by *Harvard College* v. *Amory,* what they are really asking is, "Can we be sued for doing this?" Any lawyer would answer, "It depends." One set of fiduciary duties* does not apply to all situations. The answers to the following questions can affect a fiduciary's responsibilities.

- Who are the fiduciaries holding the money for?
- With what ultimate objective are they investing it?
- For what purpose was this money put aside?
- Who gets hurt if the fiduciaries lose money?
- Who has the ultimate responsibility for investment decisions?

For advocates of socially responsible investing, the important question is the first: Who are the beneficiaries? The answer determines which fiduciary duties apply, which in turn define how the trustees must handle the trust's assets.

Those asset management duties significantly change the terms of the debate over whether trustees may engage in socially responsible investing. We believe that an examination of the trust's social and ethical obligations should always be at the core of the resolution of this debate as to a particular trust. However, a court will look at the resolution from the perspective of a fiscal disaster—one that has occurred, one that threatens, or one that was conjured up behind a fevered legal brow. A disaster that someone with a bit less than 20-20 hindsight could see coming all the way can mean large financial penalties for trustees and

---

*Fiduciary duties are ones relating to property that the law interprets very strictly in favor of the interests of the person for whose benefit the fiduciary holds it. Not all relationships in which one person holds another's property are fiduciary. If you find a bicycle and take it home, you have an obligation of ordinary care.

their insurers. Prospective liability makes most fiduciaries cautious
which is why you are supposed to be able to trust them in the first place.

Today, the classification of a trustee's duties as to the trust assets
determines the outcome of a debate over social investing. Under the
Clinton administration, we hope that the results will become uniformly
favorable.

STANDARDS APPLIED TO FIDUCIARIES

Where investments are concerned, fiduciary duties are usually catego-
rized according to the laws that define them. These are: the prudent-
person (or investor) rule; the business-judgment rule; and the Employee
Retirement Income Security Act of 1974 (ERISA). Unlike the Ten Com-
mandments, these laws are not short; a modern formulation of the
prudent-person rule runs 100 pages. Nor are they straightforward; ERISA
is widely believed to be the most complex, confusing, and contradictory
statute ever enacted by Congress.

The Prudent-Person Rule.   The "prudent-person" or "prudent-
investor" rule is the rule of *Harvard College* v. *Amory* which we quoted
at the beginning of this section. In general, it applies to persons who
manage money for the benefit of a person or persons (as opposed to a
library). The custodian for a child, the guardian of a severely ill person,
or a trustee named in a trust would be expected to run the funds the way
persons "of prudence, discretion, and intelligence manage their own
affairs."

The prudent person is an ideal, and the courts have held fiduciaries
to what amounts to a "perfect-person" standard. To avoid judicial second guessing, fiduciaries have found conservatism and the tried and true
to be the safest investment practices. Fiduciaries, if not the courts, have
defined a prudent investment as one that preserved capital with as little
risk as possible. They have traditionally believed that if they did not lose
money, they were all right, since courts have the power to force trustees
to reimburse beneficiaries for losses. The advent of permanent inflation
in the 1960s has forced a reappraisal of what it means to preserve capital,
but the basic attitude remains.

The Business-Judgment Rule.   When fiduciaries—especially the
boards of small not-for-profit institutions—do not know which standard
of care governs their conduct, usually the answer to the question, "For
what purpose was the money put aside?" resolves everything. In a
not-for-profit corporation, the people who call themselves trustees are in

fact the governing board. Examples might include a food coop or a trade association. For them, the appropriate standard is not the prudent-person rule, but the business-judgment rule.

The business-judgment rule holds that members of the board will not be held liable for actions they took with due care and in good faith. Unlike the prudent-person rule, the business-judgment rule does not hold the fiduciary to a nearly superhuman ability to avoid losses. So long as they act after carefully considering their decision and so long as the procedure and the action are not tainted by, say, self-dealing, the fiduciary will not be responsible for the not-for-profit's losses.

The acid test of liability under the business-judgment rule is whether the action furthered the purpose for which the board holds the funds. Social investment advocates point to this standard and to the state statute that governs the actions of boards of not-for-profit corporations as indications that investments with social criteria may in fact be *more* appropriate than conventional ones. For example, a religious order with a central commitment to bringing peace to humankind should not hold stock in a weapons manufacturer such as General Dynamics.

ERISA.   The Employee Retirement Income Security Act of 1974 (ERISA) applies to pension funds sponsored by a private-sector employer. The ERISA standard for trustees of pensions subject to the act has been described as a "prudent-expert" standard.[24] A fiduciary must administer a pension plan "with care, skill, prudence and diligence under the circumstances then prevailing that a prudent man acting in a like capacity and familiar with such matters would use in the conduct of an enterprise of a like character and with like aims."[25] The ERISA standard's stringency and the opposition of regulators with direct and indirect authority over these pensions have made trustees extremely reluctant to venture into socially responsible investing.

At this point, private trustees and others subject to prudent-person standards do not rely on ERISA as a standard. Still, some fiduciaries believe that ERISA previews the general trust law of the future. However, democratic administrators in the Departments of Labor and the Treasury could change their interpretations of the ERISA standard to make it consistent with the standards applying to other fiduciaries.

THE DEBATE OVER SRI

For a generation Richard Posner has argued for approaching law from the standpoint of economics. His approach has made him a leader of conservative legal thinkers. Formerly a law professor at the University of Chicago, he now sits on the U.S. Court of Appeals in Chicago. In 1980, while still teaching, he coauthored a highly influential law-journal article on social investing and fiduciary duties. In it, he defined social investing as:

> excluding the securities of . . . otherwise attractive companies from an investor's portfolio because the companies are judged to be socially irresponsible, and including the securities of . . . otherwise unattractive companies because they are judged to be behaving in a socially laudable way.[26]

Posner's definition of social investing can lead to only one conclusion. And he reached it. "[A] trustee who sacrifices the beneficiary's financial well-being for any other object breaches both his duty of loyalty to the beneficiary and his duty of prudence in investment."[27] Well, who can disagree with that? But, social investing does not require a fiduciary to breach either duty.

As we have seen, a body of data exists that Posner could not have had in 1980, when modern social investing was in its infancy. Even then, Posner grudgingly admitted, "there is no reason to expect a portfolio constructed in accordance with the usual principles of social investment to yield a below average return."[28] In this he was correct.

Then-Professor Posner tacitly acknowledged that outside of ERISA his negative view of social investing was already a minority position.[29] Indeed, Harvard professor Austin Scott, the most respected trusts scholar of his generation, had entered the fray on the side of social investing two years earlier, in 1978.

Scott was unequivocal: In the investment decision-making process, trustees subject to the prudent-person rule may consider a corporation's social performance. Trustees may reject corporations "whose activities . . . are contrary to fundamental and generally accepted ethical principles. They may consider such matters as pollution, race discrimination, fair employment, and consumer responsibility."[30]

The law of trusts, until recently, was defined by the common law; that is, by the decisions of judges rather than by legislative acts. Over the years scholars such as Professor Scott have worked to compile the common law into what are called "Restatements." These extremely influential volumes have succeeded in making the common law more uniform from state to state. In 1990 the *Restatement (Third) of Trusts* noted that under its prudent-investor (person) rule a trustee may not advance his or her personal views concerning social issues or causes in managing investments. But, "such considerations . . . may properly influence the investment decisions of a trustee to the extent permitted by the terms of the trust or by the consent of the beneficiaries."[31]

THE QUESTION OF PRUDENCE

The *Restatement* should put to rest legal objections to social investing in the private trust arena. What it does not address are practical issues of prudence: How does a trustee implement social guidelines? What are the standards against which the trustee must evaluate an investment decision?

That brings us to *Board of Trustees v. Baltimore.*[32] In 1989 the Baltimore City Council had adopted an ordinance that required its four pension funds to divest themselves of securities of companies doing business in South Africa. The ordinance gave the trustees the discretion to cease divesting for an unlimited number of ninety-day periods, if they found divestiture imprudent under the circumstances.

The trustees sued to have the ordinance declared unconstitutional. The ground cited was impairment of contract, the adoption of a law that materially alters an existing contractual obligation. The trustees argued that divestiture might cost them so much that they could not pay the pensions—the beneficiaries. The trustees lost. Maryland's highest court held that a trustee's duty is not necessarily to maximize the return on investments but rather to secure a "just or reasonable" return while avoiding undue risk. The court quoted approvingly a commentator who noted, "A trustee is under no duty to open a brothel in Nevada where prostitution is legal in order to maximize return to beneficiaries."[33] The court concluded: "Thus, if . . . social investment yields economically competitive returns at a comparable level of risk, the investment should not be deemed imprudent."[34]

The court further held that trustees could incur additional costs in order to implement a social investment policy. The maximum costs the plaintiffs had proven were minimal, in the court's view:[35] an initial cost of $750,000 (one-sixteenth of 1 percent of the funds' value) and afterward $1.2 million per year (one-tenth of 1 percent of the funds' value).[36]

The Maryland court's opinion has not swayed the Internal Revenue Service, which has signaled its unwillingness to countenance "social investing" criteria in pension plans subject to ERISA. The IRS now views with disfavor pension funds whose trustees may make investment decisions based on "continuing job security of company employees and future employment opportunities," as well as investments "in projects providing community and social benefits but at a rate of return lower than market rates."[37] The IRS did not have the question of screening a portfolio before it.

CHOOSING TO LIMIT RETURN

In some very particular and limited circumstances, fiduciaries may choose social investment vehicles that they know will produce significantly less than a market rate of return. Most community-based investments fall into this category. However, individuals who have control over their own money may freely make the choice to earn less than the maximum they might. As Joan Shapiro, senior vice president of South Shore Bank of Chicago and of its holding company, Shorebank Corporation, has said, "Every socially responsible investment portfolio must include community investments. We SRI investors must apply the same standards of accountability to our investments as to corporations' investments."[38]

The choice to limit investment returns on a part of the assets one controls in exchange for high and immediate social impact is an increasingly attractive one to social investors. The person who chooses to buy a three-year certificate of deposit from South Shore (a bank with a remarkable community-development record) may not get as good an interest rate as would have come from a corporate bond coming due in three years. However, the investor will be an important part of Shorebank's effort to revitalize its neighborhoods.

An increasing number of farsighted fiduciaries recognize that they are being prudent if they are acting consistently with the purposes for which the institution was established. For example, faith-based institutions and those created to alleviate human hardships extend their mission by investing in community development opportunities, a subject we will discuss in chapter 7.

Defined-benefit pension funds are somewhat constrained in doing community investing. Their trustees must make the highest financial return that they can. However, even these funds have found that they can structure community investments to meet both their financial needs and high social betterment goals. The New York City Employee Retirement System (NYCERS) program creates hundreds of units of low-income and affordable housing within the city each year.

It is only with community-development investments that the investor should accept below-market returns. Screening for social criteria when picking stocks or bonds need not result in low returns. In 1984, when we wrote our first book, we could only assert that socially responsible investing would not damage your wealth. Today the Domini Social Index and studies based on real performance seem to be proving us right.

Now the question for individuals and institutions alike is, "What *ought* we to do with our money?" Since the answer is a matter of conscience, we can't supply it. What we will do in the next eight chapters is to illustrate how moral choices can be implemented through screening and how these choices impact society.

3

Screening: Separating the Good from the Not-So-Good

NOT LONG AGO AN ADVISER COULD SAY to a client who suggested social screens, "You tell me what companies not to buy, and I won't. But don't expect me to track them down." Today the competition for business is such that even advisers opposed to the concept of social investing will not refuse to do the research. In early 1992, *NBC Nightly News* did a feature on socially responsible investing. They looked for someone who would appear on camera to criticize the practice but couldn't find anyone who would.[1] Now, this does not mean that the field or the people in it are perfect. It means that social investing has arrived as a major factor in financial services.

This chapter briefly introduces the mechanics of the social-screening process. In the chapters that follow we will explore the substance of the main screens and how they affect your choices of companies. We will also look at how social investing has affected companies.

FROM BELIEF TO SCREEN

Socially responsible investing is the incorporation of ethical or moral criteria into the investment decision-making process. Socially responsible investors translate their ethical and moral concerns into screens—financial and nonfinancial criteria applied by investors to companies being considered for an investment or a loan.

A social screen alone, such as operations in South Africa, may exclude a company from your consideration. But passing a social screen should never be the sole ground for investing: An investment *must* make financial sense. Social screens must *always* be integrated with financial screens. However, in this book we do not look at financial criteria, except peripherally. Our goal is to enable you to articulate your nonfinancial criteria so that you can implement them in your financial decision making.

DEVELOPING SCREENS

Social screens express an investor's often highly nuanced objectives. Many of these objectives cannot be expressed in numbers, calculations, or formulas—the common ways of stating financial screens. They must be simple enough so that an adviser, who knows less about the client's specific concerns than the client, can implement them. For example, you might define your environmental screen as follows:

I want to invest in companies that:

- provide innovative and forward-looking solutions for aspects of environmental problems through products, processes, and services, or
- demonstrate their commitment to conduct themselves within or above generally accepted environmental standards.

I do not want to invest in companies whose practices fall below generally accepted environmental standards.[2]

As clear and well stated as that screen is, it provides little guidance to an investment adviser about what you might accept. You and your adviser will have to define specific boundaries within your screen. And it is especially important that the results reflect the spirit of your efforts.

Begin the process by asking a series of questions. How do you want to treat companies in the business of cleaning up pollution? What if a company such as Browning-Ferris also has environmental negatives, such as nontechnical violations of waste-handling regulations? Another tough area for many investors is natural resource companies. Some investors believe that a socially responsible natural resource company is an oxymoron. But firms such as Consolidated Papers have strong positive qualities. (In the Appendix you will find the criteria we apply to companies when we evaluate them.)

Most SRI advisers have a statement of the screens they use. One of us, Amy Domini, argues that she also has social-criteria standards and

TABLE 3-1. U.S. SRI MUTUAL FUNDS: EXCLUSIONARY SCREENS

Fund	Exclusionary Screens
Calvert-Ariel Appreciation Fund	South Africa Weapons Nuclear Power
Calvert Social Investment Funds	South Africa Weapons Nuclear Power
Calvert World Values Global Equity Fund	South Africa Weapons Nuclear Power Polluters Alcohol; Tobacco
Covenant Investment Management	Covenant rates the behavior of the 1,000 largest U.S. companies. The fund is based upon the 200 companies who rate the highest. No company is automatically excluded based upon any single criteria.
Domini Social Index Trust	Weapons Tobacco; Alcohol; Gambling Nuclear Power South Africa
Dreyfus Third Century	South Africa Allows Weapons Investment
Green Century Balanced Fund	Poor Environmental Record Nuclear Energy Nuclear Manufacturing and Equipment Nuclear Weapons South Africa Tobacco
Muir California Tax-Free Fund	Junk Bonds Nuclear Power Short-Term Solutions or Low-Priority Needs
New Alternatives	Nuclear Power South Africa Weapons
Parnassus Fund	Alcohol; Tobacco; Gambling Weapons Nuclear Power South Africa
Pax World Fund	Weapons Production Alcohol; Gambling; Tobacco Nuclear Power South Africa
Rightime Social Awareness Fund	South Africa Weapons

TABLE 3-1.—continued

Fund	Exclusionary Screens
Schield Progressive Environmental Fund Working Assets Common Holdings	EPA Violators/Polluters South Africa Military Contractors Nuclear Power Pollution and Environmental Violations Labor Violations Poor Equal Opportunity Record including Sexual Orientation Screen Alcohol; Tobacco Israeli Boycott Exportation of U.S. Banned Agricultural Chemicals Animal Testing AFL-CIO do not Patronize

Source: Social Investment Forum, prepared from Fund Prospectuses, July 1992.

that not to state them for the client would be misleading. "As a trustee, my clients need to know that weapons manufacturers do not pass my screens. I am never, under any circumstances, going to know whether or not Lockheed is a good purchase, because I am never going to look at it." Amy and many other professionals will allow a client to be more strict or more comprehensive than she is, but not less.

All the SRI mutual funds have written statements of their screens. These can serve as models for the investor. See Tables 3-1 and 3-2 for which funds screen on which issues.

If an adviser or a mutual fund's social screens are not a perfect match, social investors usually take a "better than" approach: It is better than not screening to invest in a socially responsible mutual fund with standards that are slightly off. At least your investments are standing for something. At least the adviser to that mutual fund is clearly committed to SRI, and at least the ongoing dialogue between SRI advisers and corporations is strengthened by your contribution.

If, however, you are working out your own set of social screens, you can start with a clean slate and come up with anything. The criteria in Appendix A are quite standard. Getting to the point of being able to address issues need not be an agonizing process. But it does take seven steps.

1. You articulate a clear and comprehensive statement of your social concerns. At this point, you should not be "realistic" and try to

TABLE 3-2. U.S. SRI MUTUAL FUNDS: QUALITATIVE SCREENS

Fund	Qualitative Screens
Calvert-Ariel Appreciation Fund	Environmentally Sound
	Companies with secure market segments and strong reputations with customers, competitors, and employees.
Calvert Social Investment Funds	Environmental Protection
	Employee Relations
	Women and Minority Advancement
	Product Safety
Calvert World Values Global Equity Fund	Environmental Protection
	Environmental Soundness
	Human Rights
	Health Care
Covenant Investment Management	Company Behavior in the Community
	Product Quality and Safety Record
	Environmental Record
	Employee relations record, including equal opportunity for women and minorities.
	Behavior with respect to employees, shareholders, customers, competitors, suppliers.
	Involvement in social issues such as, but not limited to, South Africa, Northern Ireland, and the defense industry.
Domini Social Index Trust	Product Quality
	Environment
	Corporate Citizenship
	Employee Relations
	Women and Minorities
Dreyfus Third Century	Environmental Protection
	Occupational Health and Safety
	Equal Employment Opportunity
Green Century Balanced Fund	Environmentally Sound Companies
Muir California Tax-Free Fund	Environment
	Education
	Housing
New Alternatives	Alternative Energy
	Environmental Protection
	Resource Recovery
Parnassus Fund	Out of favor companies with quality products, employee relations, community participation, progressive and enlightened management.
	Opportunities for Women and Minorities
Pax World Fund	Life-Support Products and Services

TABLE 3-2.—continued

Fund	Qualitative Screens
	Equal Opportunity for Women and Minorities
	Pollution Control
	Some International Development
Rightime Social Awareness Fund	Employee Relations
	Corporate Citizenship
	Alternative Energy
	Environmental Practices
Schield Progressive Environmental Fund	Environmental Protection
	Environmentally Sound
	Alternative Energy
Working Assets Common Holdings	Affordable Housing
	Equal Opportunity
	Education
	Farming
	Small Business
	Charitable Contributions
	Economic Development
	Environment, Conservation, and Renewable Energy

Source: Social Investment Forum, prepared from Fund Prospectuses, July 1992.

guess what screens would be "reasonable." Simply say what is in your heart.

2. The adviser drafts screens, which you review and refine.
3. With a draft in place, the adviser applies the screens to your portfolio or a list of suggested companies.
4. You and the adviser discuss the companies that are borderline. This discussion should refine the screens and show how they will work in practice.
5. The results of the screening become the basis for deciding whether the screens are too restrictive or too lax. At this point you may have to make hard choices about the rigor of the screens if they too greatly restrict the investment universe.
6. The adviser formulates the final screens and begins implementing them, with your approval.
7. Thereafter, once a year, you and the adviser should review the screens to make sure they still reflect your objectives.

This process should minimize the chances of mistakes. For example, an environmental group gave its adviser a list of the kinds of industries it wanted to avoid. It had no further discussions about its screens. Later the group objected when its adviser bought Eastman Kodak stock for its portfolio. Because it had not articulated screens that covered the types of pollution problems Kodak had, its adviser had felt free to buy the stock. This kind of problem will arise when advisers and clients do not discuss the spirit of the screen.

Screens can be idiosyncratic. The Church Commissioners of England, who administer £2.65 billion for the Church of England, eliminate companies whose main business is newspapers because "many newspapers are associated . . . with a particular party or political view."[3] However, this chapter and the book as a whole focus on the screens for the Domini Social Index, which are intended to represent the mainstream of social investment.

THE UNIVERSE AND BUY LISTS

The screening process usually begins with the financial vehicles an investor already holds or that an investment advisor recommends. Even the largest institutional investors and money managers consider investments in only a small percentage of the issuers of publicly traded securities.

In the United States, mutual funds number at least three thousand. Over ten thousand companies' common stock trades on public exchanges. At least that many companies (with some overlap) issue publicly traded bonds or commercial paper. Perhaps fifty thousand government units issue bonds. These make up the universe of investments available to most investors. Obviously, it is not practical to work with, say, thirty thousand investment possibilities. The most common way of limiting that number is by doing business with an investment adviser.

An investment adviser is a person in the business of advising others on how to allocate their assets, and particularly whether to buy, sell, or hold securities. An adviser may deal directly with clients or indirectly with the public through a newsletter. Investors seek advisers to clarify their options, to present them with choices consistent with their financial and social objectives, which the adviser has used successfully before. The range of investments, including securities, from which the adviser draws recommendations makes up his or her investment universe. The investments that an adviser has researched and recommends routinely make up a buy list.

Often the number and types of vehicles in an adviser's buy list vary with the amount of assets the adviser has under management. The largest institutional investors may have five or six hundred companies on their buy lists. An individual financial planner may work with perhaps fifteen or twenty mutual funds.

In the last chapter we noted a common objection to socially responsible investing: "If you limit your adviser's universe (and therefore buy list), you limit his or her capacity to make you money." We've seen that limiting universes does not necessarily limit return. But if you have an adviser who specializes in defense stocks, your military-weapons screen is going to affect your adviser's universe, perhaps not to your financial benefit. Therefore, the argument, while not true in the abstract, can be true in the particular. Choose your adviser with that in mind.

PUBLICLY TRADED COMPANIES

A publicly traded company is one whose securities may change hands on an exchange and are therefore registered with the Securities and Exchange Commission (SEC). Most social investors have some of their money in either publicly traded securities or mutual funds made up of these securities. The same screens and screening techniques apply in both instances. Usually screens—but not the techniques—can be applied to companies that are not publicly traded. The Vermont National Bank Socially Responsible Banking Fund applies essentially the same screens to its investments and its potential borrowers.

The differences in the screening techniques for publicly traded and nonpublicly traded corporations lie primarily in the greater availability of information on the former.

The United States has the most stringent—and stringently enforced—reporting requirements for publicly traded corporations. A corporation's public documents—its annual report, its Securities and Exchange Commission Annual Report on Form 10-K, its proxy statement, and its quarterly reports to shareholders mark the starting point in researching companies. But much of what one learns about a particular company comes from reading general literature. We've found relevant information magazines ranging from *Archaeology* to *Sky & Telescope*.

"Once a company goes off your list for social reasons, can it ever come back?" Every social researcher has heard that question. In general the answer is yes. We review the companies in our universe at least annually. Each case of a nonqualifying company is unique. Consider Armstrong World Industries. As of 1990, some 57,000 persons had brought legal actions claiming injuries from Armstrong's manufacture and sale of asbestos products. Armstrong has not produced asbestos products since 1969, but most social investors continue to avoid it because of questions about how long management had known of the problem and how the lawsuits have been handled.

The Annual Report

An annual report is a financial statement that state laws require every corporation to supply its shareholders. It includes "a balance sheet as of the end of the fiscal year, an income statement for that year, and a statement of changes in shareholders' equity for the year."[4]

For publicly traded corporations and a few that are not, the annual report also serves as a promotional piece designed to convince shareholders, potential shareholders, customers, and the world at large of the company's worth. Relentlessly upbeat, the annual report's tone often makes it difficult to gather substantive information.

But beyond financial information, one can often obtain something else from the annual report that may be just as important—insight into how the company wants to portray itself to the world. The 1990 annual reports of the Hechinger Company (a home-repair retailer) and Herman Miller, Inc. (an office-furniture firm) emphasize people and personal relationships. In contrast, Tesoro Petroleum (an integrated oil and natural gas corporation) uses only ocher-tinted, hazy pictures of oil refineries, leaving the company image without an identifiable human shape.

The 1991 Bristol-Myers Squibb annual report contains a fascinating ten-page essay on infectious diseases. Nowhere in the main text of the article or its accompanying pictures does the company's name appear. One can interpret this article as a statement of Bristol-Myers's confidence in its name recognition, a sign of its respect for the reader's intelligence, or an indication of its capacity to produce brilliant "infomercials," or all three. In any case, only those who closely follow epidemiology would not benefit from reading the article.

The Form 10-K

The annual report on SEC Form 10-K is a report by securities issuers to the Commission. Written primarily for regulators and investment professionals, the Form 10-K, is indispensable because it provides a straightforward, fairly complete description of what the company does. Usually, it contains a more complete explanation of pending litigation than do the footnotes to the financial statement in the annual report, especially for environmental cases.

In the mid-1980s, the SEC permitted companies to eliminate redundancies by referencing in the 10-K to the annual report. Eliminating this "unnecessary" paperwork reduced the information available to investors. In some instances companies have forgotten to include in their annual report the coverage promised in the 10-K. In almost every case, the annual report's coverage is now skimpier and more image-oriented.

Du Pont's 1990 10-K refers readers to its annual report for information on its industry segments. Du Pont has six, ranging in terms of sales from $1.8 billion (coal) to $15.9 billion (oil). Each segment receives one 8½-by-11-inch page, which includes a 3½-by-3¾-inch photo with caption, a graph of sales and operating income, a three hundred-word description of the segment's prospects, and wide margins.

Describing a $3.6 billion segment, such as Du Pont Chemicals, under these constraints produces wondrous results:

> **Outlook** In 1991, economic conditions in the United States and other countries may adversely affect demand in many of Chemicals' core businesses. However, the diversity of the segment's portfolio should moderate the impact of the recession on overall performance.[5]

Not fair, one might say. We haven't been given the context. How can we know what "Chemicals' core businesses" are or what "the diversity of the segment's portfolio" is? One wouldn't know any more about Chemicals' core businesses or its diverse portfolio if the quotation included the whole annual report and 10-K.

Du Pont lumps four areas—agricultural products, electronics, imaging systems, and medical products—into one three hundred-word note on "diversified businesses." All four are of concern to social investors. (Electronics and imaging—military and oppressive regimes; agricultural products—environment; and medical products—biotechnology and environment.) If these were minor operations, one could not quibble. But $6.6 billion in sales does not scream "insignificant." Here is what Du Pont says about its imaging systems:

> Acquisitions in 1989 performed below expectations but have been reorganized and consolidated. Their contribution to earnings in 1990 was hindered by severe recession in the capital goods market.[6]

The more times you read those two sentences, the more baffling they become.

Our intention here is not to pick on Du Pont. It is not the worst offender. Besides, it is only doing what the SEC has invited it to do: tell investors a lot less about its businesses. But it is fair to ask: If Wertheim Schroeder & Company, a brokerage firm, produces a report[7] for its clients on Du Pont that is sixteen pages longer (without photos) than the combined length of Du Pont's then-current annual report and 10-K, should not the company be required to report to the public in the same depth? The social investor picks up part of the tab for the SEC's shirking of its statutory responsibilities by paying a premium for SRI funds and managers because of their research expenses.

Proxy Statement

The proxy statement, described in chapter 1, details who runs a company and how they are compensated. It notes whether a company has profit sharing for its employees (including top officers), a savings plan, or an employee stock-ownership plan (ESOP). Pay and perks for top managers and directors also appear. And of course, it includes the resolutions shareholders will vote on at the annual meeting.

Getting Information

A postcard or a telephone call is all it usually takes to get a company's public documents. If you want information on a few companies at a time, *Barron's Finance & Investment Handbook* (described in Box 3-1) has directories of all companies traded on the major U.S. and Canadian stock exchanges. If you are ordering documents on twenty-five or more companies at a time and have a PC, you may want to consider one of the computer programs that provides the names and addresses of all publicly traded companies. You can use these programs to generate mailing labels and your word processor to produce form postcards.

Social screening is a process both of elimination and of seeking out. Taken as a whole, the process defines what a responsible corporation is. Because social investing is frequently motivated by a desire to add one's voice to those demanding greater corporate accountability, the process of screening has developed strong links with progressive and activist groups in each issue area. These groups are excellent sources of information. In later chapters when we examine screens in detail, we will identify many of them. In the Directory, we list a number of sources of social-investment information. The publications profiled in boxes throughout the book will also help you screen.

EXCLUSIONARY SCREENS

An exclusionary social screen, as we have seen, is an ethical criterion that, if not satisfied, eliminates companies from consideration for an investment universe.

Box 3-1. Indispensable Resource: *Barron's Handbook*

Barron's Finance & Investment Handbook, edited by J. Downes and J. E. Goodman, contains more useful information for its price ($21.95) than any book we know. Start with the best short (four hundred pages!) investment dictionary on the market. Then turn to the exceptionally clear descriptions of thirty personal investment opportunities. Want an address for a publicly traded company? You'll find it, and hundreds more for regulatory agencies, the exchanges themselves, and major institutions. Looking for historical data on an index's performance? It's there for all the major indexes from the time of their origins. Trying to find just the right business publication? No list is more complete than the one you'll find here.

The essay on how to read an annual report is exceptionally well done. You can pay $13.95 for a book on how to read the financial pages that isn't as good as the explanation you'll find here. If you're going to have any book—besides ours!—in your financial library, you must have *Barron's Finance & Investment Handbook.* What a deal!

Exclusionary screens seem clear-cut and therefore easy to apply. Philip Morris manufactures cigarettes and alcohol, but McKesson no longer distributes alcoholic beverages. Standard Commercial can only improve its evaluation under a tobacco-free screen by leaving the tobacco-leaf business, but a company that has never been in the gaming business does not merit a positive.

But what about a company, like Raychem, that sells to civilians a product that it designed for the military? Or a company whose kitchen equipment goes into submarines? As we will see in chapter 4, nuclear power and military-weapons screens can be quite difficult to implement.

It seems obvious that you should apply exclusionary screens—financial or social—before any other screens and certainly before buying the securities. But in the real world, things are not always logical. According to *Pensions & Investments,* from February through June 1991 Schroeder Capital Management International bought 666,000 shares of Matsushita Electric Industrial for the $500 million South Africa–free portfolio it managed for the California Public Employees' Retirement System (CalPERS). Matsushita appears on the authoritative list of companies in South Africa maintained by the Investor Responsibility Research Center in Washington. Six months after the last purchase, Schroeder spotted its error, sold the stock, and paid CalPERS $662,974 in restitution for its error. It seems that a computer program that spots barred companies is frequently run after—not before—the stock is bought.[8]

ALCOHOL, TOBACCO, AND GAMBLING

Very few investors with an alcohol, tobacco, or gambling screen will tolerate any involvement in these businesses. They tend to have similar views on gambling—casinos, race tracks, lotteries, and the like. Fortunately, these screens are easy to research. Since these are not industries in which companies dabble, the public documents are usually sufficient. Brokerages with analysts who follow these industries may have lists of all the players in each field.

Culling alcohol, tobacco, and gaming companies in the U.K. is a much more difficult process. The Ethical Investment Research Service (EIRIS) estimates that "one in seven companies in the All-Share Index . . . a third of the entire stock market value" has some involvement, albeit tenuous, in one of these areas.[9] The explanation for the exponentially greater effect of the sin stock screen on British portfolios lies in the definition of the screen. In the United Kingdom, the tobacco and alcohol screens almost never extend to incidental purveyors, such as supermarkets. As here, other screens with the same names can have very different definitions, and therefore, very different impacts on portfolios. You must always ask for detailed definitions of a manager's screens.

NUCLEAR POWER

A nuclear power screen is often two screens. The first excludes electric utilities that own nuclear-generating capacity. The second excludes companies that design or build nuclear power plants or supply elements necessary to the nuclear fuel cycle.

Electric utilities' public documents list the percentage of their generating capacity derived from nuclear fuel. During the nuclear industry's brief heyday, the costs of constructing plants often dictated multiple-ownership interests, many of which were small. So the percentage of generating capacity ranges from less than .05 percent nuclear for companies like Pacificorp to more than 60 percent for Commonwealth Edison.

Some social investors also eliminate companies that serve nuclear utilities by constructing plants or providing materials used in the nuclear fuel cycle. Since the nuclear industry is not flourishing, it can be hard to ferret this information from public documents. Fortunately, *Power*'s annual directory of companies servicing electric utilities provides a comprehensive overview of what companies are involved in the construction or design of nuclear reactors or in the nuclear fuel cycle. General Electric and Westinghouse have had major roles in nuclear-plant design. Always ask engineering and construction companies what they do for the industry. Sometimes participation comes from unexpected quarters. For instance, IMC Fertilizer Group and Freeport McMoRan sell uranium oxide—a byproduct of their phosphate-fertilizer operations—to nuclear utilities.

MILITARY CONTRACTS

Many social investors have military screens. Very few investors exclude all companies that sell anything—be it bagels or ball bearings—to the military. Very few large companies would pass this screen. In most cases, military screens eliminate only companies that sell weapons or weapons systems. The least strict military screen—because it fails the fewest companies—is a nuclear-weapons manufacturers screen. Most military screens permit some level of tolerance, because identifying contractors below a certain size is difficult.

Many companies that provide the military with goods or services or both, usually contract with the Department of Defense (DoD) or the Department of Energy (DoE) (mainly for nuclear weapons). The most complete single source for information on weapons-related contracting is a CD-ROM data base published by Nuclear Free America and Eagle Eye in Washington. It provides detailed information on all prime contracts over $25,000.

The Department of Defense's public-affairs office issues an annual list of the top one hundred prime contractors and the top five hundred contractors for research and development work (R&D). The National Technical Information Service (NTIS) supplies data on all DoD prime contracts over $25,000, but provides much less detail than Nuclear Free America's data base.

Companies that provide goods or services to the military may be either prime contractors or subcontractors. Prime contractors sell directly to the government; subcontractors sell to another business that incorporates its goods or services into a product sold to their ultimate customer. In 1989, for example, E-Systems, Inc.'s weapons-related prime contracts totaled 14.6 percent of sales, but its military systems unit—which acts as both a prime contractor and a subcontractor—accounted for 81 percent of its sales. Because E-Systems sells to weapons-manufacturing companies, as well as directly to the DoD, their weapons work is far more important to the company than a search of the prime contractors' data base would indicate.

Company documents are the only reliable source of information on subcontracting work, but they often require close reading. For instance, keep an eye out for retired military or intelligence officers among the company's board members and officers. Their presence often indicates military contracts.

With the demise of the Soviet Union, U.S. defense budgets are being cut. Lacking U.S. markets, arms makers are looking overseas. Data on these sales can be hard to come by. Witness the Bush administration's refusal to reveal who sold arms and war-related materials to Iraq before the Gulf war. Social investors will have to maintain closer contacts with foreign social researchers who can help track global arms sales.

SOUTH AFRICA

U.S. corporate involvement in South Africa is the most thoroughly researched of the issues that concern social investors. Church involvement has long been synonymous with the Interfaith Center on Corporate Responsibility (ICCR) in New York. It coordinates shareholder actions on South Africa. ICCR's expertise and resources are unmatched in this field.

Each year the Industrial Support Unit publishes its report on signatory companies to the Statement of Principles for South Africa. U.S. corporations with employees in that country are asked to endorse these guidelines—formerly known as the Sullivan Principles—for employment practices and community relations. Those that endorse them are rated each year on compliance. The report is available from Arthur D. Little, Inc., in Cambridge, Massachusetts.

The U.S. State Department annually releases a list of companies doing business in South Africa. The New York–based Africa Fund periodically issues a detailed list of companies with present and past ties to South Africa. As we noted earlier, the Investor Responsibility Research Center (IRRC) publishes a South Africa service.

EMERGING ISSUES

The types of exclusionary screens we have just described are fairly standard in the United States, United Kingdom, and Canada. However, some other exclusionary screens promise to become important.

Northern Ireland. The Investor Responsibility Research Center (IRRC) has followed for a number of years the employment practices of U.S. corporations with operations in Northern Ireland. At issue is employment discrimination on religious grounds. For some years church groups and several institutional investors have filed shareholder resolutions urging corporations to sign the MacBride Principles for fair labor practices in that part of the United Kingdom.

Reproductive Rights. Many Roman Catholic dioceses and institutions screen out companies that make birth control devices or drugs, manufacture products used in abortions, or operate facilities that perform the procedure. There is no single reliable source for this screen.

Oppressive Regimes. Two U.S. mutual funds and several U.K. unit trusts screen for human rights violations or "oppressive regimes." This screen affects companies whose operations, through the taxes they pay, support governments, like that of Myanmar (née Burma). Freedom House in New York and *The Ethical Consumer** in Manchester, England, are good sources here. Company-specific information is very hard to gather. Human rights and religious groups are the most likely sources.

Animal Rights. Animal rights activists have targeted companies that use laboratory animals in experiments. This screen is more common in the United Kingdom than it is in the United States. A substantial number of groups (People for the Ethical Treatment of Animals, Friends of Animals, and so on) have publications covering current issues. Among the most active in working directly with corporations on programs to reduce the use of live animals in product research and development is Henry Spira of Animal Rights International. Lists of companies using animals in experiments have in the past proven unreliable.

QUALITATIVE SCREENS

Social investing began with exclusionary screens. It will always use them. But the movement's present and future belong to qualitative screens. Qualitative screens are screens that companies can fail, but they are also used to identify companies of merit.

Qualitative screens are far more difficult to research than exclusion-

---

The Ethical Consumer is discussed in more detail in chapter 9.

Box 3-2. Indispensable Resource: *In These Times*

When *In These Times* arrives in our office, it rarely waits fifteen minutes to be read. Its quirky, unpredictable articles fill our issue and company files.

No general-interest publication comments as intelligently and broadly on issues of concern to social investors. From environmental regulation to labor issues to national health, *In These Times* gives free reign to first-rate commentators. Among its regulars, Joel Bleifuss, whose column has the best title in journalism—"The First Stone"— kept alive the "October surprise" and Dan Quayle drug-use stories until the national press and Congress had to deal with them.

Sometimes the latitude given its writers leads to incoherent editorial judgments. One issue contained an article advocating public investment in the domestic infrastructure as the best cure for the then-current recession. Six pages later, a regular columnist bashed the Bush administration for failing to put millions into exhibits at the 1992 World's Fair in Seville to stimulate the U.S. economy.

Books that might escape your notice, such as Athan Theoharis's *From the Secret Files of J. Edgar Hoover,* get insightful reviews. However, arts coverage ranges from the pedantic to the shrill, particularly where issues of sexism and racism strike the eyes of the reviewers. But it is politics, not the arts, that makes *In These Times* compelling and mandatory reading.

In These Times costs $34.95 per year and is available from *In These Times,* 1912 Debs Avenue, Mount Morris, Illinois 60154.

---

ary screens. So, we must apply a different methodology which we call the bellwether approach. In the middle ages, shepherds simplified finding their flocks by putting a bell on the sheep—the bellwether—its companions followed. Find the bellwether and find the flock. A similar principle applies in screening on qualitative issues. Experience has shown that a combination of bellwether issues indicate companies' overall performance in a screening area. For instance, a company's relations with its unionized workers often reflects its record generally on employee and employment issues. Xerox has excellent relations with its unions and a very good record on employment issues generally.

Bellwethers are critical to effectively implementing qualitative social screens. Fully evaluating even a smaller S&P 500 constituent, like Bassett Furniture, would require a horde of Ph.D.'s riding high-powered

PCs. Certain standards stated as objectively as possible must stand for the company's performance generally. They help sort and organize a vast quantity of data. Thus, bellwethers are to the social side of investing what ratios, like the price/earnings ratio, are to the financial side. Reliance on bellwethers should never close other areas of inquiry. Other information—particularly negative—may override a conclusion based on bellwether issues. And bellwether issues change over time.

The Environment

The first rule of environmental screening is never to judge a company green because of its name. Environmental Systems Research Institute supplies geographical information services to the Pentagon.[10] Environmental Control Group is in the asbestos-abatement business. Peter Camejo of Progressive Asset Management in Oakland, California, has criticized some mutual funds for using "environmental" in their names. In his view, these funds bought securities issued mainly by companies in the cleanup business—regardless of their actual performance—rather than companies with good environmental records or proactive products and services.[11]

Defining the Issues.   In no other area in social investing is it as hard—and as important—to define the issues the investor cares about. So many issues come under the environmental heading: surface mining; cutting forests to create cattle ranches; whale hunting; manufacturing and applying pesticides; disposing of municipal waste; and dozens more.

Numbers, technology, and law take over when investors move from the visceral issues toward the everyday matters of legal emissions of a pollutant into the air or discharges of a pollutant into a stream. The SEC requires companies to report on the Form 10-K any environmental liabilities the company deems significant. Companies have widely different views on what is significant and report accordingly.

No company likes to report environmental failings because they reflect badly on the company. In the 10-K, companies tend to minimize or define away their liabilities. The annual report will mention only positives unless the potential for loss requires disclosure in the "Legal Proceedings" footnote to the financials.

Nonetheless, "Legal Proceedings" is the best place to start the research process. The legal data bases—WestLaw and Lexus—offer access to legal proceedings at every level and to news sources. As they pick up more administrative agency reports, their value for social research will increase. Unfortunately, the costs of using these online data bases are exorbitant. The person who comes out with a lower priced CD-ROM service will make a fortune. The legal arms of the environmental movement—especially the Natural Resources Defense Council, the Sierra Club, and the National Wildlife Federation—regularly report on their activities, which often focus on specific corporations.

If one is monitoring this issue area, there is no substitute for the publications of environmental groups. For instance, investors concerned about hazardous-waste issues should be subscribing to *Everybody's Backyard,* a publication of the Citizens Clearinghouse for Hazardous Waste in Falls Church, Virginia, and *The Toxic Times* from the National Toxics Campaign in Boston.

Applying the Screen.   Only in rare instances does an environmental screen lead to a quick "no" and never to a quick "yes." Usually its application demands careful study of complicated questions. Evaluations include a close look at the company and the industry or industries in which it operates. While each screen has minimum standards, relative performance plays a key role. The call on some companies is agonizingly close.* The Calvert Group went through this twice, first with Arco and then with Amoco.

In the case of Amoco, Calvert drafted a case study of the company and presented it to those attending the Calvert Social Investment Fund's 1990 annual shareholders meeting. The attendees met in small groups to discuss the company and then regrouped to describe their conclusions. They focused on Amoco's mixed environmental performance and its strong record of community involvement. Afterward, Calvert polled the participants. They narrowly voted against including Amoco in the Social Investment Fund—the conclusion the fund's managers had reached.

Laurie McClain, an investment adviser with Progressive Securities in Eugene, Oregon, attended as someone who both owned and sold Calvert. "Discussing Amoco for an afternoon made me realize how a thoughtful portfolio manager must balance the financial and social bottom lines. Here's a good company financially. But socially, it's all shades of gray. Amoco definitely has positives. But I kept coming back to its fight to avoid liability for the huge *Amoco Cadiz* spill. That spill is the kind of broad stroke on which my clients judge companies." That spill occurred in 1978, yet many social investors still screen Amoco on it and its aftermath.

---

*Social-research houses such as ours generally submit the reports they propose to publish to their subjects for review. The companies usually review them carefully. They sometimes suggest changes or supply additional information that affect the conclusion. This dialogue is critically important to the social-investment research process.

COMMUNITY RELATIONS

Social investors have not tended to give much weight to corporations' efforts to be good neighbors. And they have not made community relations a formal screen. This is a mistake, because how a company deals with the community in which it resides often reflects its attitude toward the public generally. Coca-Cola has made Atlanta a much better place to live through financial and human contributions to education and the arts.

Corporations live in the communities in which they are located. Their behavior toward their neighbors spreads across the entire spectrum. The key bellwethers here are:

- whether a company restricts its giving to traditional channels such as local higher education and summer ballet; or
- whether a company has a broad view of what will make society better and is acting upon it.

One of the major factors propelling a community screen toward front-rank importance has been an acknowledgment of the central role of banks in community life, and what a lousy job they have done. The banks' failure to serve their communities was becoming apparent before the Reagan administration freed them to become repositories for bad real estate loans and junk bonds. That banks were bleeding money out of depressed communities and investing it elsewhere was a common complaint. Two of the best sources of information on banks are the Southern Finance Project and the California-Nevada Center on Corporate Responsibility. Unfortunately, as their names imply, they restrict their studies to their regions.

Some corporations have responded to the deterioration of urban life by moving to the suburbs. J.C. Penney fled New York for suburban Dallas. Others, like BP America (née Standard Oil of Ohio) and Ætna Life & Casualty have stayed and spent considerable sums on systematic efforts to make their cities better. Companies with foundations or giving programs usually focus on education (50 percent of all corporate giving) and human services (30 percent). For most companies, good corporate citizenship begins—and ends—with the United Way and its constituents.

Companies often publish a foundation or community-relations report. These can range from excellent (Affiliated Publications, for example) to uninformative. From reports that list all grantees by name one obtains a sense of the nature, as well as the dollar value, of the giving.

Other sources of information on corporate giving include directories

(the *Taft Corporate Giving Directory* is particularly good) and foundation libraries in cities like New York, Boston, and Cleveland. *The Chronicle of Philanthropy* provides news on corporate philanthropy and lists
of grants. In newspapers, most local business coverage consists of re-
printing press releases and reporting on Chamber of Commerce events.
So once you leave large corporations, covered by national papers such as
the *Wall Street Journal,* research depends on each company's responsiveness to your queries.

EMPLOYEE RELATIONS

Another good indicator of a company's quality is how it treats its employees. In a real sense, it defines a corporate culture. Since 1984, a
trio of authors—Milton Moskowitz, Robert Levering, and Michael
Katz—have done much to publicize companies they consider the best
employers. Their books* are good starting places for an employee-
relations screen because the authors apply clear, comprehensible standards and have sharp eyes for telling details. The common thread
throughout this team's books is employee empowerment. Among the
indicators of a commitment to this goal are: job security; an egalitarian
work environment; genuine employee involvement in decision making,
budgetary discretion, employee stock-ownership plans, and cash
profit-sharing plans.

Most companies making systematic efforts in these areas record their
progress through their annual and quarterly reports, in-house newsletters, and press coverage. More than on any other issue, companies are
willing to share information here. But never take employee programs at
face value. Ask cynical questions. For instance, what good is a company's profit-sharing plan if the directors have not acted on the plan and
distributed shares to employees? Employee "suggestion programs" can
be so informal and laxly executed that they lead to no true sense of
involvement.

On union issues, a good starting point is the AFL-CIO's *Labor Letter*
boycott listings. Various unions have newsletters, such as the United
Paperworkers International Union's *The Paperworker,* that offer excellent pictures of companies' relations with their unionized work force.
Trade publications are also extremely useful sources of information on
union relations.

---

*M. Moskowitz, R. Levering, and M. Katz, *Everybody's Business* (both the 1980 and 1990
editions); and *The One Hundred Best Companies to Work for in America* (1993); and R. Levering,
A Great Place to Work (1988).

PRODUCT QUALITY AND ATTITUDE TOWARD CONSUMERS

Most social screens have far more to do with common sense than with ideology. Product screens are particularly common sensical. Many investors look for companies with reputations for first-class products and services. "Quality" has been the management buzzword for a decade, and companies will eagerly send you masses of material on their approaches. Thus this screen is not unique to social investors. However, political and social objectives do come into play when the products are war toys, agricultural chemicals, or fast foods.*

What a company highlights in its image-making can reveal both its self-image and its weaknesses. Companies with reputations for product quality and good consumer relations let people know about them. The Maytag repairman became a cultural icon because he gently spoofed the public's high regard for his company. Companies that need a better rapport with consumers tend to create Mr. Goodwrenches.†

Advertising is a good indicator of both product quality and responsiveness to consumers, but litigation is even better. Many businesses rail against product liability suits, but when you see a company with a lot of them, you can bet a gap exists between a company's representations about a product and the public's perception of its performance. The SEC requires companies to disclose potential liabilities arising out of court actions. So, the annual report and Form 10-K are your starting point. The legal data bases discussed earlier are absolutely essential to producing a clear picture of a company's products but also its attitudes toward remedying problems. An early warning of A. H. Robins's Dalkon Shield‡ debacle was to be found in the *Federal Rules Decisions Reporter* (West Publishing), a series that reports decisions on arcane matters of court procedure. Long before the press began reporting the story, the decisions covering documents Robins was obligated to turn over to opposing parties revealed a shocking pattern of deception and abuse of the courts.[12]

---

*Most exclusionary screens—except South Africa—are product screens. They require separate treatment because those who adopt negative screens usually do not care whether, for instance, Anheuser-Busch is the best alcoholic beverage company. In their view, beer has no positives as a product, and the promotion of drinking is wrong.

†"Goodwrench"—only a series of committees could have given GM's spokesman a name and blow-dried presence that reminded customers of the gap between auto-maker promises and auto-dealer reality. Consider Mr. Goodwrench's contemporary, the Fram Oil Filter man. This rough-looking grease monkey offering practical advice ("You can pay me now or . . . pay me later") stood for what Americans wanted from mechanics.

‡In the 1970s, A. H. Robins manufactured an intrauterine birth control device called the Dalkon Shield. A wave of product liability actions brought by injured or maimed users swamped Robins. The company was forced to seek protection in bankruptcy from the Dalkon Shield claims.

Marketing issues figure in this screen. Often the question becomes not whether a product is good or bad but whether it is appropriate for the target market. The fifteen-year infant-formula controversy centered on whether European and American manufacturers should encourage poor women in Third World countries to use formula instead of their own milk. American Home Products, which now owns A. H. Robins, and Nestlé were the most notable combatants here. As on the continuing infant-formula controvery, church groups are excellent sources of information on marketing issues. And the Interfaith Center for Corporate Responsibility (ICCR) is the logical place to start.

Women and Minorities

While company employees have become more diverse, their boards have not. Many boards and executive suites remain all white and all male. A screen that eliminates all companies without a woman and a minority on their boards—with no allowance for double counting—would drastically limit one's investment universe. Perhaps a third of all publicly traded companies would pass that screen. Some investment advisers have begun protesting all-white, all-male slates by withholding their proxies and letting the company know why.

Identifying the exceptional boards is easy 90 percent of the time. The proxy statement briefly describes each candidate for a board seat. Some even have pictures of the board candidates. Annual reports, too, contain lists—and often pictures—of board members and senior executives. When looking at these lists, you should distinguish positions such as vice president of operations or senior v.p. of marketing from less influential staff positions such as corporate communications or human resources. Occasionally a list of officers includes "assistant secretaries" and "assistant treasurers." These positions have little authority, which is why women often fill them. Often pictures in the annual report hold all the information a company will divulge about its adaptation to a workplace where women and minorities have an important role.

Much good research is being done in this field and reported in the popular press. Every few years *Black Enterprise* publishes its list of the best workplaces for blacks. The Chicago-based *Dollars and Sense* frequently highlights companies making substantial progress in promoting blacks. In January 1990, *Hispanic* magazine published its list of the one hundred best companies for Hispanics. The most thorough of the surveys of the best workplaces for women has been appearing annually in the October issue of *Working Mother* magazine. Baila Zeitz and Lorraine

Dusky's book, *The Best Companies for Women* (Simon and Schuster, 1988), provides many anecdotes about fifty-three firms.

A few companies (Ford and Sara Lee, for example) put in their annual reports the percentage of women and minorities in all job categories. Others (such as Bristol-Myers Squibb and GM) publish these figures separately. Although difficult to evaluate in themselves, these figures can be compared with industry averages as published by the U.S. Equal Opportunity Commission (EEOC) to provide some perspective. Press accounts, the Form 10-K, and the legal data bases are the primary sources for information about sex-, race-, or age-discrimination suits.

SCREENING COMMUNITY-BASED INVESTMENTS

You can apply the same social screens to community-based investments that you do to publicly traded securities. Indeed, Vermont National Bank's Socially Responsible Banking Fund (SRB Fund) uses the same screens for both its portfolio investments and its borrowers. The SRB Fund's tobacco screen would bar both a bond issued by RJR Nabisco and a loan to a tobacco farm.

By its nature, a community-based investment should pass most common social screens. Most such investments occur in the areas of housing and the environment. The offering circular and descriptive materials should explore the impact of the project in some detail.

One of us, Amy Domini, specializes in community-based investing. She says, "I try to diversify my portfolios in terms of not only risk and return but also social impact. Most of my clients are looking for answers to desperate problems. They do not discriminate between answers for a reservation or ghetto. Need is need. The most frequent request I receive is to narrow down need geographically. Sometimes I'm asked to narrow it down by issues that tend to be in the form of qualitative screens."

One of the most commonly applied qualitative screens is for solutions to women's needs. The Low Income Housing Fund of San Francisco operates a national fund through which investors can earmark loans for women's housing projects. For those who target the needs of Native Americans, Blackfeet National Bank, First American Credit Union, and the Lakota Fund offer three opportunities. Both Blackfeet and First American are federally insured and offer close to market rates of interest. Lakota, as a community-development loan fund, offers neither insurance not market rates, but it works in the nation's poorest county to provide a financial infrastructure where there is none.

Those targeting investments in appropriate farming techniques should investigate deposits in the First Alternative Credit Union in Ithaca, New York, or the Cascadia Loan Fund in Seattle, or (for California residents only) Santa Cruz Credit Union. Investors seeking worldwide economic solutions might consider the Ecumenical Development Society in Hamilton, Ontario, which operates microeconomic lending programs throughout the world, or ACCION International in Cambridge, Massachusetts, which operates them in Central and South America.

CONCLUSION

In this chapter we have looked very briefly at how you might research and apply screens. Screens express your aspirations for the way you want to live and for society. They will evolve as you change.

For the balance of the book we will look at issues that will affect you and possibly your screens. We will explore issues that concern social investors and see how they changed companies in eight subject areas.

4

The Exclusionary Screens: "Sin," Nuclear Power, and Military Contracts

FOR MOST OF THIS CENTURY, socially responsible investors have focused on negatives, on what they did not want in their portfolios or did not want companies doing.

As we have noted, modern social investing began with alcohol and tobacco-product screens in the 1900s. In the 1970s came South African investment, military weapons, nuclear power, and gambling. Hand in hand with divestment—the elimination of securities from a portfolio for moral reasons—have come proxy resolutions. On each of the issues except gambling, social-issue shareholder activists have played key roles.

The moral imperative now goes beyond consumption issues to issues of justice and peace. In the process, social investors seem to have lost sight of the important distinction between issues of personal consumption and those of social justice. In this chapter, we will examine that distinction as we look at how social investors implement negative screens on consumption issues. We will then explore the more global negative screens: nuclear power and military weapons. South Africa, because of its central role in social investing's history, rates a chapter to itself.

THE EFFECTS OF EXCLUSIONARY SCREENING

"What's the point of divesting our stocks? Someone else will just buy them and make money on them. And it won't affect the companies a bit." Every time a negative screen has been suggested to an institution, someone has raised a variant of that argument.

The argument is half right and half wrong. Consider an incident described in *Barbarians at the Gate,* the tale of RJR Nabisco's leveraged buyout. Warren Buffett, America's premier investor, at one time had been the largest stockholder of R. J. Reynolds Industries. In 1988 he owned 12 percent of Salomon Brothers, the investment house. Salomon was considering bidding for what had become RJR Nabisco—the nation's second-largest cigarette manufacturer and second-largest brewer. Salomon's management wanted to clear the venture with their most important director and invite him to participate as an investor. As a Salomon director, Buffett approved. "I'll tell you why I like the cigarette business. It costs a penny to make. Sell it for a dollar. It's addictive. And there's fantastic brand loyalty." But as an investor, Buffett declined. "I'm wealthy enough where I don't need to own a tobacco company and deal with the consequences of public ownership."[1]

As with RJR, someone *will* buy the stock and may well make money on it. But not everyone who might have bought it before the movement against tobacco products gathered strength will buy it today. How much would RJR have gone for if Buffett had entered the bidding? Were other potential purchasers similarly put off? We will never know.

The Buffett story is unique in illustrating the decisive effect on a private-investment decision of a movement associated with an exclusionary social screen. Much more common are stories about institutions and government bodies that decide to divest. But those stories treat divestment as an end rather than the means to an end that it is. The end is a change in public policy and private behavior.

Portfolio investors who apply exclusionary screens do so, first, to make their own portfolios consistent with their beliefs and, second, to make others aware of the social costs of the issuer's products or actions. At no point do social investment and social activism intertwine more closely.

Cleansing a portfolio benefits the investor's psyche, but it has little or no larger effect unless the divestment is publicized. Except in unique circumstances, like the RJR Nabisco buyout, a decision not to own a company's stock—for nonfinancial reasons—will not affect the pocketbooks of the company or its management. Even if many investors take the same action, as they have on military weapons, financial effects on the corporations are not documentable. As we saw in chapter 1, the combination of public divestment and shareholder activism adds muscle to political movements. However, it is important to keep in mind that the objective of these movements is social change. What companies do or do not do is only a part of much larger issues. Those larger issues define how we as humans live together.

Thus it really does not matter that there is little chance that companies will leave lucrative businesses, such as alcoholic beverages and cigarettes, or abandon viable plants, such as nuclear power stations. Nor is it likely that companies whose culture has been shaped by military contracts will leave the defense business. The objectives of shareholder actions and divestitures are to affect private beliefs, public thinking, and ultimately public policy.

"SIN": ALCOHOL, TOBACCO, AND GAMBLING

> I learned everything I know not from intelligent people, but from imbeciles. It's automatic. You don't do what they do.
>
> —MINNESOTA FATS ON WHY HE NEVER DRANK OR SMOKED.[2]

In the United States, the first social screens applied to securities were negative, barring investments in companies that manufactured alcohol or tobacco products.* Much later, investors applied the same screen to gambling. Collectively, the three screens became known as the "sin stocks" screen. Investors who apply a sin stock screen rarely accept a company with any involvement in either the alcoholic beverage, tobacco product, or gambling businesses—depending on their beliefs. The history of these screens and their impact on social investing—much of which we looked at in chapter 1—holds some critical lessons for the movement.

PIONEERS, PROGRESS, AND PROHIBITION

In the 1910s some mainline Protestant denominations barred alcohol and tobacco-product manufacturers from their portfolios. These screens squared their investment policies with their teachings on the personal

---

*Some companies offer programs to help their employees deal with tobacco- and alcohol-related problems. Others have tobacco-free workplaces. These types of programs are discussed in chapter 10.

use of these substances and with their political support for Prohibition. Alcohol and tobacco screens were common enough in 1928 to induce a Boston money manager to start a mutual fund that explicitly adopted them. But the Pioneer Fund stood alone—the first and only socially screened fund—until 1969, when the same manager introduced the Pioneer II fund.* Social investing itself did not advance during this period, largely because of its identification with Prohibition, which criminalized conduct of which many disapproved but few regarded as a crime.

As a screen, gambling has a much shorter history than its venal companions. Until the 1960s there were almost no gambling stocks to buy. From the early 1900s until the mid-1970s casino gambling was banned virtually everywhere in the United States except Nevada. In the mid-1960s, speculators such as Huntington Hartford developed casino resorts in the Caribbean, and the stock in these companies did appear on U.S. exchanges. With the opening up of Atlantic City as a gambling center and the wild expansion of Nevada resorts, investors have had a number of domestic companies from which to choose.

After huge scandals in the late nineteenth century, both public and private lotteries disappeared until 1964 when that pillar of Puritan rectitude, New Hampshire, introduced one to skin the tourists. Today, most states run them.

The continuing illegality of many forms of gambling—such as bookie shops—is another holdover from the age of reform that brought us Prohibition and the first antidrug laws. No one can argue that these criminal schemes have worked. Nor can one convince a reasonably smart ten-year-old we should legalize, tax, and encourage the consumption of some drugs—alcohol and tobacco—and some forms of gambling, while imposing horrific penalties for indulging in others.

For social investors the sin screens may be easy to implement, but the underlying issues of a person's right to a private vice or two versus the desirability of a vice-free society are not easy to resolve. But it may well be better to address individual behavior rather than supply. Making alcohol difficult—even illegal—to obtain only heightened its desirability. The emergence in several states, most notably New Jersey, of smokers'-rights laws forbidding employers to discriminate against people who smoke off the job are a fair warning.

Redefining socially acceptable consumption habits is one thing; fin-

---

*There are indications that other socially screened funds were launched during the forty-one years between the two Pioneer funds, but they did not last long enough to make a permanent impression.

ing or jailing those who do not comply is another. Prohibition and all it came to stand for—small-mindedness, obscurantism, political corruption, street violence—tarred the movements against alcohol and tobacco consumption for more than two generations. (The politicians whose drug laws led to the doubling of the U.S. prison population between 1981 and 1990 should be required to study Prohibition.) *The Economist*[3] is not alone in scenting a new move toward prohibition—this time of tobacco. There is no reason to believe this prohibition will work better than the prohibition of liquor did.

DRINK SCREENS

Without question, an alcohol screen bars beer, wine, and spirits producers. But who else is in the alcohol business and should be excluded? That is a much tougher call, and one that in the United States, at least, investors do not show any inclination to make.

Alcoholic-beverage manufacturers tend to be very large companies, like those listed in Table 4-1, or small companies, like many of the California wine makers. In this industry, medium-size companies have largely disappeared because they could not compete.

Some social investors eliminate distributors of alcoholic beverages, too. Larger publicly traded corporations tend not to have these businesses. For example, McKesson, the consumer-products company, shed its small alcoholic-beverage distributorship in 1988. Extending an alcohol screen to distributors would not be much more restrictive than applying one limited to producers, but a screen that extended to retailers would be significantly more limiting. A retailer screen on alcohol and tobacco is fairly common among U.K. social investors, but is virtually

**TABLE 4-1. SOME PUBLICLY TRADED COMPANIES WITH
ALCOHOL BUSINESSES**

Company	Alcohol-related Business
American Brands, Inc.	Spirits
Anheuser-Busch Cos., Inc.	Beer
Brown-Forman Corp.	Wine and spirits
Adolph Coors Co.	Beer
Philip Morris Cos., Inc.	Beer
The Seagram Co. Ltd.	Wine and spirits
UST Inc. (*née* United States Tobacco)	Wine

Source: Kinder, Lydenberg, Domini & Co., Inc.

unknown here. Many types of retailers carry beer. Virtually all grocery chains sell alcoholic beverages in states that permit supermarkets to carry them. For instance, in Ohio, Kroger's carries beer and wine.

SMOKE SCREENS

In general, alcohol has been treated more as a social evil than as an individual vice. With tobacco, the emphases have been reversed. However, as health care costs come to dominate the national agenda, the social costs of tobacco consumption will become more of an issue.

The tobacco industry is even more concentrated than the alcoholic beverage industry. Therefore, it is even easier to screen. Table 4-2 lists major companies in the industry.

Unlike their U.K. counterparts, U.S. social investors have not focused on retailers of tobacco products. It is difficult to rationalize the sale of cigarettes in drug stores, like Melville Corporation's CVS chain, except on the grounds of profit. In 1992, the Marianist Society filed a shareholder resolution with Rite-Aid, one of the nation's largest drugstore chains, asking the company to divest itself and its pensions of tobacco stocks and to make its pharmacies smoke- and cigarette-free.[4]

Encouraging people to smoke seems outrageous, given what medical researchers have proven about tobacco's health effects. But that is the objective of cigarette advertising—Joe Camel, et cetera—and tobacco-

TABLE 4-2. SOME PUBLICLY TRADED COMPANIES WITH
TOBACCO-RELATED BUSINESSES

Company	Tobacco-related Business
American Brands, Inc.	Cigarettes
Borden, Inc.	Adhesives and glues for cigarettes
Calgon Carbon Corp.	Carbon for cigarette filters
Culbro Corp.	Cigars
Dibrell Brothers, Inc.	Leaf-tobacco dealer
Eastman Kodak Co.	Filter tows
Kimberly-Clark Corp.	Cigarette papers
Mobil Corp.	Cellophane wrap
Philip Morris Cos. Inc.	Cigarettes
Shorewood Packaging Corp.	Cigarette packages
Standard Commercial Corp.	Leaf-tobacco dealer
UST Inc. (*née* United States Tobacco)	Smokeless tobacco
Universal Corp. (*née* Universal Leaf Tobacco)	Leaf-tobacco dealer

Source: Kinder, Lydenberg, Domini & Co., Inc.

company sponsorship of sporting events, like the Virginia Slims tennis tournaments. Social-issue activists have filed shareholder resolutions with UST Inc., American Brands, Loews, and Philip Morris seeking voluntary restraints on advertising that makes tobacco use seem appealing. (Philip Morris received a similar resolution on beer advertising.) Loews also got a resolution on its targeting of advertising to African-Americans for its Newport cigarettes.[5]

Because of the billings they represent, advertising agencies eagerly compete for alcoholic-beverage and cigarette accounts. Large advertising firms tend to have numerous subsidiaries, and brand accounts can flit from subsidiary to subsidiary with astonishing speed. As the advertising issue expands, shareholders may begin looking at the activities of publicly traded agencies like Saatchi & Saatchi, WPP Group, the Interpublic Group, Omnicom, and Young & Rubicam. Already media companies such as Gannett and Time-Warner are receiving shareholder resolutions asking for reports on the cigarette advertising they take and whether corporate policies should change.[6]

Social-issue activists have pressed insurance companies—specifically the Ætna, Cigna, Travelers, and Sears, Roebuck (Allstate)—to divest their holdings in tobacco companies.[7] The inconsistency between owning these securities and insuring lives and property (against cigarette-related fires, for instance) seems clear. Advocates of tobacco-stock divestiture scored an unexpected victory when Harvard's then-president, Derek Bok, responded affirmatively to a medical researcher's request that the university sell its tobacco holdings. (By contrast in 1992, Harvard marked twenty-three years of resisting South Africa divestiture.)

Of special concern to antitobacco activists are the effects of "environmental tobacco smoke," tobacco smoke inhaled by people who happen to be around smokers. It is fitting that a target for a shareholder resolution seeking a smoke-free environment was Humana, the nation's largest hospital chain.[8] It happens to be based in Louisville, Kentucky, long a tobacco-industry center.

Over the past decade or so, domestic tobacco consumption has fallen on a per capita basis. Recognizing that growth lies overseas, the companies have moved aggressively into foreign markets, particularly in the Third World, where people lack information about smoking's health effects and tobacco is a luxury for many. The companies have even gotten the U.S. government to pressure countries to drop bars to tobacco imports so they could sell more. Church groups have responded with shareholder actions.[9]

Gambling Screens

As with the other two sin-stock screens, investors who use a gambling screen usually want companies with no involvement whatsoever. Luckily for those trying to identify players, gambling is another business in which few publicly traded companies dabble. The downfalls of amateurs such as Donald Trump have proven that only professionals can play successfully. There are no small-timers in Table 4-3, which lists some of the publicly traded casino owners and other gaming specialists. But with legalization's steady progress, many companies may soon see a fit between their businesses and aspects of the gaming industry.

Casino gambling, video poker, and lotteries have become the politicians' panaceas for unemployment and fiscal stability. Officials have proposed casinos for depressed areas as diverse as: New Orleans; Deadwood, South Dakota; Vicksburg, Mississippi; Lorain, Ohio;[10] and North Adams, Massachusetts. Native Americans are opening gambling facilities on reservations in New York and Connecticut. Iowa has reintroduced riverboat gambling on the Mississippi. Neither Las Vegas nor Atlantic City offers much assurance that the politicians have hit on a cure-all.

TABLE 4-3. SOME PUBLICLY TRADED COMPANIES WITH INTERESTS IN GAMBLING

Company	Gambling-related Business
Aztar Corp. (*née* Ramada Inc.)	Casinos
Bally Manufacturing Corp.	Casinos and gaming equipment
Caesar's World, Inc.	Casinos
Circus Circus Enterprises, Inc.	Casinos
Control Data Corp.	Computer services to lotteries
Golden Nugget, Inc.	Casinos
GTECH Corp.	Computer services to lotteries
Hilton Hotels Corp.	Casinos
International Game Technology	Gaming equipment
Jackpot Enterprises, Inc.	Gaming machines
Mirage Resorts	Casinos
Ogden Corp.	Racetracks and off-track betting
Promus Cos. Inc.	Casinos
Santa Anita Realty Enterprises	Racetrack
Showboat, Inc.	Casinos
Video Lottery Technologies	Video-gaming machines
WMS Industries, Inc.	Gaming machines and casinos

Source: Kinder, Lydenberg, Domini & Co., Inc.

Despite its glittering pleasure palaces, Las Vegas is a "sleazy town that never sleeps." Bugsy Siegel, a hit man turned hotelier, founded its casino business.[11] Few of the benefits casino promoters promised Atlantic City residents have arrived, but public corruption has. Nonetheless, by the end of the decade few Americans will be more than a few hours' drive from a gambling facility.

It is unlikely that many new casino operators will emerge as the industry expands. Small operators will not be able to afford entry so long as regulators restrict gambling to pleasure domes. And it is in the interests of the current members of the industry to limit competition in the new venues.

Where we will see great growth will be in firms servicing the gambling industry. Casinos and transportation services to them are major advertisers, especially in cities within an hour's flight of Las Vegas and Atlantic City. Among gambling-equipment companies, the aptly named Jackpot Enterprises and International Game Technology are the best known. Several smaller equipment companies are also publicly traded.

Since most casinos are part of hotels or resorts, companies specializing in lodging and food services might come under an investor's screen. Indeed, you should check any hotel chain for gambling interests. Hilton Hotels is a major casino operator. Municipalities traditionally go to great lengths to attract new industry and with it, they hope, jobs. The gambling industry is no exception, though its image and cash flow inhibit direct subsidies. Investors should look carefully at municipal bonds issued to fund infrastructure—sewerage, water mains, roads, and so forth—where gambling operations are opening up.

Racetracks rarely appear on the board. And unlike lotteries and casinos, horse racing is a dying business. Here and in Europe, tracks are more valuable for the land they take up than as going concerns. The 1991 proxy battle for control of Hollywood Park centered on development, producing some of the raciest takeover stories of the year. Among those with racing interests is Ogden, which also has significant interests in environmental services.

Privately operated, for-profit lotteries, like "the numbers," remain illegal. So the only way for an investor to play the numbers is to invest in companies that service state-run lotteries. The largest of these are GTECH and Control Data. State lotteries are supposed to benefit education and keep taxes down. Lotteries appeal to precisely the people who can least afford to play them—the people who buy tickets at the same corner store where they once played the numbers. Lotteries amount to the most regressive tax since the abandonment of the poll tax. As things stand now, some states spend hardly any money on communications with the people they are supposed to serve except to promote their lotteries.

Small-shop owners want lottery franchises because they bring in a steady stream of customers. Large grocery chains in some states also have lottery franchises, as do chain convenience stores. Advertising for lotteries tends to go to local agencies with good political connections, not to the publicly traded houses. Lotteries depend on computers, and as we noted at least one major firm, Control Data, provides computer services to them.

Some states that have had lotteries for some time are finding that ticket purchases have plateaued. But revenue enhancers have learned that many people think little of spending a dollar or two on lottery tickets. Generalizing from that experience, they are considering systems that will attract dollars from tourists. If video poker comes to tourist cities like Boston, which is considering it, a new generation of "high-technology" slot machines will not be far behind. So gambling screeners should keep a weather eye on game firms.

NUCLEAR POWER

For many social investors, power companies that own nuclear generating capacity fall into the same classification as cigarette manufacturers. No matter how small a company's participation in a nuclear power venture, it is not welcome in their portfolios. In addition, major companies in the nuclear power service industry are unwelcome.

AND THE NUKE SHALL MAKE YE FREE

Perhaps the most arresting prediction in U.S. history was that nuclear technology would make electricity so cheap it would be practically given away. When the government made that guess in the mid-1950s, atomic energy looked pretty good—especially in contrast to coal. No one under thirty—apart from those who have traveled in eastern Europe—can imagine the level of visible air pollution and soot cities endured into the 1960s. The social and environmental ravages of coal mining, too, made "clean" atomic power seem a godsend.

By the late 1960s or early 1970s, the dangers of nuclear power were growing apparent. The environmental movement blossomed—in part because of nuclear plant construction. Once plants were up, operating them proved more difficult and dangerous than had been thought. Then came the near-disasters—Brown's Ferry and Fermi—and the disasters—Three Mile Island and Chernobyl.

Worst of all from the utilities' standpoint, electricity customers went into rate shock when they learned—at about the same time as the utilities did—how much "free" atomic power would cost. When they recovered, they entered rate rage. So fell Public Service Company of New Hampshire in 1988, now part of Northeast Utilities.

Although far cleaner in their operations than coal-fired plants, nuclear units are sources of ongoing pollution. Primarily, the pollutants take the form of steam vented into the air from cooling towers and hot water discharged into a nearby body of water. Occasionally radioactive gases and water escape, but usually at well below lethal levels.

Aside from the possibility of a meltdown, the real environmental problem with nuclear power comes with the marvelously named "back end of the fuel cycle," the disposal of spent nuclear fuel and contaminated water used to cool the reactor. Much of this material will remain toxic for tens of thousands of years. At present, the utilities store it in on-site temporary facilities because no permanent repository exists. Nor is one likely to come into operation until at least 2005, if then. No state wants the facility, and the technologies for permanent disposal are, to some, highly questionable.*

Nuclear power opponents waged a war of attrition, which they have apparently won. No utility has ordered a new nuclear plant since 1974, and most of the ones proposed at that time were never built. But no administration has slowed research on nuclear power or deterred the Nuclear Regulatory Commission. In 1992, the Bush administration succeeded in gaining passage of a program for streamlining plant applications as part of its energy legislation. In June 1992, Westinghouse became the first company to file for preapproval of a new generation of reactors. Still, no utility has expressed an interest publicly in building one.

No Nukes

Most social investors' rationales for screening out nuclear utilities rest on two distinct bases. First, because the development of nuclear power went hand-in-hand with weapons development and use, it is profoundly

---

*Nuclear power advocates argue that the plants now in existence should have been the first stage in a chain of reprocessing plants and new generation reactors that would have closed the fuel cycle. Despite billions of dollars in research and a demonstration project at Savannah River, nothing indicates these facilities would produce what they promised, much less in a cost-effective manner.

TABLE 4-4. SOME PUBLICLY TRADED NUCLEAR UTILITIES
(% of fuel sources represented by nuclear)

Centerior Energy Corp. (*née* Cleveland Electric and Toledo Edison) (31%)
Central & South West Corp. (6%)
Commonwealth Edison Co. (79%)
Detroit Edison (11%)
El Paso Electric Co. (36%)
Entergy Corp. (*née* Middle South Utilities) (44%)
Gulf States Utilities Co. (16%)
Houston Industries Inc. (6%)
IE Industries (*née* Iowa Electric Light & Power) (43%)
Midwest Resources Inc. (22%)
Pacific Gas & Electric Co. (18%)
Portland General Corp. (20%)
Public Service Co. of New Mexico (25%)
SCEcorp (*née* Southern California Edison) (20%)
San Diego Gas & Electric Co. (20%)
WPL Holdings, Inc. (*née* Wisconsin Power & Light) (18%)

Sources: Companies; *Value Line Investment Survey.*

tainted. The second basis, its environmental effects, confirms the evil of the first in many people's minds. Neither rationale leaves a principled basis for including even the best of the industry.

How long should a company remain off an investor's list after it abandons nuclear power? Cincinnati Gas & Electric and DPL, Inc. (née Dayton Power & Light) abandoned the Zimmer nuclear station in the face of revelations of massive construction defects. Public Service Company of Colorado shut down its Saint Vrain nuclear plant in 1989 and began converting it to gas. These companies bear watching at least for a time.

Social investors often ask how they can be sure the power they use does not come from nuclear utilities. After all, utilities in densely settled parts of the country have joined together to form "grids," networks of power generators that allow utilities to buy and sell power among themselves. This system has worked well in terms of limiting the number of plants that have to be built to serve a region. However, it is usually impossible for consumers to determine whether their power comes from coal or gas or nuclear fuel. They can know only the types of plants operated by the company to whom they send their checks.

Many social investors also apply their nuclear power screen to the nuclear power service industry. This category includes companies such as General Electric and Westinghouse, which built and now maintain plants. Table 4-5 lists some prominent publicly traded companies in the industry.

TABLE 4-5. PUBLICLY TRADED COMPANIES IN THE NUCLEAR POWER SERVICE INDUSTRY
(Subsidiary)

Michael Baker Corp.	McDermott International, Inc.
General Electric Co.	Westinghouse Electric Corp.
Halliburton Co. (Brown & Root)	

Source: Kinder, Lydenberg, Domini & Co., Inc.

Nuclear energy has proven to be like Bilbo's ring in Tolkein's *Lord of the Rings*. It seems to confer superhuman powers, but in reality it makes its possessor a slave—or worse. But no epic quest will lead us to Mount Doom into whose volcano we can toss it.

MILITARY CONTRACTS

The third socially screened mutual fund (following Pioneer and Pioneer II) appeared in 1971 just after the Vietnam War protests peaked. As its name implied, Pax invested only in "non–war-related industries."[*] Its founders reflected a belief whose strength has ebbed and flowed over the ensuing twenty years: Weapons contribute only to war. Investments in weapons add little to sustaining the civilian economy. The Quakers and the Mennonites represent another, much older tradition. They do not invest in weapons makers because they equate war-making with sin. For them, weapons makers stocks are sin stocks.

As we've just described it, a military screen seems simplicity itself: Just identify weapons makers and avoid them. But it's not that easy.

WEAPONS-RELATED SCREENS

Three adjectives—weapons-related, war-related, and military—suggest the levels of screening available to an investor. Precise definitions for them are impossible to give, but here are some suggestions:

> *weapons-related:* of or relating to any goods that are capable of inflicting physical harm in a conflict between nations or peoples;
> *war-related:* of or relating to any goods or services that could be used in or to sustain an armed conflict between nations or peoples;

---

[*]As we noted in Chapter 1, Pax was the first multiply screened mutual fund and the first to apply qualitative screens. Pax was at least ten years ahead of its time.

military: of or relating to responsibilities of the Department of Defense (DoD) or defense-related activities of the Department of Energy (DoE) or the Central Intelligence Agency (CIA).

"The sisters really aren't too concerned about military issues, and we want a screen that let's us keep, oh, GM, GE—you know what I mean." We did, but why have a screen if it allows you to include the number-three and four defense contractors, according to the Department of Defense's list of the one hundred companies receiving the largest dollar volume of prime contract awards in fiscal year 1990?[12] (The list is reproduced in Table 4-6. The number in parentheses following a company name below indicates its rank on this list.)

A weapons-related screen is both the least stringent military screen and the most common. Often the screen is phrased in terms of avoiding "companies that derive a substantial portion of their income from weapons-related military contracts." We've already seen that defining *weapons* isn't easy. "Substantial" poses problems, too. The Domini Social Index (DSI) chose to define "substantial" in terms of companies that derive either:

- more than $10 million in sales from nuclear weapons–related contracts, or
- more than 2 percent of gross revenues from prime contracts for military weapons or weapons-related materials, or
- more than 4 percent of gross revenues from sales that may have military weapons-related uses or origins.

Thus the DSI's screen eliminates the major defense contractors, such as McDonnell Douglas (1), Martin Marietta (7), Grumman (9), and Loral (31). It also keeps out large firms whose military sales may be less than 4 percent of total revenue but who are among the larger contractors for nuclear weapons. IBM (18) and AT&T (23) fall into this category.[13]

Many social investors screen out companies subcontracting substantial amounts of military work. For example, Intergraph, an Alabama firm specializing in computer-aided design, had no unclassified weapons-related prime contracts in 1989, but the firm did substantial subcontracting on weapons design.

Of course, the problems with a weapons-related screen don't become apparent so long as you deal with companies that are clearly in the weapons business. The problems come when you have to draw lines.

As the DSI screen shows, you can define "substantial" either in

TABLE 4-6. TOP 100 DEFENSE PRIME CONTRACTORS, FISCAL YEAR 1990

Rank	Parent Company	Rank	Parent Company
46	Aerospace Corp.	27	International Business Machines Corp.
25	Alliant Techsystems Inc.	87	International Shipholding Corp.
29	Allied-Signal Inc.	22	ITT Corp.
84	Amerada Hess Corp.	44	Johns Hopkins University
93	American President Cos. Ltd.	59	Johnson Controls Inc.
28	American Telephone & Telegraph Co.	70	Kaman Corp.
69	American Trans Air Kalitta JV	13	Litton Industries Inc.
65	Amoco Corp.	9	Lockheed Corp.
40	Arco Products Co.	96	Logicon Inc.
73	Astronautics Corp. of America	16	Loral Corp.
53	Avondale Industries Inc.	17	LTV Corp.
67	Bahrain National Oil	8	Martin Marietta Corp.
23	Bath Holding Corp.	45	Massachusetts Institute of Technology
76	Bell Boeing JV	1	McDonnell Douglas Corp.
79	Black & Decker Corp.	100	MIP Instandsetzungsbetric
63	Boeing Co. & Sikorsky Aircraft JV	41	Mitre Corp.
18	The Boeing Company	64	Mobil Corp.
75	Booz, Allen & Hamilton Inc.	74	Motor Oils Hellas Corinth Refineries
97	CAE Industries Ltd.	57	Motorola Inc.
94	Caltex Petroleum Corp.	78	National Steel & Shipbuilding Co.
88	Carlyle Group	99	Norfolk Shipbuilding Drydock Corp.
56	CFM International Inc.	6	Northrop Corp.
66	Chevron Corp.	31	Olin Corp.
61	Chrysler Corp.	39	Oshkosh Truck Corp.
48	Coastal Corp.	54	Penn. Central Corp.
43	Computer Sciences Corp.	72	Philips Gloeilampenfabrieken
52	CSX Corp.	5	Raytheon Co.
91	E. I. Du Pont de Nemours & Co.	12	Rockwell International Corp.
38	Dyncorp	68	Rolls-Royce PLC
32	E-Systems Inc.	49	Royal Dutch/Shell Group of Cos.
90	Eaton Corp.	36	Science Applications International Corp.
77	EG&G Inc.	82	Sequa Corp.
55	Esco Electronics Corp.	71	Shore Management Inc.
33	Exxon Corp.	83	Ssangyong Oil Refining Co. Ltd.
24	Federal Express, Pan Am, Northwest et al.	92	Sun Company Inc.
14	FMC Corp.	37	Teledyne Inc.

TABLE 4-6.—continued

Rank	Parent Company	Rank	Parent Company
42	Foundation Health Corp.	51	Tenneco Inc.
34	Gencorp Inc.	21	Texas Instruments Inc.
2	General Dynamics Corp.	20	Textron Inc.
80	General Electric Co. PLC	60	Thiokol Corp.
3	General Electric Co.	89	Tracor Inc.
4	General Motors Corp.	95	Trinity Industries Inc.
10	Grumman Corp.	19	TRW Inc.
26	GTE Corp.	62	Unaka Co. Inc.
81	Halliburton Co.	15	Unisys Corp.
58	Harris Corp.	98	United Industrial Corp.
30	Harsco Corp.	7	United Technologies Corp.
86	Hensel Phelps Construction Co.	85	Vinnell Corp.
50	Hercules Inc.	11	Westinghouse Electric Corp.
35	Honeywell Inc.	47	World Rosen Key Amer Etal JV

Source: Department of Defense.

terms of dollars or of a percentage of some measure of a company's income. Neither approach is problem-free. Take Raychem, for example. This diversified specialty chemical company announced in 1990 that it was reducing its military work. Though it has almost no prime DoD contracts, it derives around 8 percent of gross revenues from sales of electrical connectors, insulation, and communications equipment to weapons manufacturers. The company also sells the same products in considerable volume for nondefense purposes. The volume of sales alone might not eliminate Raychem. But Raychem designed these products originally for weapons systems, and, for some, that tips the scales against them.

AMP manufactures electrical connectors. Approximately 5 percent of its sales end up in weapons systems. But of this amount, only half comes from connectors designed for weapons systems. Because this volume of sales falls below many investors' percentage limit, because the connectors themselves resemble AMP's off-the-shelf products, and because the firm has a high reputation for quality and service, it passes most weapons-related screens.

In fiscal year 1989, Digital Equipment Corporation (DEC) had weapons-related contracts totaling $20 million (0.12 percent of sales).[14] Like Hewlett-Packard (89),[15] DEC asserts its military sales consist of off-the-shelf computers not tailored to military specifications. However, DEC has long sold computers to Raytheon (5) for use in weapons systems. And DEC ranked 88 on the 1990 list of DoD prime contractors.[16] It is very much on the borderline.

Zurn Industries designs small power plants and manufactures wastewater equipment—both products with environmental positives. In 1987 Zurn announced that it intended to seek military markets for its clutches and crankshaft lines. It won a contract to develop specialized components for the Osprey vertical takeoff and landing aircraft. In 1990 Zurn announced that it had ended active pursuit of these markets, although it would honor past commitments. With the fate of the Osprey still in doubt, Zurn's long-term involvement in this market is difficult to project, but it will not be more than 4 percent of sales in the foreseeable future.

Zurn illustrates the problems with military screens in general. Many companies hop in and out of the business as their sales volume in other lines dictates. Prime contracts can make up a small percentage of a company's business, and subcontracts can involve nearly invisible parts.

WAR-RELATED SCREENS

A war-related screen, like Pax World Fund's, encompasses any weapons-related screen but is significantly broader. This screen turns on a determination of what advances war. In some instances, the question is quite literal. For instance, Amoco (72), Chevron (73), Coastal Corporation (51) and Royal Dutch/Shell (46) sell fuel to the Defense Department.[17] While they pass many weapons-related screens, they would not pass a war-related screen.

Most semiconductor manufacturers sell off-the-shelf products that end up in military systems. The aerospace industry can account for from 10 to 20 percent of these companies' sales.

"An army runs on its stomach," runs the old truism. Is food, then, war-related when it's sold to the military? The U.S. garrisons its military around the world in enclaves that resemble nothing so much as small suburbs centered on a shopping center, the post exchange. Philip Morris (90) sells $140.8 million in goods to the Defense Department, more than half of which are food items.[18] How should one classify these goods? Even when a good seems more closely related to fighting, the line can be hard to draw. For instance, is kitchen equipment on an aircraft carrier war-related? After all, there is no conceivable nonmilitary use for such a ship.

Investors who want a military screen must define it for themselves and then work out the boundaries. Very few investment advisers have sufficient experience in this area to probe preferences very deeply. Relatively few large companies outside the financial-services sector are free of contracts with the Department of Defense. So the more tightly drawn the screen, the fewer investment-grade companies will pass it.

MILITARY SCREENS

A military screen would bar companies that have any contracts with the Department of Defense, the Department of Energy's noncivilian programs, and the Central Intelligence Agency. Close scrutiny of a company's relationships with the Departments of Agriculture and Commerce would also be in order, since those agencies serve as conduits and facilitators for concealed military aid. Our former ally, Saddam Hussein, received help this way during his diplomacy by other means with Iran.

Virtually all large companies would either fail such a screen or could not be monitored. (Corporations only have to disclose in their public documents significant lines of business and customers whose loss would significantly affect business.) Even with dollar/percentage tolerance levels, investors would have to limit themselves to very small companies whose sales could be monitored. They would probably have to forego money-center and super-regional banks, too, because of their inability to identify the recipients and the purposes of loans. Thus for practical purposes, a total military screen is impossible for any conventional securities investor.

A DISARMING FUTURE?

With the demise of the Soviet Union, it appeared a large part of the world could begin to disarm. Instead, the arms industry broadened its marketing to peoples, like the Croats and Serbs, who were now free to buy modern weaponry. Some U.S. weapons makers, McDonnell Douglas for one, have gained government approval for huge foreign arms sales as a way to keep employment up. In contrast, Lockheed, Olin, and McDermott International have formed Disarmament Inc. to profit from the Defense Department cuts.

The timidity of Western leaders, especially ours, in aiding the emerging countries of the former Soviet sphere may have cost the world its greatest opportunity to reduce armed conflicts. Instead, swords are being beaten into Uzis and spears into TOW missiles. It will be a long time before the military screen disappears from social investors' repertoire.

SIMPLE, THEY'RE NOT

The exclusionary screens have the virtue of clarity: Investors usually know how they feel about them. In some instances, like the sin stocks, investors can even implement them easily. But the issues surrounding them are not simple. If their screening is to have any meaning, investors must not only impose the screen but articulate why. And most importantly, they must advocate an alternative vision.

5

South Africa:
The Defining Issue

> To measure the effectiveness of an ethical sanction by whether it
> caused a country to make a U-turn makes as little sense as to
> describe sanctions against South Africa as futile because they
> have failed to destroy apartheid before now. The aim is to influ-
> ence for the better. And opportunism as well as absolute values
> must play a part.
>
> —*FINANCIAL TIMES* EDITORIAL, APRIL 14, 1990[1]

IN THE EARLY 1980s, some argued that when South Africa disappeared
as an issue, social investing would disappear with it. That prediction will
prove false. But there can be no doubt that South Africa transformed
social investing, and indeed investing as a whole.

Before South Africa emerged as an investment issue, social screens
were mainly a matter of religious concern. Now a screen had primarily
a political dimension, although with strong moral and religious over-
tones.* Purely exclusionary screens—alcohol, tobacco, and later, military weapons—had initially defined socially responsible investing. South
Africa expanded the range of options for investors. The first step was
divestiture—selling securities out of repugnance for their issuers' actions, in this case, their tacit support of apartheid. Universities such as

---

*We have already noted the critical role of the Interfaith Center on Corporate Responsibility
(ICCR) in shareholder activism and social investing generally. It is no exaggeration to say that ICCR
and the religious groups that make up its membership shaped the South Africa movement and
thereby defined modern social investing.

Princeton first had divestiture pressed on them in the late 1960s. Then in the mid-1970s came the Sullivan Principles for companies that did business in South Africa. Signing the Principles committed companies to do something affirmative. More importantly, by compelling companies to act, investors had acted affirmatively. And finally came disinvestment—the withdrawal of corporations from South Africa by not investing new capital or by selling or closing existing operations. Disinvestment began when shareholders frustrated with the slow pace of change in South Africa demanded it. But as a shareholder action, it moved too slowly. So the movement turned to Congress which, in 1986 and 1987, coerced corporations into leaving.

This evolution marked something new: the progression of the development of a code of conduct—albeit imperfect—and the mobilization of forces to compel legislative action. What made the South Africa issue different from the exclusionary screens described in the last chapter was the motivation behind the campaign. The will to force *positive* change drove the issue, not the desire to avoid association with something sinful. Political and social change both in South Africa *and* here—that is what it was about. Social investors showed that they could further that objective. This experience has shaped and will shape social investing's response to issues as diverse as Northern Ireland and the environment. For that reason—though we hope South Africa will soon cease to be a screen—a close look at the history of this issue is in order.

APARTHEID THEN AND NOW

On February 11, 1990, the South African government granted an unconditional release to the most famous political prisoner of the late twentieth century, Nelson Mandela. He had been in jail for twenty-seven years and three months for his involvement with the banned African National Congress (ANC).

The release of Mandela and other political prisoners, the "unbanning" of the ANC, and the March 1992 referendum that gave President F. W. de Klerk a mandate to proceed with the dismantling of apartheid gave the world hope. But if South Africa has come far since 1990, it still has a very long journey ahead. For even people with the best of wills cannot erase 350 years of oppression in two.

Segregation and subjection of blacks in Southern Africa arrived with the first permanent white settlers. In the 1650s, the Dutch established a trading outpost on the Cape of Good Hope. Dutch settlers considered blacks a separate species, calling them *skepsels* (creatures).[2] From the earliest days of colonization Europeans practiced slavery, until it was abolished in the early nineteenth century. Slavery at least in part rests on the denial of the slave's humanity. So do apartheid and segregation. As early as 1773 the Cape Colony even had separate gallows, "one . . . on which Europeans are hanged, and the other . . . on which slaves and Hottentots are executed."[3] The first pass laws—regulations controlling the movement of nonwhites—were enacted two hundred years ago.*

The intense mutual dislike of the original Dutch or Boer settlers for the new arrivals from Britain (after the British permanently assumed control of the Cape in 1806) only made matters worse for blacks.

The British may have had a more enlightened attitude on race until the discovery of gold and diamonds. The need for cheap labor ended that impulse. Beyond that, the British recruited Indians to come to South Africa to supply agricultural skills. With these workers came an entrepreneurial class whose competition threatened the white middle class. The long struggle between Indians and whites added sharpness to the movement for racial separation. It also changed world history by training Mohandas K. Gandhi in the techniques he would use to free India of British rule.[4]

Apartheid (literally, "apartness") is a legal system that enforces separation of the races. After the National Party won control of the South African Parliament in 1948, it institutionalized over the next eight years long-standing systems to control the nonwhite majority and extended apartheid with a number of repressive measures including:

- banning racially mixed marriages;
- requiring all citizens to register by racial groups (Population Registration Act); and
- assigning residential and commercial districts to individual racial groups (Group Areas Act). In later years, black Africans would be assigned as citizens of any one of ten "homelands" (bantustans), a convenient way of making them aliens in South Africa proper.[5]

AMERICA SHUTS ITS EYES

Until the late 1960s, the United States—both its government and its people—ignored the South African government's internal policies. South Africa had been an ally in both world wars. J. C. Smuts, the prime

---

*Even after making allowances for different cultural and geographical manifestations, the "separate but equal" policy in the United States and South African apartheid seem quite close. Both denied civil rights to nonwhites while using—often forcing—them to work under conditions of peonage.

minister who lost the crucial 1948 election, had played a prominent role in establishing the League of Nations and the United Nations.

In the nervous days of the cold war, South Africa was staunchly anticommunist. (Nelson Mandela received his life sentence under South Africa's Suppression of Communism Act.) South Africa was also the source of strategic minerals such as gold, platinum, chromium, and uranium. American and European investments in the country caused its economy to expand impressively during the 1950s and 1960s.[6]

The Sharpesville massacre (1960), when police killed sixty-nine black Africans during a peaceful demonstration, drew some American attention. So, too, did the writings and speeches of Alan Paton, whose novel *Cry, the Beloved Country* was an international best-seller. But in the main, Americans saw South Africa as just another country—one of many—with problems.

Of course, the United States had its own apartheid system in the South and de facto segregation in the North. In the 1960s and early 1970s Americans had their eyes fixed on matters nearer home. Freedom Riders, sit-ins, and marches made headlines; the war in southeast Asia polarized the country; a president was assassinated in 1963, then his brother and Martin Luther King, Jr., were murdered in 1968; antiwar protestors took over campuses in 1968 through 1970; and in the Cambodia Spring of 1970 the environmental movement took wing.

In a curious way, these upheavals laid the ground work for what became a powerful movement in the United States for change in South Africa. Awareness of their own failings made Americans sensitive to injustices abroad. In 1971 the presiding bishop of the Episcopal Church in the United States went to the shareholders meeting of General Motors and asked that the company get out of South Africa. This was the first public effort to use economic power to attack apartheid.

The Sullivan Principles

In chapter 1, we noted that the happiest consequence of round one of Project GM was the appointment of the Reverend Leon Sullivan to the auto maker's board. At the 1970 annual meeting, shareholders had defeated a resolution seeking minority (and other) representation on the GM board. Three months later, the first African-American* to serve on the governing body of what was then America's largest corporation took his seat.[7]

At the 1971 GM shareholders meeting, Sullivan, too, demanded that

---

*We will return to this fact in chapter 11, for—beyond Sullivan's own accomplishments—it has enormous significance to institutional investors in the 1990s.

the company withdraw from South Africa. Over the next five years, he revised his views and eventually opposed withdrawal. U.S. corporations acted as an internal force for reform, he and others reasoned, and their departure would harm the interests of the black majority.[8]

Sullivan began to work with twelve major corporations, including GM and IBM, to develop a statement of principles for companies doing business in South Africa. Its signatory companies would commit themselves to try to end racial separation and to promote fair employment practices.[9] The document came to be known as the Sullivan Principles. Its tenets have evolved over the years. Box 5-1 summarizes the current iteration.

The Principles did not meet with universal approval. Some activists saw them as a license to continue business as usual with the South African government.[10] And in the short run, they were right. But what the critics did not foresee was the Principles' long-term significance.

The signatories—at one time, seventy companies—had agreed to do *something* about an evil. The nation's largest international companies acknowledged that they had moral obligations, duties not quantifiable on financial statements. For one hundred years, corporations had wrapped

---

Box 5-1. Statement of Principles for South Africa (Abridged)*

1. Nonsegregation in the workplace.
2. Equal and fair employment practices for all.
3. Equal pay for all doing equal or comparable work.
4. Training programs to prepare blacks, coloreds, and Asians for managerial, clerical, and technical jobs.
5. Increasing the number of blacks, coloreds, and Asians in management and supervisory positions.
6. Improving the quality of employees' lives outside the workplace.
7. Working to eliminate laws and customs that impede social, economic, and political justice.

Source: "Fourteenth Report on the Signatory Companies to the Statement of Principles for South Africa," November 9, 1990 (Cambridge, Mass.: Arthur D. Little, Inc.), p. vi. Reprinted by permission.

*The Reverend Leon Sullivan, the Principles' original author in 1976, became increasingly dissatisfied with the ways in which the Principles came to be implemented. In 1987, he disassociated himself from them. They are now officially called the Statement of Principles.

themselves in the doctrines of social Darwinism and substantive due process* to argue that they were purely economic entities. Their only role, they argued, was to maximize their shareholders' wealth. This view grossly misrepresented the historical role of corporations. A discussion of this topic exceeds our scope here, but we will touch upon it again in chapter 11.

The Principles themselves stated standards by which corporations could be appraised. Here was a first step toward a system of corporate accountability. It showed the way for later statements of principles that apply to Northern Ireland, *maquiladoras*—the industrial zones in Mexico along the Rio Grande, and the environment. The Sullivan Principles also provided a framework for reasoned dialogue between activists and corporations. The parties had a structure for negotiation and compromise. These negotiations set a pattern later applied to the infant formula debate, tobacco marketing, and many other issues.

A key element in the Principles' success was more than twenty years of shareholder initiatives. These resolutions were effective in both getting U.S. companies to disinvest in South Africa and building public support for action against apartheid. In 1991 alone, churches, public pension funds, and individual shareholders submitted ninety-one resolutions regarding South Africa to eighty-two U.S. companies.[11]

The resolutions followed a pattern. Typically, the company was first asked to report on an aspect of its business in South Africa. In response to a church-sponsored resolution, Mobil became the first company to prepare such a report—on employment practices—in 1972.[12] There could be a series of information-seeking resolutions. Resolutions would also ask the recipient to sign or comply with the Sullivan Principles. Later resolutions would ask for reports on progress toward the Sullivan goals. Finally, companies were asked to disinvest. In 1991, Pfizer and Westinghouse received such resolutions.[13]

The importance of the information-seeking and the code-of-conduct resolutions cannot be overstated. They led to de facto standards for evaluating and comparing corporate behavior.

DIVESTITURE

For perhaps eight years before the Sullivan Principles appeared, concerned people had urged institutions—especially universities and public

---

*Substantive due process was a legal doctrine used to knock down much of the early social legislation, such as wage and hour laws. It dominated constitutional law for fifty years ending in the 1930s. As we will see in chapter 11, substantive due process has had something of a rebirth in the last twenty years.

pension funds—to sell their stock in companies with operations in South Africa. The divestiture movement flowed and ebbed with the nation's attention to South Africa. But in June 1976, an event took place that horrified people of conscience worldwide. Twenty thousand schoolchildren had marched in Soweto to protest government orders that Afrikaans be the language of their schools. Police opened fire on the children, killing two. Six months after the shootings and the ensuing riots, Madison, Wisconsin, passed what appears to be the first ordinance restricting purchases by that city from companies doing business in South Africa. East Lansing, Michigan, followed with a similar measure the following year.

Dissatisfaction with the progress made by the Sullivan signatories impelled many to take a more active approach. The Cambridge (Massachusetts) Retirement Board voted to divest in February 1980, making it one of the first institutions to do so. Many others followed suit: the states of New Jersey, California, Minnesota, and Michigan, the New York City Employee Retirement System, TIAA-CREF, and the Episcopal church prominent among them. Michigan State University and others divested their endowments.

Disinvestment

The loud public arguments over divestiture in city halls and state houses and on college campuses kept the relationship between apartheid and American business in the news for more than fifteen years. The impact of the divestiture movement on the government of South Africa may

TABLE 5-1. SOME PUBLICLY TRADED COMPANIES WITH EQUITY INTERESTS IN SOUTH AFRICA

Abbott Laboratories	Johnson & Johnson
American Cyanamid Co.	Kellogg Co.
Borden, Inc.	Minnesota Mining and Manufacturing Co.
Bristol-Myers Squibb Co.	Monsanto Co.
Chevron Corp.	Nalco Chemical Co.
Colgate-Palmolive Co.	Pfizer, Inc.
Deere & Co.	Schering-Plough Corp.
Du Pont Co.	Texaco Inc.
Eli Lilly and Co.	Upjohn Co.
Gillette Co.	Warner-Lambert Co.

These companies have an equity interest in a company doing business in South Africa. All data are current as of August 1, 1992.
Source: Kinder, Lydenberg, Domini & Co., Inc. the KLD Social Investment Database.

never be known. Not so with disinvestment—the diminishing or elimination of business operations and investment in South African ventures. From 1985 through 1987, over half of the 230 U.S. corporate operations in South Africa were either sold or dismantled. Many corporations complained that in pressuring them to leave South Africa, social activists in the United States would be leaving thousands of black South Africans unemployed—or employed by white South Africans who were not committed to enlightened practices. But by 1989, many U.S. firms—Mobil, Goodyear, International Paper, RJR Nabisco, Caltex Petroleum, and Johnson & Johnson among them—had disinvested. Why?

In 1985 the international banking community cut off new capital and credit.[14] In 1987, a U.S. tax law suspended the credit for taxes paid to foreign governments if the payments were made to the Republic of South Africa. This act hit the remaining firms hard. The biggest U.S. employer in South Africa—Mobil—damned that "foolish legislation" but tossed in the towel, selling its operations to Gencor, a white South African firm, for $150 million. To its credit, Mobil conditioned the sale on Gencor's continuing to fund at $3 million per year a foundation to provide nonwhites with opportunities in education and business and with home-ownership assistance.[15]

Like Mobil, Fluor Corporation, the giant engineering firm, resisted disinvestment. The firm's charismatic CEO, J. Robert Fluor, believed that

> business should not take moral stands in a world that is—by U.S. standards—highly immoral. "I think we have a lot of crazy standards," he told The [Los Angeles] Times in an interview in 1979. "I would a hell of a lot rather be a black in South Africa than be a Russian of any kind."[16]

In 1986 when Fluor disinvested, it sold its subsidiary but continued to directly employ workers, allowed its name to be used, and retained an option to buy the sub back.[17]

Nelson Mandela believes the economic pressures put on South Africa—in large part attributable to social investors—gained him freedom.[18] He may be right. According to the Interfaith Center on Corporate Responsibility (ICCR), between 1985 and 1990 South Africa "suffered a net capital outflow of $12 billion . . . and [saw] 40 percent of foreign-owned companies withdraw assets." Two-thirds of the U.S. companies in the country in 1984 had left by 1991.[19] Another source estimates that sanctions caused South Africa's gross domestic product to be from 20 to 35 percent lower than it otherwise would have been.[20]

U.S. statutes may have been a critical element to the collapse of apartheid. Shareholder activists aided their passage by keeping up the pressure on corporations and adding to the publicity barrage. In addition to the 1987 Tax Act, Congress enacted over President Reagan's veto the Comprehensive Anti-Apartheid Act of 1986. It banned further investments and bank loans, ended air links between the two nations, prohibited some imports, and enabled the U.S. government to cut off military aid to countries that were in violation of previous arms embargoes aimed at South Africa. As the third-largest investor in South Africa's economy (behind Britain and Germany), the United States had recognized, finally, that economic sanctions could persuade the South African government to change its ways.

The Comprehensive Anti-Apartheid Act defined the changes required in terms of five conditions for lifting economic sanctions:

- ending the state of emergency;
- releasing all political prisoners;
- unbanning all political parties;
- repealing of the Group Areas and Population Registration acts; and
- making a good-faith commitment to enter into negotiations with black African leaders.

These conditions fell well short of those in the Harare Declarations adopted by South African antiapartheid groups, most notably by failing to call for "one person, one vote."

Nonetheless, the sanctions imposed by the United States and other nations certainly compounded the economic difficulties South Africa experienced during the 1980s. The cutoff of foreign capital, embargoes against its products abroad, and disorder and uncertainty at home poisoned the atmosphere for investment for South African business people and foreigners alike. The annual rate of inflation rose rapidly through middecade: 11 percent in 1983; 13.2 percent in 1984; 16.2 percent in 1985; and 18.6 percent in 1986. Economic growth declined, and unemployment rose dramatically.[21] By 1987, South Africa could claim one of the world's moribund economies. Economic pain propelled the movement toward reform that began in 1989 under the leadership of F. W. de Klerk.

But remember: the divestiture/disinvestment movement was never —and is not now—the real story here. Rather, the movement was only *a way of making the public aware of the U.S. role in South Africa.* As part of a much larger movement to push South Africa toward a democratic society, its means may be financial but its objectives are political. So the measure of the movement's success is not the billions divested but the vast number of people who have forced businesses, institutions, and governments to take action.

IS IT TIME TO REINVEST?

By late winter of 1992, Americans thought the possibilities for democratic change and the end of apartheid seemed enormously hopeful, if not unstoppable. This progress prompted some to call for an end to economic and moral sanctions against South Africa. Indeed, President Bush had announced in 1991 the end of economic sanctions under the Anti-Apartheid Act. Some leaders representing public pension funds and endowments voiced interest in reinvesting in South Africa to signal their satisfaction with the course events were now taking. Jean Mayer, president of Tufts University, argued that progress in South Africa was threatened by economic disintegration. Citing violence provoked by 30 percent unemployment, Mayer told the *New York Times,* "Unless there is reinvestment soon . . . all political progress is going to be wiped out."[22] Little money flowed from the United States back into South Africa. However, some British institutions—including the socially screened Merlin Ecology Fund—have begun gradually reinvesting in selected progressive companies, such as Reckitt & Coleman.[23]

So when will it be time for U.S. companies to go back into South Africa? When there is a multiracial government in place. Some put the answer more simply: when Desmond Tutu and Nelson Mandela say it's time. And neither Tutu, the Anglican archbishop of Cape Town, nor Mandela has said financial sanctions should be relaxed, much less eliminated.

From seven thousand miles away, democracy for South Africa seems inevitable. Undoubtedly, it looks less so from Tutu's and Mandela's perspective. The apartheid system did not appear out of nothing in 1948. Ending that system marks only a first step in the process of creating a new social fabric for the country. Tutu and Mandela know this, and they will not succumb to enthusiasm. Neither should social investors.

THE CURRENT SCREENS

Until black African leaders say that outside investment is welcome, most social investors will not buy stocks of companies that have equity interests or operations in South Africa. An "equity interest" is an ownership interest in a South African company. Kimberly-Clark and Kellogg have them. An "operation" is a physical presence in South Africa. It might consist of as little as a one-person sales office.

Companies such as Eastman Kodak that cut all ties when it aban-

**TABLE 5-2. SOME COMPANIES WITH NONEQUITY, NONSTRATEGIC
INTERESTS IN SOUTH AFRICA**

Coca-Cola Co.	PepsiCo Inc.
FMC Corp.	Sensormatic Electronics Corp.
Honeywell, Inc.	Tektronix, Inc.
Lotus Development Corp.	Weyerhauser Corp.
Microsoft Corp.	

These companies appear to have, or to have had recently, nonequity interests
in nonstrategic industries in South Africa. All data are current as of December
30, 1992.
Source: Kinder, Lydenberg, Domini & Co., Inc., the KLD Social Investment
Database.

doned the country are rare. As many as half of all U.S. firms that have
disinvested have retained some nonequity links.

A nonequity link usually takes the form of a licensing or sales agreement, which is a contract between a South African company and a U.S.
company. A licensing agreement might permit a local firm to use technology or copyrighted material. A sales agreement might permit a local
company to import and sell goods. Apple Computers has sales agreements that permit locals to service its computers sold in the country
before Apple withdrew. Most social investors will not buy the securities
of companies that have substantial nonequity involvement in strategic
areas within the South African economy. The industries generally regarded as strategic are mining, energy, computers, and transportation—
activities that greatly benefit the current South African economic and
social infrastructure.

THOSE WHO NEVER LEFT

Assuming that Archbishop Tutu and Mr. Mandela do one day invite
foreign corporations to return to South Africa, social investors will find

**TABLE 5-3. SOME COMPANIES WITH STRATEGIC INVOLVEMENT
IN SOUTH AFRICA**

Chase Manhattan Corp.	Hewlett-Packard Co.
Citicorp	International Business Machines Corp.
Ford Motor Co.	Manufacturers Hanover Corp.
General Motors Corp.	Unisys Corp.
Goodyear Tire & Rubber Co.	

These companies appear to have, or to have had recently, a substantial nonequity involvement in South Africa in areas of strategic importance to the South African government. All
data are current as of August 1, 1992.
Source: Kinder, Lydenberg, Domini & Co., Inc., the KLD Social Investment Database.

themselves confronted by another sticky problem: what to do about the companies that stayed. Some investors may decide to forget the past and bring these companies back into their portfolios. But to many that seems wrongheaded. At the very least, some believe investors must take a corporation's response to the apartheid system as an indication of its attitude toward issues of business ethics in general. But for how long?

One approach may be to look at what the company did in South Africa. So for companies like Kellogg, the answer to how long they should remain on probation may be very briefly, since it dealt only in foodstuffs. Other companies not tied to consumer products or pharmaceuticals may not return to social investors' universes for a long time, depending on their connections to the apartheid system. The precedent is limited. For Britain's Barclays Bank, which left in 1986, the sanctions remained until its president, Sir John Quinton, approached Bishop Trevor Huddleston, a white South African who has spent most of his life fighting apartheid. "I said I thought that Jesus Christ told the sinner to go away and sin no more. He didn't put him on good behaviour for another six months. Huddleston laughed, and a few days later they took off the sanctions."[24]

In the end, who stayed and who left may not matter. The need for reinvestment might be so great that it overwhelms any moral considerations, at least on the South African end.[25] How the individual social investor reacts may be another matter.

HELPING POSTAPARTHEID SOUTH AFRICA

Even with the best of political outcomes, the economic outlook for South Africa does not appear good for the decade ahead. The country suffers from the problems common to all of southern Africa: low economic growth, high birth rates, rampant AIDS, and dependence on commodities—metals, diamonds, and agriculture products—in a world dominated by services and manufactured goods. Furthermore, South African industries have more in common with the state-owned industries of eastern Europe than with their free-market counterparts.

Years of apartheid have done nothing to win friends for free-market capitalism among the blacks who would dominate the government if full democracy were accomplished. According to The Economist, a survey of black and mixed-race university students indicates that one-third considered themselves social democrats, another third Marxists, and the final third Trotskyites.[26] Indeed, South Africa seems to be the only place on the globe where reformers are unabashed in their support of socialist economic programs.

A postapartheid government will be under tremendous pressure to upgrade housing, schools, and medical facilities for the 80-plus percent of the population that is black. With the economic pie actually shrinking, government will have to either slice it differently or plead for international aid to fund its social programs. Given the skimpy portions doled out to Russia and the other former Soviet states—which have thirty thousand nuclear warheads—one wonders what the West and its bankers will have for South Africa. The investment attraction for foreign firms will also be problematic.

SOCIAL INVESTING AFTER APARTHEID

Social investing predated apartheid, but will it survive its demise? Some institutional investors required by law to divest will take a signal to go back into South Africa as a sign that they may once again ignore social concerns. Tens of billions of dollars will no longer reside in socially screened portfolios.

However, social investing now has a broad base of support for a variety of causes, as we will see in the following chapters. The South Africa issue has spawned a generation of shareholder activists and investors motivated not by laws or single issues, but by deep social concerns. They are applying its lessons to a spectrum of issues ranging from employee relations to smoking to the relationship between corporations and their communities.

Take one example: 1991 marked the twentieth anniversary of the Interfaith Center for Corporate Responsibility (ICCR), the coalition of religious institutional investors that has been the backbone of shareholder actions on South Africa. Rather than celebrate past successes, ICCR used its anniversary to look forward to new challenges, especially regarding protection of the environment.

Socially responsible investing grew up on the South Africa issue. No issue will ever again dominate the social investor's agenda the way it has because social investment has taken its place as a technique used by many movements for change. Social investing is here to stay.

6

The Environment

"AFTER DONATING TO ENVIRONMENTAL GROUPS, recycling their trash, and reducing their waste, people are now demanding that their investments be consistent with their environmental values," says Mindy Lubber, president of the Green Century Funds. "They are insisting on environmentally responsible companies and environmentally screened mutual funds."[1]

In terms of the number of socially responsible investors, the environment has become the dominant concern though it ranks well behind South Africa in terms of the dollars screened. Since the mid-1980s, social investors and the institutions that serve them have added or repeatedly tightened environmental screens. For instance, in 1992 the nation's largest pension fund, TIAA-CREF, adopted a rigorous environmental screen for its Social Choice Account. And new funds focusing on the environment, like the Green Century family, have opened their doors.

Social investors are not alone in emphasizing their environmental concerns. Seventy-five percent of the respondents to a 1989 Gallup poll described themselves as "environmentalists"[2] and expressed a willingness to pay for environmental protection through higher taxes and higher prices.[3] An even better barometer than Gallup is the world's largest restaurant company, McDonald's. In the late 1980s, as many environmentalists pointed out, McDonald's clamshell boxes accounted for 80 million of the 12 billion pounds of disposable plastic packaging used each year. In August 1990, McDonald's and the Environmental Defense Fund (EDF), one of America's most influential environmental groups, announced they would jointly study how McDonald's disposed of solid wastes. Their association would be informal, with EDF paying its own expenses. But both were committed to finding practical solutions to a large problem. Three months later, McDonald's and EDF announced that the restaurant chain would eliminate their foam box in favor of a quilted paper wrapper.[4]

Whether paper is the best solution—something some critics question—is less important than the fact that a major generator of solid waste responded to public opinion—and its own sense of what was right—and acted. In the 1970s, when environmentalism was newly born, the McDonald's-EDF partnership would have seemed revolutionary. In the 1990s, the public and some segments of the corporate world were prepared, if not eager, for it.

How did this happen? What can social investors do to keep up the momentum? Those are our themes for this chapter.

NEPA AND ENVIRONMENTAL AWARENESS

Public awareness of the environment's frailty can be dated to 1961, the year *The New Yorker* published excerpts from Rachel Carson's landmark book, *Silent Spring*. In it Carson, a marine biologist, warned that pesticides were poisoning our fellow beings—and ourselves. *Silent Spring* changed our perception of the world, but the environmental movement in its broadest sense probably dates to 1969, to something that drew directly on Carson's book.

THE NATIONAL ENVIRONMENTAL POLICY ACT

Controlling the mosquito with DDT—widely regarded as a success of American technology—had had unintended consequences for all forms of life, including humans, Carson showed. In 1969, Congress responded with the National Environmental Policy Act (NEPA), requiring federal agencies to study the environmental impact of a proposed action in its full context. If the Nuclear Regulatory Commission receives an application for construction of a new power plant, it must consider matters such as the potential for releases of radioactive gases and the effects on neighboring wetlands. But NEPA does not require the agency to choose the best option from an environmental standpoint. Its purpose is only to ensure that the decision-makers factor in ecological considerations. Box 6-1 lists what an agency must consider.

NEPA has been described as an environmental full-disclosure law. But it is much more than that. It demands a new approach to decision

Box 6-1. The National Environmental Policy Act (NEPA)

In its effects on American society, NEPA probably ranks with the Northwest Ordinance (1787), which defined how the United States would expand and with what forms of government, and the Morrill Act (1862), which through land grants funded public higher education west and south of the Appalachians. Like many of our most important laws, the National Environmental Policy Act (NEPA) made an enormous change with a very few, undistinguished words. What follows is the part of the Act that specifies what federal agencies must do before they take a proposed action.

The Congress authorizes and directs that . . . all agencies of the Federal Government shall—

(A) utilize a systematic, interdisciplinary approach which will insure the integrated use of the natural and social sciences and the environmental design arts in planning and in decision making which may have an impact on man's environment;

(B) identify and develop methods and procedures, in consultation with the Council on Environmental Quality . . . , which will insure that presently unquantified environmental amenities and values may be given appropriate consideration in decisionmaking along with economic and technical considerations;

(C) include in every recommendation or report on proposals for legislation and other major Federal actions significantly affecting the quality of the human environment, a detailed statement by the responsible official on—

(i) the environmental impact of the proposed action,

(ii) any adverse environmental effects which cannot be avoided should the proposal be implemented,

(iii) alternatives to the proposed action,

(iv) the relationship between local short-term uses of man's environment and the maintenance and enhancement of long-term productivity, and

(v) any irreversible and irretrievable commitments of resources which would be involved in the proposed action should it be implemented.

Source: 4/2 U.S.C. §4332 (NEPA §102(2)).

making. Most members of Congress who voted for NEPA probably did not realize how radical a change they were launching. The key elements are the "systematic, interdisciplinary approach" to decision making and the factors to be described in the "detailed statement." American business had flourished—from the cotton gin to the Model-T by looking at the elements of a process and reducing them to mechanical segments, not by looking at the world as an integrated whole.

From the province of a few dedicated academics, such as Eugene Odom at the University of Georgia, the analysis of environmental consequences became overnight something all government agencies and the businesses that worked on government projects had to master. Throughout the 1970s, they learned by doing. Meanwhile, academic institutions began offering courses in environmental studies across the entire spectrum of disciplines from engineering to English. But it was not until the 1990s that top business schools began to consider courses on environmental management.

THE CORPORATE REACTION

Over the past twenty-five years, some industries and companies have fought environmental regulation and enforcement every step of the way. In a war against the growing environmental ethic, some held local economies hostage with threats of plant closings and frightened workers into serving as their foot soldiers.

Take, for example, the long fight between a coalition of public interest groups and the state of Minnesota on one side and Reserve Mining, a company originally owned by Armco and Republic Steel on the other. Reserve operated a huge plant on Lake Superior, in Silver Bay, Minnesota, where it crushed taconite rock and extracted iron ore for shipment to steel mills. The remains, hundreds of thousands of tons of "tailings" (powdered rock containing asbestos fibers), went into Lake Superior. In the early 1970s, the damage to the lake became apparent to the Minnesota Department of Natural Resources, which moved to force Reserve to stop dumping. Reserve argued that any changes in their operation would make the plant uneconomic and force its closing. Silver Bay had no other major source of employment. Steel-union officials and rank and file members took Reserve's side.

The Reserve battle set a pattern that continued from the 1970s into the 1990s on recycling initiatives, efforts to preserve forest lands from logging, and disputes over mining—wherever a case can be made that environmental requirements threaten jobs. But the Reserve case has an

ending that may bode well for all concerned. Cypress Minerals now owns
the operation. The cleanup has begun. Dumping in Lake Superior has
stopped, and water-quality levels are very good.[5] If the domestic steel
industry comes back—and that is a big if—the Silver Bay plant will again
employ a lot of workers.

Other corporations have taken a different approach. For instance,
starting in the mid-1970s, 3M faced rising costs for disposing of the many
toxic byproducts of its tape, adhesives, and specialty chemical businesses. The company responded with its Pollution Prevention Pays programs, which systematically incorporated reduction of wastes into its
product design and manufacturing processes. However, despite the apparent success of the program, the Citizens Fund, using 1989 EPA data,
ranked 3M second on its list of the largest legal emitters of toxic chemicals into the air, second on its list of legal dischargers of toxic chemicals
into water, and first on its list of legal releasers of chemicals suspected
of causing birth defects.

By the early 1990s, more and more companies were trying to address environmental issues. Computer companies—including Apple,
Digital Equipment (DEC), and Compaq—developed innovative alternatives to manufacturing processes that had required ozone-depleting
chemicals. Hundreds of "green" products had appeared in recent
years. Some, like Ecover's household chemicals, were genuinely new.
Others were old products in new "green" bottles. Procter & Gamble
has replaced plastic shampoo bottles with refill cartons made of biodegradable materials and redesigned Sure deodorant containers to eliminate shipping cartons. Both approaches have positive environmental
impact.

ENVIRONMENTAL EVALUATIONS

A sure gauge of the environment's importance to U.S. corporations is
the attention they call to their green initiatives. Social investors have
learned never to take these at face value. Businesses now know that
their claims are likely to be checked, as Mobil learned when it had to
withdraw its "biodegradable" claims for its Hefty™ trashbags. As we
will see when we discuss environmentally beneficial products, some
rating services now exist to guide consumers and investors through the
"green or not green" determination. But the question is often not an
easy one.

If it is difficult to evaluate the greenness of a single product, judging
the environmental performance of even the smallest *Fortune* 500 com-

pany is a Herculean task. Since 1989 a coalition of social-investment professionals, church groups, and institutions have advanced the cause of environmental accountability through a code of conduct. The Coalition for Environmentally Responsible Economies' CERES Principles* describe aspirational standards and a commitment to report on environmental performance. Joan Bavaria, president of Franklin Research & Development Corporation and CERES cochair, has said that the Principles stand for the proposition that social issues are every bit as important as financial data in understanding a company.[6] The Principles are reprinted in Box 6-2.

The Principles serve two purposes: First, they are a vehicle for asking businesses to commit themselves to minimum standards of behavior toward the environment. In February 1993, the Sun Company (Sunoco) became the first *Fortune* 500 company to sign the Principles. Forty smaller companies had signed the Principles, including publicly traded companies such as Ben & Jerry's, LecTec, and Ringer. But support for the Principles is growing.

Second, the CERES Principles provide a mechanism for evaluating corporate behavior against measurable standards. As with the Sullivan Principles discussed in chapter 5, they are a code of conduct. A social investor can ask initially whether the company has subscribed to the Principles and after signing whether it has lived up to them.

Social-issue shareholder activists are playing a key role in the effort to convince corporations to subscribe to the CERES Principles. From the 1990 through the 1992 proxy seasons, approximately fifty companies each year received resolutions asking them to adopt the CERES Principles. The sponsors included members of the Interfaith Center on Corporate Responsibility (ICCR)—the Evangelical Lutheran Church in America, the Maryknoll Fathers and Brothers, the United Methodist Church, and several others—and three New York City pension funds. The vote in favor of these resolutions in 1992 ranged from 5.7 percent to 12.2 percent. The average vote for adoption was 8 percent.[7]

In 1991, CERES began circulating draft policy statements and report forms that companies would use. The process of devising the reporting mechanisms will be a long one. But, when the Principles are adopted broadly and the coalition implements its reporting system, social investors and the public at large will have a much better means of evaluating companies' assertions. For now, socially responsible investors must rely on bellwethers. The balance of this chapter will explore those we use.

---

*Until 1992, the Principles were called the Valdez Principles because the coalition came together in response to the *Exxon Valdez* grounding.

PUBLIC CONTROVERSIES AND REGULATORY PROBLEMS

Social investors tend to avoid companies that have recently paid significant fines or civil penalties or have been involved in major controversies involving some form of environmental degradation. The key words here are *significant* and *major*. Ultimately, you will have to define what they mean for yourself.

The range of environmental regulations makes it likely that a large company will, at some point, run afoul of either the public or the regulators. Companies like Disney that develop large tracts of land often run afoul of local environmental groups and preservationists. The larger the company, the more likely a controversy will arise. Depending, of course, on its magnitude and seriousness, an occasional problem should not overly concern a social investor. A civil violation of an air-emissions permit is not the Bhopal disaster. Rather, investors should look for patterns of controversies or violations, and study how the company responded. For many social investors, the fact that the *Amoco Cadiz* ran aground in 1978 and fouled the beaches of Brittany is of far less significance than the fact that Amoco fought the French for thirteen years over cleanup costs.

A key element to evaluating any company is its record of criminal liabilities. The law is divided into criminal and civil law. A finding of guilt under a criminal statute implies blameworthiness. Proving a criminal violation is a much more difficult proposition for a prosecutor than winning a civil case. It is the difference between establishing guilt beyond a reasonable doubt and proving liability by a preponderance of the evidence; that is, the weight of the evidence indicates responsibility.

Even when environmental enforcement is a top priority, government agencies hesitate to bring criminal cases because of the investment of time and money required. When the government takes a criminal case to trial, you can be virtually positive that the alleged violation was serious—though you cannot assume the defendant's guilt. However, look very hard at companies that plead guilty or are found guilty of criminal charges.

Although civil violations are, by definition, less blameworthy than criminal, in practice they may not be. You must look closely at the underlying events to determine whether the company is truly culpable or merely the victim of something beyond its control. Many civil violations do not require a finding of fault. Suppose a company correctly handled hazardous waste it generated, but the waste ended up in a landfill designated as a Superfund site. The innocent company will

Box 6-2. The CERES Principles

INTRODUCTION

By adopting these Principles, we publicly affirm our belief that corporations have a responsibility for the environment, and must conduct all aspects of their business as responsible stewards of the environment by operating in a manner that protects the Earth. We believe that corporations must not compromise the ability of future generations to sustain themselves.

We will update our practices continually in light of advances in technology and new understandings in health and environmental science. In collaboration with CERES, we will promote a dynamic process to ensure that the Principles are interpreted in a way that accommodates changing technologies and environmental realities. We intend to make consistent, measurable progress in implementing these Principles and to apply them in all aspects of our operations throughout the world.

1. *Protection of the Biosphere.* We will reduce and make continual progress toward eliminating the release of any substance that may cause environmental damage to the air, water, or the earth or its inhabitants. We will safeguard all habitats affected by our operations and will protect open spaces and wilderness, while preserving biodiversity.
2. *Sustainable Use of Natural Resources.* We will make sustainable use of renewable natural resources, such as water, soils, and forests. We will conserve nonrenewable natural resources through efficient use and careful planning.
3. *Reduction and Disposal of Wastes.* We will reduce and where possible eliminate waste through source reduction and recycling. All waste will be handled and disposed of through safe and responsible methods.
4. *Energy Conservation.* We will conserve energy and improve the energy efficiency of our internal operations and of the goods and services we sell. We will make every effort to use environmentally safe and sustainable energy sources.
5. *Risk Reduction.* We will strive to minimize the environmental, health and safety risks to our employees and the communities in which we operate through safe technologies, facilities, and operating procedures, and by being prepared for emergencies.
6. *Safe Products and Services.* We will reduce and where possible eliminate the use, manufacture, or sale of products and services that cause environmental damage or health or safety

hazards. We will inform our customers of the environmental impacts of our products or services and try to correct unsafe use.

7. *Environmental Restoration.* We will promptly and responsibly correct conditions we have caused that endanger health, safety or the environment. To the extent feasible, we will redress injuries we have caused to persons or damage we have caused to the environment and will restore the environment.

8. *Informing the Public.* We will inform in a timely manner everyone who may be affected by conditions that might endanger health, safety or the environment. We will regularly seek advice and counsel through dialogue with persons in communities near our facilities. We will not take any action against employees for reporting dangerous incidents or conditions to management or to appropriate authorities.

9. *Management Commitment.* We will implement these Principles and sustain a process that ensures that the Board of Directors and Chief Executive Officer are fully informed about pertinent environmental issues and are fully responsible for environmental policy. In selecting our Board of Directors, we will consider demonstrated environmental commitment as a factor.

10. *Audits and Reports.* We will conduct an annual self-evaluation of our progress in implementing these Principles. We will support the timely creation of generally accepted environmental audit procedures. We will annually complete the CERES Report, which will be made available to the public.

DISCLAIMER

These Principles establish an environmental ethic with criteria by which investors and others can assess the environmental performance of companies. Companies that sign these Principles pledge to go voluntarily beyond the requirements of the law. These Principles are not intended to create new legal liabilities, expand existing rights or obligations, waive legal defenses, or otherwise affect the legal position of any signatory company, and are not intended to be used against a signatory in any legal proceeding for any purpose.

This amended version of the CERES Principles was adopted by the CERES Board of Directors on April 28, 1992.

Contact: National Environmental Law Center (NELC), 29 Temple Place, Boston, MA 02111; (617) 422-0880; Coalition for Environmentally Responsible Economies (CERES), 711 Atlantic Avenue, Boston, MA 02111; (617) 451-0927.

be liable for cleaning up the site along with the people whose misfeasance caused the problem. So you must study the substance of civil liabilities before making a judgment about a company's environmental performance.

HAZARDOUS SUBSTANCES AND CONTROVERSIAL CHEMICALS

Social investors look for companies that have instituted substantial, company-wide changes in production processes to eliminate the use of hazardous substances in the course of normal operations. Called "source reductions," these efforts can mean less environmental harm to workers and consumers.

Hazardous substances include any substance that poses a threat to human health or the environment.[8] By reducing the use of hazardous substances, companies reduce the need to dispose of hazardous wastes. The U.S. Environmental Protection Agency (EPA) defines wastes as hazardous if, because of their quantity, concentration, or physical, chemical, or infectious characteristics, they cause or significantly contribute to an increase in mortality or serious illness, or if they pose a present or potential hazard to human health and the environment when improperly managed. Toxic wastes are hazardous wastes that are "directly poisonous to humans."[9] Asbestos, lead, and mercury are three substances whose presence in wastes can have them classified as toxic, as are radioactive materials and many of the seventy thousand chemicals industry uses regularly.[10] We know very little about most chemicals' toxic

TABLE 6-1. SELECTED COMPANIES WITH MAJOR POLLUTION
CONTROVERSIES

Atlantic Richfield Co.	Occidental Petroleum Corp.
Bethlehem Steel Corp.	Pfizer Inc.
Bristol-Myers Squibb Co.	Potlatch Corp.
Browning-Ferris Industries, Inc.	Royal Dutch Petroleum
Du Pont Co.	Safety-Kleen Corp.
Eastman Kodak Co.	Union Pacific Corp.
Exxon Corp.	Unocal Corp.
International Paper Co.	Upjohn Co.
Louisiana-Pacific Corp.	Waste Management, Inc.
Maxus Energy Corp.	

These selected companies have a recent record of fines, civil suits, or major controversies relating to air, water, noise, or land pollution. Data are current as of August 1, 1992.
Source: Kinder, Lydenberg, Domini & Co., Inc., the KLD Social Investment Database.

effects. According to one estimate, no toxicity data is available on 79 percent of these compounds.[11] And yet they end up in our homes, workplaces, food, water, and landfills.

Our bellwether here is straightforward. We reject companies with potential hazardous-waste liabilities that exceed $100 million, and we look very carefully at a company with potential liabilities that exceed $20 million or extend to more than twenty sites, or cover one or more sites located at a company facility.

FEDERAL REGULATIONS

In order to apply this standard, you need some background on three federal laws. They define a company's liabilities for the hazardous wastes it generates and require the government to make public what hazardous substances a company may legally release into the environment. More importantly from your standpoint, they determine what you can find out easily.

CERCLA and SARA.   Investors' main source of information about a company's liabilities for disposal of hazardous wastes is the SEC Form 10-K. An increasing number of companies provide thorough reports, but overall the coverage is inadequate. Fortunately, alternative sources, such as EPA data bases, are available.

Two federal statutes referred to as CERCLA and SARA determine what a company tells you about its hazardous waste–disposal liabilities—and how the company says it. The laws are extremely complex and jargon-laden, and therefore so are the 10-K descriptions.

The Comprehensive Environmental Response, Compensation, and Liability Act of 1980 (CERCLA) gave EPA authority to clean up hazardous substances released into the environment and to prevent such releases in the future. It compels responsible parties to fund cleanups and, if they do not, authorizes the EPA to recover the costs of remediation. Hazardous-waste generators have cradle-to-grave liability, meaning a company cannot avoid responsibility by selling or transferring the waste to someone else. CERCLA also established the Superfund, a $1.6 billion trust for cleanups. The Superfund Amendments and Reauthorization Act of 1986 (SARA)* added $8.6 billion to the trust fund.

CERCLA requires the EPA to identify and evaluate disposal sites

---

*The two acts are often called "the Superfund statutes." We have not used this term because it implies that a taxpayer-subsidized fund will take care of the remediation problem. The fund pays only when waste generators cannot or will not take care of a site.

containing potentially hazardous wastes. As of 1991, the EPA had identified approximately 34,000. In assessing a site, the EPA considers the quantity and toxicity of the wastes involved, the number of persons potentially or actually exposed, and the importance and vulnerability of underlying groundwater sources.

Of the sites it evaluates, the EPA adds a relatively small number—about one hundred per year—to the National Priorities List (NPL), a list of sites that qualify for long-term cleanup under CERCLA and SARA. For each site, the EPA tracks down "potentially responsible parties" (PRP), anyone who might have contributed to a National Priorities List site and who may be liable for some or all of its cleanup. Just because a company that has no liabilities for an NPL site does not mean it is free of all hazardous waste liabilities. A company may also be liable for sites designated by state or local authorities as requiring cleanup or sites on their properties that regulators have yet to designate.

A company's estimates of its hazardous waste–disposal liabilities in the Form 10-K can serve as a measure of the risks its manufacturing processes pose to the environment and of the environmental harm it has caused in the past. A broad PRP gauge has advantages. CERCLA and state regulatory proceedings provide a mechanism for allocating responsibility in often complicated situations.

A PRP gauge, however, has drawbacks. For the most part, the disposal practices that resulted in these liabilities were legal. Also, many companies become PRPs because of the disposal practices of parties with whom they contracted or because of the acquisition of properties

TABLE 6-2. HAZARDOUS WASTE–SITE LIABILITIES—SELECTED COMPANIES

Aluminum Co. of America	Niagara Mohawk Power Corp.
Atlantic Richfield Co.	NL Industries, Inc.
Browning-Ferris Industries, Inc.	Occidental Petroleum Corp.
Chevron Corp.	Panhandle Eastern Corp.
Dow Chemical Co.	Reynolds Metals Co.
Du Pont Co.	Rockwell International Corp.
Eastman Kodak Co.	Royal Dutch Petroleum
Ford Motor Co.	Union Pacific Corp.
General Electric Co.	Unocal Corp.
General Motors Corp.	Waste Management Inc.

These companies face liabilities for hazardous-waste sites that exceed $20 million, or for more than twenty sites, or for Superfund sites at their facilities. Data are current as of August 1, 1992.
Source: Kinder, Lydenberg, Domini & Co., Inc., the KLD Social Investment Database.

on which third parties had disposed of hazardous wastes. Thus, liability does not *necessarily* bear any relation to blameworthiness. Not a few innocent parties have found themselves with substantial CERCLA liabilities.

CERCLA imposes on a site's PRPs "joint and several liability," which means in practice that any PRP who contributed waste to the site is liable for the entire cleanup. But that party has a right to be indemnified by the other PRPs in proportion to their deposits in the site. Suppose one hundred generators sent waste to a site. The EPA can prove that Megacompany sent a small amount of waste to the site, while Minicompany contributed 30 percent. The EPA can demand payment for the entire site from Megacompany and leave it to Mega and its insurers to collect from the other PRPs. From the regulators' standpoint, this "deep-pockets" approach is wonderfully efficient and shifts the focus of PRP hostility to big companies—which explains why GM—not the EPA—got mugged in the press for attempting to extract a contribution from a Girl Scout camp that had sent garbage to a site later found to contain toxic wastes.[12]

In 1992, the NPL includes 1,245 sites. Manufacturing companies are responsible for approximately 39 percent of these sites. Since 1980, just eighty-four NPL sites have been completely cleaned up. The cost to taxpayers and private business of CERCLA through 1991 was $11.1 billion.[13] EPA estimates *its* cleanup costs for sites currently on the NPL at $27 billion. Those parties responsible for the hazardous wastes, however, perform roughly 65 percent of the cleanup work and will spend billions more. On average, cleanup costs $26 million per NPL site and takes six to eight years to complete. Congress has consistently underestimated the entire hazardous-waste cleanup task, if some critics are right, by a factor of one hundred. And the EPA has proven incapable of achieving the act's goals. Congress will have to revisit CERCLA soon.[14]

Toxic Release Inventory. One of the most cited sources of information on the release of hazardous substances into the environment is the Toxic Release Inventory (TRI). It came into existence after Union Carbide's Bhopal catastrophe as part of the Emergency Planning and Community Right to Know Act of 1986.

The emissions reported on the TRI are either authorized by permit or do not require a permit. The TRI is supposed to inform the public who is emitting what, and in what quantities. Because the EPA reports the information on a plant-by-plant basis, it would be very difficult to get national figures if Citizens Fund did not do the job for us each year. Table 6-3 is their 1989 list.

**TABLE 6-3. TOTAL RELEASES OF TOXIC CHEMICALS:
TOP FIFTY MANUFACTURING COMPANIES, 1989**

Company	Total Releases (tons)
1. Du Pont Co.	343,648,629
2. Monsanto Co.	293,831,577
3. American Cyanamid Co.	201,958,338
4. BP America	123,747,517
5. Renco Holdings Inc.	119,141,675
6. 3M	108,574,134
7. Vulcan Materials Co.	93,145,699
8. General Motors Corp.	85,833,092
9. Eastman Kodak Co.	79,461,625
10. Phelps Dodge Corp.	77,417,192
11. BASF	76,670,606
12. Elf Aquitaine	73,322,120
13. Asarco Inc.	70,808,110
14. Inland Steel Industries Inc.	57,273,300
15. Allied-Signal Inc.	52,851,716
16. Occidental Petroleum	49,538,291
17. Hoechst Celanese Corp.	48,536,583
18. National Steel Corp.	47,160,875
19. Courtaulds Fibers, Inc.	45,827,522
20. Amoco Corp.	41,501,998
21. Freeport McMoRan Inc.	40,427,833
22. General Electric Co.	36,901,904
23. Ford Motor Co.	35,194,199
24. Unocal Corp.	32,466,516
25. Akzo Chemicals Inc.	30,131,205
26. Union Carbide	28,600,898
27. Arcadian Corp.	28,342,033
28. Dow Chemical Co.	27,255,557
29. First Mississippi Corp.	27,009,143
30. Eli Lilly & Co.	26,756,305
31. Westvaco	26,084,978
32. Scepter Industries Inc.	25,730,388
33. USX Corp.	25,464,557
34. Upjohn Co.	25,040,576
35. Pfizer Inc.	24,022,019
36. Air Products and Chemicals, Inc.	23,938,056
37. International Paper Co.	23,156,341
38. Texaco Inc.	22,067,700
39. PPG Industries	21,251,073
40. Reynolds Metals Co.	21,020,394
41. Agricultural Minerals Corp.	20,596,587
42. Sterling Chemicals Inc.	20,574,970
43. Witco Corp.	20,472,323
44. Shell Oil	20,369,649
45. Chrysler Corp.	19,168,728

TABLE 6-3.—continued

Company	Total Releases (tons)
46. Wheeling Pittsburgh Steel	19,105,375
47. Royster Co.	18,746,357
48. Coastal Corp.	18,370,404
49. James River Corp.	18,322,309
50. Union Camp Corp.	18,115,018

Source: EPA data and Citizens Fund calculations. *Manufacturing Pollution: A Survey of the Nation's Toxic Polluters* (Washington, D.C.: The Citizens Fund, 1991), p. 27. Reprinted by permission of the Citizens Fund.

SOURCE REDUCTIONS

CERCLA's harsh penalties have inspired source reductions. Some companies face greater challenges than others. CFCs (chlorofluorocarbons) in cleaning compounds are easy to eliminate. But what about ending the use of chlorine in making paper? A much more difficult problem.

Many companies have announced ambitious waste-reduction goals. AT&T decided it would be safer and cheaper to minimize its use of several chemicals in its production processes. An aggressive program begun in 1990 at thirty-five AT&T plants produced a 55 percent reduction in CFCs; a 60 percent reduction in toxic air emissions; and an 8 percent drop in manufacturing waste. Encouraged by these successes, the communications giant set a number of demanding goals for the future, By 1994, it would:

- eliminate CFCs entirely
- reduce waste from manufacturing by 25 percent
- reduce paper usage by 15 percent
- recycle 35 percent of all paper used.

By 1995, the company hopes to cut its total toxic air emissions by 95 percent. Use of environmentally benign substitutes, more efficient processes, and new methods of manufacturing will make these goals achievable. Economics makes it worth doing.[15] Table 6-4 lists some other companies that have made similar reductions in wastes.

Evaluating corporate claims on source reductions is hard because one must rely on company reports that are not standardized in any way and are not audited by an impartial third party as their financial reports are. One of the real values of the CERES Principles is its attempt to establish standards of reporting and a mechanism for auditing.

FOREIGN OPERATIONS

Large U.S. corporations have increasingly acquired operating units scattered around the globe. For reasons we will explore in the final chapter, social investors with environmental screens have found it difficult to gather and evaluate data on overseas operations.

Two rules of thumb may help you. First, you should regard a company with U.S. environmental problems as likely to have problems with its foreign operations. Second, companies that have migrated within the U.S. from high-wage and intensely regulated states to those with a "better business climate" tend to do so globally. These rules apply generally, not just to problems of hazardous wastes.

The nations of western coastal Africa—Sierra Leone, Congo, Guinea, and Nigeria—have proven vulnerable to the disposal of toxic wastes from industrialized countries.[16] Closer to home, American companies have moved manufacturing operations to Mexico, to the industrial zones just below the U.S. border known as *maquiladoras*. There, companies such as General Motors, Zenith, Ford, and General Electric have established plants to take advantage of low-priced labor and lax regulations. No small part of the opposition to the U.S.–Mexico Free Trade Agreement stems from the living conditions in these *maquiladoras*. The Coalition For Justice in the Maquiladoras, which consists of church groups, labor unions, and others, has begun filing shareholder resolutions.

TABLE 6-4. COMPANIES ELIMINATING TOXIC OR HAZARDOUS CHEMICALS

Apple Computer, Inc.	International Business Machines Corp.
B.F. Goodrich Co.	Johnson Controls, Inc.
Boeing Co.	Merck & Co., Inc.
Digital Equipment Corp.	Minnesota Mining and Manufacturing Co.
Dow Chemical Co.	Monsanto Co.
Du Pont Co.	Motorola, Inc.
General Dynamics Corp.	Procter & Gamble Co.
Gillette Co.	United Technologies Corp.
Hewlett-Packard Co.	Vulcan Materials Co.
Hunt Manufacturing Co.	Watts Industries

These companies have made substantial progress toward eliminating at least one category of toxic or hazardous chemicals from their production processes. Data are current as of August 1, 1992.
Source: Kinder, Lydenberg, Domini & Co., Inc., the KLD Social Investment Database.

AGRICULTURAL CHEMICALS

Some social investors screen out companies that are major producers of agricultural chemicals. Agricultural chemicals are artificial chemical substances that are used in farming. Fertilizers, herbicides, insecticides, and pesticides are the most important types of agricultural chemicals.

The danger of agricultural chemical residues in the foods humans consume is hotly debated. But their presence is not debatable. Food and Drug Administration (FDA) inspections of commodity food produce indicated widespread pesticide residues on apples (58 percent), carrots (39 percent), lettuce (66 percent), and strawberries (82 percent).[17] U.S. companies export to produce growers overseas agrichemicals, such as chlordane,[18] that the FDA deems unsafe for use domestically. Since the United States imports about 25 percent of its fruits and vegetables, traces of those exported chemicals may appear in our grocery stores.

Concerns about agricultural chemicals extend well beyond food. They include: contamination of underground water supplies, runoff—particularly of phosphate fertilizers—into lakes and waterways, destruction of wildlife by pesticides, and direct hazards to farm workers. However, some believe that the use of agrichemicals began to slow in the early 1980s as their negative effects became better known, and alternative measures for tilling and pest control became available.[19] Table 6-5 lists some major producers of agricultural chemicals.

Genetic Engineering.   Genetic engineering is the modification of the information content of a cell to alter its characteristics. While few social investors eliminate a firm solely because it is in genetic engineering, many regard a presence in the business as a sign they must look hard at the company's operations.

TABLE 6-5. SOME PUBLICLY TRADED PRODUCERS OF AGRICULTURAL CHEMICALS

American Cyanamid Co.	Freeport McMoRan Inc.
Dow Chemical Co.	Great Lakes Chemical Corp.
Du Pont Co.	Monsanto Co.
First Mississippi Corp.	Rohm and Haas Co.
FMC Corp.	Upjohn Co.

These selected companies are among the leading producers of agricultural chemicals. Data are current as of August 1, 1992.
Source: Kinder, Lydenberg, Domini & Co., Inc., the KLD Social Investment Database.

The idea of producing genetically engineered varieties of corn, soybeans, and other food crops that are resistant to viruses, drought, and insects has great appeal. Such crops might produce better yields with which to feed a hungry planet. But environmentalists fear the unseen effects of genetically engineered products. And they worry that private individuals or firms developing genetically engineered plant and microbe varieties could release them into the environment without proper testing.

Genetically engineered plants that facilitate the use of particular agricultural chemicals have caused great concern. Scientists at several chemical firms are working on new varieties of food crops that are no more resistant to pests than existing types but *are* more resistant to pesticides—in Monsanto's case, to its powerful herbicide Roundup.[20]

OZONE-DEPLETING CHEMICALS

Social investors typically screen out companies among the top legal emitters or producers of ozone-depleting chemicals, such as chlorofluorocarbons, hydrochlorofluorocarbons, bromines, halons, or methyl chloroform. "Ozone depletion" refers to the elimination of some part of the layer of ozone that surrounds the earth in the upper atmosphere. While ozone at ground level is a serious health menace, in the upper atmosphere it absorbs cancer- and cataract-causing ultraviolet rays.

The first public warning of depletion of the earth's ozone layer came in 1976 in a report by the National Academy of Sciences. The report identified the chlorofluorocarbon (CFC) gases commonly used in aerosol cans, refrigerators, and air conditioners as major villains. The 1985 discovery of a hole in the ozone layer over the Antarctic led to a 1987 international agreement (the Montreal Protocol) to eliminate the use of CFCs by 1999.[21] Du Pont and Allied-Signal, two of the top CFC producers, have pledged to stop producing CFCs by the turn of the century. Table 6-6 lists the top emitters or producers of ozone-depleting chemicals.

USING AND PRODUCING ENERGY

No other human activity has as much impact on the planet as the production and conversion of energy. Some energy sources create major environmental problems, while others are relatively benign. Fossil and nuclear fuels—the problem fuels—account for 70 percent and 20 percent, respectively, of U.S. domestic consumption. Roughly 85 percent of

**TABLE 6-6. EMITTERS OR PRODUCERS OF
OZONE-DEPLETING CHEMICALS**

Allied-Signal Inc.	Ethyl Corp.
Dow Chemical Co.	Great Lakes Chemical Corp.
Du Pont Co.	

These companies are among the top emitters or producers of ozone-depleting chemicals. Several of those listed are preparing to produce CFC substitutes, even though environmentalists have questioned the dangers of the new substances. Data are current as of December 30, 1992.
Source: Kinder, Lydenberg, Domini & Co., Inc., the KLD Social Investment Database.

the energy used in North America and the European Community (EC) comes from fossil fuels.[22]

As befits an extremely complex area, social investors cannot be said to be of one mind on energy issues. Social investors have come to judge fuels by whether they have environmental advantages. A fuel has environmental advantages when the sum of its harvesting, conversion, and waste products have minimal impact on the environment. By this standard coal and nuclear fuel (see chapter 4) are at best suspect. Oil has lost favor with social investors as a result of controversies about exploration and production in and off Alaska and along the east and west coasts of the United States. Natural gas is clearly the fossil fuel of choice for social investors. Alternative-energy sources have great appeal. Indeed, one of the older socially screened mutual funds, the New Alternatives Fund, specializes in such companies. But pure plays in this area tend to be small and risky.

Fossil Fuels

Fossil fuels—primarily coal, oil, and natural gas—were formed by decaying plants millions of years ago. They are nonrenewable energy sources because once they are used it will take millions of years to replace them. When burned, coal and oil release gases that contribute to acid rain and to the overall warming of the earth known as the greenhouse effect.

Old King Coal.   No industry has resisted environmental regulation more than coal. Since the Surface Mining Act's enactment the year after President Ford's veto in 1976, the industry—with the cooperation of the Reagan-Bush Administration—has hamstrung its enforcement. The same team has turned Occupational Safety and Health Act (OSHA) enforcement, black lung compensation programs, and union health and pensions programs into nightmares for the people they were intended to benefit.

William Ruckelshouse, the first director of the EPA, is said to have commented: "There are only two problems with coal: You can't dig it and you can't burn it." Environmentalists and shareholder activists, such as the Sisters of Loretto, have fought King Coal's blight for two generations. Social investors have taken their side. Whether brought from deep within the earth or stripped from open-pit mines, coal extraction creates land use and water pollution problems. And this is just the beginning. Environmental degradation follows a long trail from the mine to the power plant and along high-tension lines.

With the notable exception of acid rain, the environmental effects of coal receive far less publicity than those of oil. Coal mining takes place in benighted regions of Appalachia and bleak expanses of the Great Plains. Most Americans can go for weeks without seeing coal consumed. Residential burning has all but disappeared, and coal-powered plants are highly centralized.

Acid rain occurs when emissions of sulfur and nitrogen compounds combine with airborne water particles and other substances. They are transformed by chemical processes in the atmosphere and then, often far from their original sources, deposited on earth in a wet form.* As a result, acidic raindrops damage vegetation and lakes. The big sinners are the coal-fired generating stations closest to the Midwest's high-sulfur coal fields. Prevailing winds bear their emissions which then fall as acid rain on the forests and fields of New England and parts of Canada. Many coal-fired utilities, such as Allegheny Power and American Electric Power, fail investors' screens for just this reason.

Oil and Water.   Oil's extraction problems are far more visible because rich oil fields lie in California's coastal waters and Alaska's pristine expanses. The debacles of the Santa Barbara Channel blowout in 1969 and the *Exxon Valdez* grounding in 1989 galvanized and regalvanized the environmental movement. Since the mid-1980s, social investors have turned away from the major oil companies. ARCO and Amoco, which used to appear in socially screened mutual funds, now appear in few. The Calvert Social Investment Fund eliminated both after considerable soul-searching.

Americans are also more aware of oil's effects because they see it consumed every day. And in one form or another—gasoline, plastics, et cetera—they consume it. When burned, oil emits about 40 percent more

---

*The dry forms of acid deposition are acidic gases or particulates.

Box 6-3. Indispensable Resource: Mineral Policy Center

The Mineral Policy Center is a national nonprofit organization dedicated to preventing environmental impacts from hardrock mining and onshore oil and gas development and to cleaning up the massive damage from these industries' pasts.

Mining for "hardrock" metal ores and oil and gas exploration and extraction are major causes of environmental damage—causes not adequately controlled by existing (outdated) laws and regulations. Each year metals mining generates three times as much solid waste, much of it hazardous, as all other U.S. industries combined. To protect the environment and natural resources from the impacts of hardrock mining and oil and gas development, the Mineral Policy Center:

- Conducts and publishes research on the environmental impacts of mineral development and on the industry's record of corporate citizenship;
- Answers inquiries from concerned individuals, citizen groups, the media, and local, state, and federal government personnel by providing technical materials, photographs, videotapes, and educational information;
- Advocates reform of the laws and agency regulations that govern hardrock mining and its wastes, including the 1872 Mining Law and hazardous mining waste controls in the Resource Conservation and Recovery Act;
- Publishes Clementine, The Journal of Responsible Mineral Development;
- Links individuals and community groups working to prevent environmental destruction from hardrock mining and onshore oil and gas development with others working on similar issues;
- Publishes and distributes Canary Calls, a newsletter on environmental-campaigns on mining and oil-field issues; and
- Collates and publishes the Mining Conservation Directory, a networking guide to local citizen action on mineral-development threats to the environment.

Contact: The Mineral Policy Center, 1325 Massachusetts Avenue, N.W., #550; Washington, DC 20005; (202) 737-1872.

carbon dioxide—the major greenhouse gas—than does natural gas. These factors have contributed to a reluctance by social investors to consider the auto industry, too.

For social investors, the questions surrounding oil are profoundly troubling. Our economy centers on petrochemicals. The dislocation of the auto industry since the mid-1970s drastically reduced the number of highly skilled—and paid—blue-collar jobs and devastated the Midwest. The consolidation of the oil industry has left scars on cities such as Pittsburgh, which lost Gulf Oil's headquarters and all the jobs that went with it when Chevron won a takeover battle against T. Boone Pickens. And yet the need for alternative fuels and modes of transportation—or social organizations that require less commuting—is obvious to most. But an era dominated by cheap oil, uninterested public policymakers, and a powerful oil-industry lobby has limited incentives to find new approaches.

Natural Gas.   Social investors tend to favor natural gas over the other fossil fuels. Companies such as Brooklyn Union Gas, Consolidated Natural Gas, and Washington Gas & Light are mainstays of social portfolios.

Natural gas may be thought of as the "transition" fuel between the age of fossil fuel/nuclear energy and the age of renewable energy. It has two advantages. First, natural gas burns relatively cleanly. Its emissions of sulfur dioxide are next to zero and carbon-monoxide emissions are small; particulates from gas are minuscule compared to those of coal. Second, transporting natural gas through pipelines poses fewer environmental risks than moving oil in oceangoing tankers.[23] However, it is not problem-free. Panhandle Eastern faces over $700 million in cleanup liabilities for PCBs used to lubricate its compressor stations.

In areas of the country where it is available, natural gas is the fuel of preference for commercial and residential heating and for process heat. Current estimates indicate that the United States has reserves of natural gas that should carry it through the next sixty years.[24]

COGENERATION

Cogeneration is a process that produces simultaneously heat and electricity or another form of energy from a single source. Before the energy crises of the 1970s, cogeneration was little used in this country. Today many electric utilities have cogeneration facilities. An interesting example is a fossil-fuel plant—originally planned as a nuclear station—in Midland, Michigan, that was designed to supply its waste heat to Dow

Chemical. Dow's partially owned subsidiary, Destec Energy, is a leader in cogeneration technology.

Large industrial companies now use cogeneration technologies, too. Merck has discovered that by installing a cogeneration system at its West Point, Pennsylvania, plant, it saves 30 million kilowatts each year, an amount almost equal to the electrical requirements of the plant.

ALTERNATIVE SOURCES

Very slowly—too slowly—alternative-energy sources are coming on-line. The technologies to convert these renewable energy resources are at various stages of development.* For the most part, companies engaged in alternative energy are small, entrepreneurial, and, as investments, highly speculative. However, a few large companies have recognized the promise of this field. Not surprisingly, many of these ventures are in California, where air pollution is a top concern.

Photovoltaic Conversion. Photovoltaic conversion changes the sun's energy into electricity. Sunlight striking photovoltaic (PV) cells, which are made of silicon, causes them to generate electricity without moving, making noise, or polluting. Homes, businesses, and factories can use PV cells for electricity, but the technology is not generally cost-effective today. In April 1991, Texas Instruments and SCEcorp (parent of Southern California Edison) formed a joint venture to produce low-cost PV panels. Virtually all large companies, such as these, with solar technology fail one or more standard social screens. The half dozen or so publicly traded solar power plays are small and highly speculative.

Geothermal Energy. Geothermal energy is derived from the heat of the earth's interior. There are over one hundred geothermal power plants in the United States. In 1990 Pacific Gas & Electric (PG&E), a California utility, generated 7.6 percent of its electricity from geothermal plants. Not coincidentally, Unocal (née Union Oil of California) is the world's largest producer of geothermal energy. Both PG&E and Unocal have significant environmental negatives in other energy-related areas. A pure play in geothermal energy is Magma Power. Its four plants sell power to SCEcorp.

Geothermal energy is not without environmental negatives. Wells

---

*It is worth recalling that an early target of Reagan's budget cuts was solar and alternative energy programs. As a result, we have lost twelve years of research. No one can say whether the research would have produced results, but we would know a lot more about our options.

can blow out, releasing steam or harmful pollutants. The siting of the wells can also lead to controversy. Hawaiian Electric Industries damaged its once-excellent reputation among social investors when it proposed buying power from sites located in a pristine area on the island of Hawaii.

Wind Power.   For hundreds of years, wind power has been used to grind grain and pump water. More recently, people have begun to use windmills to generate electricity. In California, large groups of windmills (wind farms), such as Altamont's, are connected to the electric utility grid.

Hydroelectric Power.   Hydroelectric power is created by forcing water through a turbine and causing it to spin. Large-scale hydroelectric power plants require dams to be built across rivers to build up water supply and pressure. Some environmentalists criticize hydropower plants because they interfere with the migration patterns of fish, flood or dry up areas, and alter plant growth. Idaho Power has found itself deeply involved in the complicated problem of how to preserve salmon runs. The James Bay hydroelectric project in Quebec attracted significant opposition because of the huge area that would have been affected by the its lakes and the dislocation it would cause indigenous peoples.

Biofuels.   Biofuels are produced from materials from living organisms. In the 1970s, biofuels seemed to promise reduced emissions of pollutants and greenhouse gases, because they would burn more cleanly than fossil fuels. The plants grown for these fuels would also absorb carbon dioxide (a greenhouse gas). Corn is now being processed to make ethanol, a fuel additive that is mixed with gasoline to power cars. But ethanol-blended gasoline evidently emits more nitrous oxide than does plain gasoline and therefore creates more smog. Ethanol's leading proponent is the nation's third-largest grain merchant, Archer-Daniels-Midland.[25]

Another biofuel is methane, a flammable gas that releases no hazardous air pollutants. Some farms and sewage-treatment plants change waste to methane. Landfills are also a source of methane.

Waste-to-Energy Facilities.   Waste-to-energy (WTE) facilities burn trash to provide heat energy for industrial processes and electricity. About 160 WTE plants nationwide convert about 11 percent of the country's garbage into energy. WTE's major benefits are reductions in the demand for landfill sites and the abundance and cheapness of its fuel. Two major WTE companies are Wheelabrator Technologies (a subsidiary of Waste Management, Inc.) and Ogden Corporation.

Most environmentalists regard WTE as highly suspect, at best. They question the effectiveness of controls limiting the toxicity of air emissions and on the disposal of ash byproducts. The jumbled substances found in trash make controls very difficult to implement. Also, some see WTE as a competitor of recycling because of its fuel demands. Others argue that the technology provides a disincentive to reform our "disposable" society.

ANIMAL TESTING AND ANIMAL RIGHTS

Buried in the pink pages of London's *Financial Times (FT)* in the spring of 1992 appeared an article whose lead read, "The Co-operative Bank is planning to tell corporate customers involved in blood sports and other activities of which it disapproves to change their ways or close their accounts."* After consulting its customers, the 1.5 million-customer U.K. bank had adopted a policy that also barred business with anyone involved in: using exploitive factory farm methods; manufacturing or importing furs; experimenting on animals for toiletries and cosmetics; or facilitating or participating in blood sports. The bank and its parent company also had a policy banning fox hunting over their lands.[26]

THE WAR AGAINST CRUELTY TO ANIMALS

Co-op Bank's screen is exceptional in Great Britain only in its application to its customers. In the U.S. concern about our responsibility toward our fellow mammals is not so common among social investors' screens. But there is every reason to believe that it will become a routine part of American investors' environmental screen. The definition of the emerging screen is a matter of intense debate, which is not surprising given the emotional, humanitarian, and scientific stakes.

The first official protection of animals in modern times may have been a British law of 1822 that prohibited cruelty to domestic animals. An 1835 act outlawed barbarous animal sports, such as bear baiting.[27] Victorian books like Anna Sewell's *Black Beauty* (1877) focused attention on the maltreatment of domestic animals. Opposition to dog fighting, cock fighting, fox hunting, and rabbit-coursing appeared before World War I, as did statutes protecting songbirds and other wild beasts.

---

*The *FT* also reported that the "policy stops the bank from engaging in business with manufacturers of tobacco promoted in the less developed world, with foreign regimes which are in breach of human rights, or with arms manufacturers supplying those countries."

More recent are rejections of the fur business and laboratory testing using animals, though these date in Britain to the end of World War II at the latest.

Expressions of concern for the beings that share our environment most closely found their way into the American ethos as well. Volumes of federal, state, and local laws and regulations define our legal obligations to other species. The impetus behind legislation on the treatment of domestic animals came mainly from urban and suburban reformers— the same people concerned with social welfare issues.* Laws protecting wild animals passed largely at the behest of conservationists led by hunters such as Theodore Roosevelt and Aldo Leopold.

In the early 1970s, the moral basis of our relationship to other species began to be reexamined. That debate is expressed in social investing in terms of two (not inconsistent) screens: animal testing and animal rights.

ANIMALS IN LABORATORIES

In both the United Kingdom and the United States, a growing number of social investors screen out companies that use animals in laboratory tests of consumer products that they judge frivolous. Cosmetic companies especially have responded to investor and consumer pressure by limiting such tests, and companies like The Body Shop have established a market niche with "cruelty free" products.

People for the Ethical Treatment of Animals (PETA) has presented shareholder resolutions to Procter & Gamble, Avon, Colgate, Palmolive, Bristol-Myers Squibb, Gillette, and several others. The proxy resolutions have attracted significant numbers of votes, but more importantly, the companies have acted to minimize, if not eliminate, the number of animals used in product tests.†

Many regard the use of animals in medical and scientific research as necessary. Scientists argue that computer modeling and other types of tests do not produce the same quality of results as experiments on animals. While there appears to be unanimity on the need to avoid cruelty in the laboratory, no consensus appears in sight on whether animals should be used in testing at all. It may well be time to refocus the issue on the real—and continuing—problem of outright cruelty.

---

*Indeed, legend has it that the earliest American child abuse prosecution took place under a statute for the prevention of cruelty to animals.

†Some argue that these victories are more apparent than real, since the companies abandoning testing may farm it out to independent laboratories.

THE RIGHTS OF ANIMALS

Notably missing from the Co-op Bank's screens is animal rights, the assumption that nonhuman species are sentient beings due the same consideration humans extend to other humans.[28] Adherents of this view oppose speciesism, "a prejudice or attitude of bias toward the interests of members of one's own species and against those of members of other species."[29]

Two books advocating animal rights have attracted followings in recent years. The first and probably most important is Peter Singer's *Animal Liberation* (1975), which views distinctions between species, like distinctions drawn between the sexes or races, as arbitrary. Expanding on Singer's work, Tom Regan's *The Case for Animal Rights* (1984) argues that the qualities of memory, beliefs, emotions, and the like qualify a species for the right to moral treatment by humankind.[30] For a contrasting view, see Box 6-4, which describes *The Covenant of the Wild*.

For those who oppose speciesism, genetic engineering practiced on domestic animals represents the height of human repression. The promise of genetic engineering looks like a reprise of the bright future painted by nuclear scientists in the 1950s. The most glaring example may be Du Pont's "Oncomouse," a patented strain of laboratory mice designed to be susceptible to cancer.

ENVIRONMENTALLY BENEFICIAL PRODUCTS

Social investors tend to look for companies that do not just "do no wrong," but that also provide environmentally beneficial products and services. But defining *beneficial* has provoked a major controversy.

REMEDIATION

Remediation—the cleaning up of contaminated soil or water and the prevention of further pollution—would seem to be an area of business that would automatically put companies in an environmental investor's universe. But, it is not that simple. A controversy that hit the front page of the *Wall Street Journal* highlighted the problem.

As 1990 began, the environment was a hot topic. Environmental groups were finalizing plans for the twentieth anniversary of the first Earth Day. Their activities had taken on a sense of urgency with the

---

Box 6-4. Indispensable Resource:
The Covenant of the Wild

Stephen Budiansky's *The Covenant of the Wild* (New York: William Morrow & Co., 1992) contains truths about the relationship between humans and domestic animals many will find unacceptable.

A senior science writer for *U.S. News & World Report* and a farmer, Budiansky refuses to accept the simplistic notion of nature's peaceable kingdom. The realities of forest and field put the lie to them. Nor does Budiansky accept the equally simplistic notion of humans as exploiters. Domesticated animals have gained much from their relationship with humans: regular feeding, grooming, protection from predators and parasites, and the like. (This relationship is not unique. The ant and its aphids is only the best-known example of other species working together.) And the relationship between human and domesticates cannot flow from human's dominance. Humans tried to domesticate many other species ranging from the raccoon to the ibex and failed.

A growing body of archaeological and anthropological studies is revealing that the domesticates chose us as much as we chose them. Since the end of the last ice age, horses, cows, pigs, goats, and sheep—the entire barnyard—have evolved in symbiosis with civilization. From opportunists taking advantage of food at the edges of

---

unfolding story of the *Exxon Valdez* disaster, which had occurred nine months before. Several of the large fund families—Freedom, Alliance, Fidelity, Oppenheimer, and Kemper among them—saw an opportunity to capitalize on the public's concern by offering funds made up of the stocks of companies concentrating on "environmental services," such as Waste Management, Safety-Kleen, and Browning-Ferris, which specialize in remediation. They called the funds "environmental funds."

Their use of the term aroused Peter Camejo, president of Progressive Asset Management, an Oakland, California, brokerage firm specializing in social investing.

The word *environment* could be interpreted two different ways. It could mean picking stocks out of a universe of about three hundred listed environmental services companies . . . or it could mean excluding major polluters and selecting stocks of companies that are truly helping to solve environmental problems—firms that are pro-environmental.[31]

habitations to an integral part of many human cultures, over the last ten thousand years domesticates linked their lives with ours. Our species became interdependent.

Interdependence means that we humans have responsibilities toward the animals that have evolved with us. At a minimum, we must fulfill the animals' "expectations" of what we will provide them, and we must avoid inflicting unnecessary pain. It is the latter that separates human from beast. In nature, death by predator is neither quick nor merciful, as domestic cats prove with mice. But, Budiansky argues, our responsibilities must include understanding the tragedy of nature: from death comes life. In our urban and suburban settlements, we can insulate ourselves from this reality. We can object to the violence of the opening frames of *Bambi*. But countless generations until the present understood that "there is not necessarily a contradiction between using an animal for our justifiable ends while respecting it and fulfilling our responsibilities."

Humans must regain the moral lessons of this natural ethic. Without these informing principles, we risk catastrophic errors in managing the conflicting interests of the earth's inhabitants. The responsibility is ours.

Budiansky's meditation has another virtue: It is beautifully and plainly written. The challenge of *The Covenant of the Wild* lies in its ideas, not in its prose.

Camejo rightly pointed out that some of the environmental-services companies in the funds had records of repeated environmental violations. Also, the funds had not screened out companies with ties to the nuclear power industry.[32]

Even in the absence of these problems, social investors tend to look skeptically at companies involved in landfills, deep injection wells, and the incineration of toxic wastes—standard disposal techniques. However, a proenvironmental standard does not exclude all remediation companies. For instance, Groundwater Technology Inc. specializes in cleaning up contaminated groundwater and soil through the innovative use of indigenous microbes.

RECYCLING AND SOLID-WASTE REDUCTION

Social investors look for companies that are concerned with the creation of a sustainable economy. Such companies include substantial users of recycled materials in manufacturing processes and firms that are major factors in the recycling business.

Recycled waste takes the place of raw materials that would otherwise have to be taken from nature, thus reducing impact upon the environment. For true or "closed-loop" recycling to take place, a material should be remanufactured into its original use. A glass container can be crushed, melted, and made into another container. A plastic bottle, however, cannot be made into a new bottle, but it can go into carpet fiber, park benches, tennis-ball fuzz, and sleeping-bag insulation. In some cases, as with aluminum, recycling requires less energy than does the processing of virgin materials. That is why Alcoa is a great supporter of recycling.

There are many recycling success stories. The Times Mirror Company prints its flagship paper, *The Los Angeles Times,* on 80 percent recycled papers, the highest percentage of any major U.S. newspaper. That commitment creates an important market for recycled paper—the absence of which has long held back the recycled-paper business. Times Mirror also maintains recycling programs at most of its facilities. Wellman, Inc. uses recycled plastic as a raw material for many of its synthetic fabrics and plastic resins. Currently 40 percent of its total fiber production comes from recycled materials. Chaparral Steel uses recycled scrap as its principal raw material.

In its production of antibiotics, the pharmaceutical giant Merck uses a lot of toxic solvents such as acetate, ethylene glycol, and ethanol. A solvent-recovery system has enabled Merck to reuse 90 percent of the solvents it would have had to dispose of at high cost and restock. Table 6-7 lists some major recyclers.

Social investors using waste reduction and recycling as gauges of environmental performance should not take company claims at face value. A company can reduce its waste stream by 35 percent, but recycling or waste reduction may have played less of a role than downsizing or a particular discontinued operation.

Social investors and businesses alike must also beware conventional wisdom about recycling's raw materials. *Rubbish!,* an extraordinary book by William Rathje and Cullen Murphy, reports the findings of the University of Arizona's Garbage Project that applies the tools of anthropology and archaeology to landfills and trashcans. Their findings are startling.

Take the disposable diaper controversy. Government agencies and others estimated disposables made up anywhere from 12 to 32 percent of all trash. Rathje and his team have shown that disposable diapers take up less than 1.4 percent (by volume) of all waste disposed in landfills between 1980 and 1989.[33]

TABLE 6-7. SOME PUBLICLY TRADED COMPANIES DEALING IN OR USING RECYCLED MATERIALS

Adolph Coors Co.	Media General, Inc.
Alcan Aluminum Ltd.	Mobil Corp.
Aluminum Co. of America	Nucor Corp.
Armco Inc.	Reynolds Metals Co.
Ball Corp.	Safety-Kleen Corp.
Browning-Ferris Industries, Inc.	Scott Paper Co.
Chambers Development Co., Inc.	Sealed Air Corp.
Consolidated Paper, Inc.	Stone Container Corp.
Du Pont Co.	Temple-Inland Inc.
Georgia-Pacific Corp.	Times Mirror Co.
Johnson Controls, Inc.	Tribune Co.
Knight-Ridder, Inc.	Wellman, Inc.

These companies are either substantial users of recycled materials or are major factors in the recycling business. Data are current as of March 1, 1992.
Source: Kinder, Lydenberg, Domini & Co., Inc., the KLD Social Investment Database.

Some aspects of Rathje's conclusions about our "garbage crisis" will displease almost every environmental and industry faction, as well as many concerned with social welfare. He argues persuasively for incineration as a partial solution, close environmental regulation of all disposal facilities, and the reintroduction of dump scavenging as a part of recycling efforts.[34]

SEALS OF APPROVAL

Businesses now understand the value of being perceived as pro-environment. For that reason, "green labeling"—claiming environmental compatability for a product—has become an important issue. Some companies have seen green labeling as a marketing question and have used terms like "earth-friendly" or "biodegradable" loosely in their ads. What might have been a minor marketing coup turns into a public relations disaster when the public realizes the claim was at best inappropriate. For instance in the U.K. British Petroleum claimed its "Supergreen" gasoline caused no pollution.[35]

Some organizations are attacking this problem by establishing, in effect, "seals of approval" for products and packaging that are relatively good for the environment. Green Seal, Inc., started by Earth Day founder Denis Hayes, conducts environmental-impact evaluations of products. The research is very time-consuming, and it will probably be the mid-1990s before Green Seals start appearing on packages.

Another organization, Green Cross, has already handed out nearly four hundred seals to various products. Green Cross says that its symbol is not an environmental seal of approval. Rather, it verifies a company's environmental claims, such as, "This beverage container has been certified to be made of 50 percent recycled glass." Critics of Green Cross argue that it rewards recycling but ignores source reduction. Bags made from 95 percent recycled plastic share the seal with bags made from 50 percent. Boxed bleach wears the symbol, not because the bleach is good for the environment (it is not), but because the box contains recycled fibers. Box 6-5 lists some criteria for evaluating a product's greenness.

Controversies about products' impacts on the environment are both inevitable and healthy. Green Seal and Green Cross have much to con-

---

Box 6-5. Green Product Criteria

You can easily construct a list of green criteria for products. Obtaining information to implement them is considerably more difficult. And more difficult still is convincing businesses to conform their products to them. Only evidence of demand from the marketplace will convince them. Here are our criteria for a green product.

- It is designed to meet essential human needs without being frivolous.
- It does not endanger the health of the consumer or others.
- It causes no significant environmental damage during production, use, and disposal.
- It conserves energy and resources during production, use, and disposal.
- It is not made from materials derived from threatened species or environments.
- It did not require in its development or production the unnecessary use of, or cruelty to, animals.
- It is made from recycled materials or renewable resources processed in a way that preserves the environment.
- It is durable and reusable first, and recyclable or truly biodegradable next.
- It is minimally or responsibly packaged.

Sources: D. L. Dadd and A. Carothers, Greenpeace, May/June 1990, as described in Is It Really Green? (Colchester, Vt.: Seventh Generation Publications, 1990), pp. 4–5; J. Elkington and J. Hailes, The Green Consumer Guide (London: Victor Gollancz Ltd., 1989), p. 5.

tribute in these debates. As their standards evolve, they will help investors judge companies' environmental claims. Along with the CERES Principles, their standards will provide comprehensive benchmarks by which to evaluate environmental performance.

TOUGH QUESTIONS AHEAD

"Jobs versus the environment." That is how the issue in postindustrial America is often framed—even by environmentalists—when natural resource industries contract or auto makers fight air pollution laws. But it is a false choice. There is no going back to the era dominated by heavy manufacturing and its well-paid blue-collar workers.

Robert Zevin of U.S. Trust Company in Boston has pointed out that we must redefine the concept of work and what we as a society value to fit the new circumstances. That redefinition must include humankind's relation to the environment. The late twentieth century is not the first period in which people have had to adapt to profound changes in their ways of life. When thinking about environmental issues in this era, consider the following quotations. The first is from the Hebrew prophet Isaiah, who preached around 710 B.C.E. The second was spoken by the Native American ghost-dance prophet Smohalla in the 1880s.

> And [the Lord] shall judge among the nations, and shall rebuke many people; and they shall beat their swords into plowshares, and their spears into pruning hooks; nation shall not lift up sword against nation, neither shall they learn war any more.[36]

> You ask me to plow the ground. Shall I take a knife and tear my mother's bosom?[37]

In the years when the anniversaries of Columbus's voyages will be observed, we would do well to remember that the transitions from hunter-gatherers to farmers and from farmers to urban workers were every bit as wrenching as what we are now experiencing. The difference is that we know a lot more about what is happening to us. As socially responsible investors, we have a particular obligation to put our money where it will benefit both humans and the environment in the new era.

7

Corporations and Communities:
Beyond Paychecks and Taxes

A FRIEND OF OURS RECENTLY VISITED DETROIT. The Motor City. The heart of America's automobile economy. Since the first decade of the century the city and its surrounding communities produced more motor vehicles than the rest of the world combined. The auto companies employed tens of thousands and contracted with the hundreds of suppliers that gravitated to them.

Our friend was in downtown Detroit for a one-day business meeting at the gleaming Renaissance Center. He planned to visit a cousin that evening in a nearby suburb, Royal Oak. "What's the best way to your place?" he asked. "It may not be the best," his cousin said, "but if you drive up Woodward Avenue you'll get to Royal Oak, and you'll get a cross-sectional look at Detroit."

This route took our friend through block after block of squalor and misery. Boarded-up storefronts, burned-out houses and apartment buildings, and hopeless faces on young men standing around liquor stores stretched on for mile after mile. "Where have eight decades of wealth gone to?" he asked himself. "How could so many great fortunes arise here and leave so few traces?"

WEALTH AND CITIES

The relationship between wealth and the condition of our communities has perplexed the finest minds of our times. Lewis Mumford, Jane

Jacobs, and William Cronon have grappled with the question, but if there is *an* answer, it eluded them. While wealth alone does not create a vibrant community, it does contribute to better schools, health care, and safety. Some corporations have made deep and complex commitments to the communities in which they operate. These commitments go well beyond ponying up for the symphony orchestra or assigning junior executives to the United Way for a quarter or two. They bespeak a day-to-day involvement in the civic and grass-roots organizations that make larger social units function.

Their communities are better places to live because of them. These are not company towns, like the ones mining companies ran, or single-industry cities like Scranton was. Indeed, the most impressive example is Minneapolis–Saint Paul, the home of national firms such as 3M, Pillsbury, General Mills, Honeywell, and Cargill. The Twin Cities are a com-

TABLE 7-1. SELECTED COMPANIES CONSISTENTLY GIVING MORE THAN 1.5 PERCENT OF PRETAX EARNINGS TO CHARITY

A. O. Smith Corp.	Kroger Co.
Affiliated Publications, Inc.	Lincoln National
Air Products & Chemicals, Inc.	May Department Stores Co.
American Express Co.	Media General, Inc.
AMR Corp.	Medtronic, Inc.
Analog Devices, Inc.	Mellon Bank Corp.
Apache Corp.	New York Times Co.
Bank of Boston Corp.	Nordson Corp.
Ben & Jerry's Homemade Inc.	Norwest Corp.
Brown Group, Inc.	NWNL Cos., Inc.
Burlington Resources, Inc.	ONEOK Inc.
Chambers Development Co., Inc.	PepsiCo Inc.
Claire's Stores, Inc.	Piper, Jaffray & Hopwood Inc.
CLARCOR Inc.	PNC Financial Corp.
CPI Corp.	Polaroid Corp.
Cummins Engine Co., Inc.	Rochester Telephone Corp.
Dayton-Hudson Corp.	Rouse Co.
Deluxe Corp.	SAFECO Corp.
Federal-Mogul Corp.	Sears, Roebuck and Co.
General Cinema Corp.	Stanhome Inc.
Giant Food Inc.	Stride Rite Corp.
Graco, Inc.	Tennant Co.
Hasbro, Inc.	Times Mirror Co.
Huffy Corp.	Wachovia Corp.
Hunt Manufacturing Co.	Walgreen Co.
J.C. Penney Co., Inc.	Xerox Corp.
Jostens, Inc.	Yellow Freight Systems Inc. of Delaware

Source: Kinder, Lydenberg, Domini & Co., Inc., the KLD Social Investment Database.

munity in which education, science, the arts, and civic virtues are broadly supported.

For example, since 1971 Piper, Jaffray & Hopwood, a regional brokerage headquarters in Minneapolis, has donated 5 percent of pretax profits to charity. Piper, Jaffray's commitment goes beyond passing out checks. Real progress comes as much from the dedication of people as it does from money, so the firm has made a point of involving all its employees, from the mailroom to the boardroom. In 1989, 600 of the firm's 760 employees did some sort of active community work. A company-sponsored volunteer council coordinates opportunities for its Twin Cities employees. Piper, Jaffray has expanded its contribution matching program to include nonprofit organizations where an employee is an active volunteer, as well as educational institutions.

Piper, Jaffray is a founding member of the Minnesota Keystone Program. The program began when, in 1976, the Greater Minneapolis Chamber of Commerce recognized twenty-three firms as members of the nation's first "5 Percent Club," companies that had pledged 5 percent of pretax earnings to charities. Three years later a "2 Percent Club" was established. By 1991 over two hundred Minnesota companies had become 5 percent or 2 percent members, the highest level of corporate philanthropy in a major city relative to local population in the country. The Minnesota Keystone Program has provided a model for at least a dozen others.

The Twin Cities experience demonstrates how strong communities and strong firms sustain each other. Notwithstanding fewer natural advantages than Detroit and severe winters, Minneapolis–Saint Paul is home to national companies including Control Data, Cray, Deluxe Corporation, H.B. Fuller, and Medtronic. Venture capitalists rate the area a close third behind Silicon Valley and metropolitan Boston as an incubator of high-tech firms and a magnet for a highly educated work force. In turn, corporate payrolls, tax payments, donations, and volunteerism sustain the vitality of the community. This climate of mutual support has produced a strong local economy and a good place to live.

APPROACHES TO GIVING

Corporations contribute to their communities in different ways. That is to be expected. One should also expect that corporate giving includes a fair measure of self-interest. After all, self-interest affects individual donors, too. James B. "Buck" Duke, the architect of the modern cigarette industry, offered the College of New Jersey a fabulous endowment if it would change its name to Duke. He was turned down. Trinity College in Durham, North Carolina, accepted his offer. Lest the College of New Jersey (now Princeton University) seem altruistic, its campus memorializes donors with great fortunes: Carnegie, Pyne, Murray, Dodge, Forbes, and Rockefeller, among others.

An unintended consequence of "Buck" Duke's effort to build himself a monument is that the United States now has two world class universities where it might have had one. So, it seems unwise, if not ungrateful, to look too hard at the gift horse's mouth. As we will see, there are exceptions to that rule.

A corporation's motives for what it does in the community and how it gives usually go together. For that reason, social researchers tend to focus on the "hows" of giving and to emphasize innovative and distinctive contributions as opposed to the conventional. Table 7-2 shows how 339 major corporations directed their gifts in 1990.

GIVING AND MARKETING

Conventional corporate-giving programs direct approximately 50 percent of grants to education—primarily higher education—and 30 percent to human services—primarily United Fund drives. Grants are often unimaginative. For example, in 1991 W. R. Grace & Company made a $1.5 million grant to Clemson University to endow a professorship in packaging science. Grace's specialty chemical subsidiary is in the packaging business. In contrast, Sara Lee and Northern States Power allocate

TABLE 7-2. CORPORATE DONATIONS, 1990 (339 FIRMS)

	Donations $ (in millions)	Percent (%) of Allocated Portion
Education	773.4	41.0
Health and human services	569.7	30.2
Cultural	248.2	13.1
Civic and community activities	238.2	12.6
Other	58.4	3.1
Unallocated	203.7	
Total	$ 2,091.5	

After tremendous growth in charitable giving from 1981 through 1987, corporate contributions lagged behind the inflation rate through 1991. The forecast for 1992 was not promising. Still, the amount of annual giving is considerable, $6 billion in 1990. Here is how 339 corporations, which accounted for more than a third of that total, allocated their gifts.
Source: Council for Aid to Education, as cited in J. Moore, "Corporate Giving: Still Stalled," *The Chronicle of Philanthropy*, October 22, 1991, p. 10. Reprinted with permission of *The Chronicle of Philanthropy*.

much of their giving to programs for the economically disadvantaged that encourage self-sufficiency. Talking with persons active in the non-profit world is an excellent means of discovering which corporations are most creative in their support.

Separating corporate giving from corporate marketing—or even R&D—is not simple and perhaps not necessary. If Apple and IBM donate computer hardware to schools, are these merely marketing techniques to acquaint future customers with the products of those firms, or are they genuine contributions of value to the schools? Probably both. Syntex, a major health care firm, was an early benefactor of AIDS research. A still-larger pharmaceutical firm, Bristol-Myers Squibb, has since 1977 given $27 million in unrestricted grants for biomedical research. The firm has also given doses of its seventeen heart-disease drugs to patients who cannot afford them.[1]

Even if these firms benefit from these transactions, does this reduce the value of their "donations" to society? In a letter to the National Committee for Responsive Philanthropy, Craig Smith, editor of *Corporate Philanthropy Report,* argued:

> There *should* be a creative dynamic between philanthropy and marketing. . . . They are not the same thing. . . . If philanthropy is too far away from marketing, it's not liable to get more than peanuts from the budget. If it's too close to marketing, it's schlock. But if the tension between both functions is managed properly, both the company and society can benefit.[2]

Nonetheless, some charity seems to cross the line. One example is cited in Box 7-1.

Because so much of what corporations contribute to their communities mixes altruism and advertising, social investors can find out about it easily. Corporate reports—both the annual report and the quarterlies—will often feature such activities. Many large corporations, especially those with foundations, publish separate annual reports on their programs. Offbeat events sometimes get press coverage. Ben & Jerry's gets a nice publicity boost at the beginning of ice cream season when they hand out samples at the Boston Postal Annex to mobs of last-minute income-tax filers. The ice cream mavens and a couple of Boston firms have turned trauma into an astonishing community event.

VOLUNTEERISM

Social investors often gauge a company's commitment to the community by its attitude toward volunteerism—direct involvement in charitable

Box 7-1. Partners for a Drug-Free America?

Is the "war on drugs" just a competition for market share between legal and illegal drug purveyors? Very likely, a pattern of contributions to an advocacy group indicates.

An article by Cynthia Cotts in *The Nation* took the Partnership for a Drug-Free America to task for accepting "$5.4 million in contributions from legal drug manufacturers, while producing ads that overlook the dangers of tobacco, alcohol and pills."

You've seen their ads. The fried egg—"your brain on drugs." The ten-year-old girl who's supposed to smoke an ounce of marijuana a week. (Since it would take ten thousand dollars per year to support her "habit," one wonders if she has worse problems.)

The Partnership's CEO, James Burke, took over the advocacy group in 1989 after leaving Johnson & Johnson, where he was CEO and board chair. He brought with him a $3 million grant from the Robert Wood Johnson Foundation. Other 1988–1991 contributors "with ties to the legal drug industry" Cotts identified include: "J. Seward Johnson, Sr., Charitable Trusts ($1,100,000); Du Pont ($150,000); the Procter & Gamble Fund ($120,000); the Bristol-Myers Squibb Foundation ($110,000); Johnson & Johnson ($110,000); SmithKline Beecham ($100,000); the Merck Foundation ($75,000); and Hoffman-La Roche ($50,000)."

Other contributors included: the alcohol and tobacco company American Brands ($100,000); the brewer Anheuser-Busch ($150,000); the beer and tobacco conglomerate Philip Morris ($150,000); and RJR Nabisco's cigarette arm, R.J. Reynolds ($150,000).

An unlikely group of partners for a drug-free America.

Cotts's article brings to mind Adam Smith's observation in *The Wealth of Nations:* "People of the same trade seldom meet together . . . but the conversation ends in a conspiracy against the public, or in some contrivance to raise prices." Did we double the populations of our prisons in the 1980s to maintain market share for our legal drug companies?

Source: C. Cotts, "Hard Sell in the Drug War," *The Nation,* March 9, 1992, pp. 300–302.

activities without pay or compulsion, other than good intentions, in addressing important issues in the community. Volunteering is the most common form of corporate involvement in the community. Most large companies have a volunteer program. Between 1978 to 1989, the number of formal volunteer programs sponsored by corporations appears to have tripled.[3]

One of the best corporate volunteer programs is Eastman Kodak's. Participants can take up to forty hours per year of paid leave for public-service work. This time does not count against normal sick leave or vacation time. Kodak supports this effort with a "Dollars for Doers" program that donates up to five hundred dollars to projects in which employees are actively involved.[4]

Xerox's twenty-one-year-old social-leave program guarantees job security and pays full salary and benefits for up to a year while employees work for nonprofit organizations. The Xerox Foundation provides the funding.

Adolph Coors has mustered 3,600 of its current employees and re-tirees—almost half its Colorado work force—to donate some 34,900 hours to community projects in 1991 alone. Naysayers point out that alcohol causes much of the need for many community projects. Perhaps this is the reason that producers of alcoholic beverages tend to be active in such giving.

PUBLIC/PRIVATE PARTNERSHIPS

"Public/private partnerships" is a catch-all term for a number of arrangements by which corporations, unions, universities, and government institutions form alliances to attack community problems. They take the form of a nonprofit organization to which a private corporation contributes and whose mission a government body facilitates with tax benefits, zoning variances, and the like. Thousands of public/private partnerships are now active.

One well-known public/private partnership involves the Pittsburgh Pirates baseball team. In 1985, after years of poor attendance, the family that owned the Pirates announced that it was looking for a buyer. The Pirates seemed likely to be grabbed by a sun-belt city anxious to get a big league team. But an unusual cooperative venture between the city and ten major corporations raised the money to buy the team and return it to fiscal health and division titles in 1991 and 1992.

A public/private partnership of a very different type is City Year, which brings college students to spend a school year serving communities in greater Boston. They clean and monitor playgrounds; they work with the elderly; they wash grafitti off buildings. At the end of school year, each student receives a small cash bonus. Corporations sponsor City Year students by paying for their living expenses. They also sponsor participants in City Year's annual Servathon fundraiser in which 7,000 people devote a fall Saturday to community work.

Affordable Housing Initiatives

Corporations got into the affordable-housing business as early as the mid-1800s, when they created row houses for workers near New England's textile mills. Later, entire "company towns" grew up near the coal mines of Appalachia and the Iron Range of Minnesota.* Today business, lenders, and government are working together to rehabilitate housing where it has fallen into decay in low-income areas and to build new housing where it is most needed. The Stevens Square initiative of General Mills and the city of Minneapolis rehabilitated 750 units. Ralston Purina has made similar efforts in St. Louis, and BP America has gained national attention for its program in Cleveland.

Particularly in the Northeast and in coastal California, housing is becoming a major issue for businesses. Long a problem for low-level employees, affordable housing has begun to be an issue even for midlevel employees and managers. High costs and limited supplies have made it difficult to recruit, transfer, and retain employees, driven up wages, and forced many to endure long commutes, leading to measurable productivity losses.

Over the past eighteen years, wages adjusted for inflation have declined for blue-collar and clerical workers. Were it not for working wives and second jobs, the living standards of millions of American families would have declined more than they have. The price of housing (homes and rental properties) has increased rapidly, creating an "affordability gap" that prevents employees from obtaining adequate shelter near their workplaces. Changes in the federal tax laws on real estate have limited the number of new units of low-cost housing being built, even as the stock of this housing decreases due to fire, clearance, and deterioration.

Corporations have always had programs to meet the housing needs of newly hired or transferred managers, but until recently they have done little for their low-paid workers. A few have begun to recognize that the lack of affordable housing is bad for business. During the 1980s

---

*Of course, some of these towns with their company stores served as little more than a means to keep workers in thrall, especially where the company paid in "script," notes only good at its stores and for paying rent on its houses.

boom, for example, Boston experienced a severe labor shortage for non-skilled and semiskilled jobs. As the metropolitan area with the nation's largest "affordability gap," Boston's high wages could not attract the numbers and kinds of workers employers needed. Economists warned that this condition would limit the region's capacity for further economic growth.[5]

The problems just described pale compared to those of the poor. The growing numbers living on the street are just the visible portion of the millions who live below the poverty line. For every homeless person we encounter, some estimate another two hundred live on the edge, a paycheck away from homelessness. To ameliorate these conditions, the cooperation of corporations, government, and private agencies is required. And, amazingly, it is happening.[6]

One such effort is represented by the Local Initiatives Support Corporation (LISC), a New York–based organization founded in 1980. LISC's objective is to raise corporate and foundation funding for locally sponsored and executed community-development projects. Through 1991 it raised $759.6 million from foundations and corporations such as Aetna, ARCO, Continental Illinois Bank, and Prudential—just a handful of the 873 donors, investors, and lenders that have supported its programs. These funds, plus secured leverage, put $2 billion into the hands of 833 community-development corporations by the beginning of 1992.[7]

Other organizations, such as the Enterprise Foundation and the Chicago Equity Fund, have developed similar programs. The Federal Home Loan Bank has set up several programs—the Affordable Housing Program, the Community Investment Program, and the New England Housing Fund—through which it makes financing available to those who most need it. Many other public/private partnerships operate around the nation.

The National Equity Fund (NEF), which is sponsored by LISC, presents perhaps the most popular corporate solution to affordable-housing problems. Modeled after the real estate limited partnerships so popular with individual investors in the 1980s, the Fund combines the energies and expertise of affordable-housing professionals with the cash and good intentions of corporate investors. Corporate investors are limited partners. They receive tax benefits based upon their shares of property depreciation and federal Low Income Housing Tax Credits. NEF, Inc.— the nonprofit sponsor of the Fund—is the general partner. It reviews community-based affordable-housing projects around the country and invests for the Fund in viable projects. Between 1987 and 1991, seventy-six corporations put $260 million in NEF partnerships, helping to create or rehab over eleven thousand units of affordable rental housing.* Warren Buffet, CEO of Berkshire Hathaway, has described NEF as the perfect marriage of corporate interest and social causes.[8]

While the programs outlined in this section have specific corporate appeal. LISC, Enterprise Foundation and the Chicago Equity Fund have been criticized for their bank-like attitudes, for their unwillingness to spend money on projects that do not meet very strict lending standards. In contrast, the community development lenders discussed at the end of this chapter make loans to people who are not bankable, work with them to build up their credit rating, and then turn them over to mainstream institutions.

EDUCATION AND TRAINING

In 1990, *Working Woman* reported that New York Telephone had to test 60,000 applicants to fill just 2,100 entry-level positions, while Michigan Bell found just 2 of 15 applicants for clerical jobs could pass reading and math exams.[9] Corporations that want to help themselves and their communities can make tremendous contributions in the areas of education and technical training at below-college levels. And they have every reason for doing so.

EDUCATION FOR THE WORK FORCE

To be competitive, corporations need educated, trained workers. The American educational system is not providing them. Some 13 percent of America's seventeen-year-old are illiterate, and only 73 percent of students finish high school.[10] An increasing percentage of new entrants to the labor market, as we will see in chapter 10, come from groups that traditionally have had the fewest educational accomplishments.[11] This situation is likely to get worse.

Corporate giving to education in America has been substantial. However, the overall effect of corporations on education—particularly public education—is difficult to measure. Harvard public policy professor Robert Reich has warned that what corporate America gives with one hand, it takes away with the other. Corporations have never been reluctant to extract tax concessions from communities, using either the carrot of new jobs or the stick of plant closings. Look, for example, at what happened

---

*The thousands of units built or rehabbed mean not only housing but jobs.

when Hyster Corporation notified officials in five states and four nations where its plants were located that some would be shut down.

> The governments were invited to bid to keep local jobs. Several American towns . . . surrendered a total of $18 million to attract or preserve around 2,000 Hyster jobs. The biggest give up was offered by Danville, Illinois, a city of 39,000 people, which agreed to provide Hyster with roughly $10 million in subsidies and tax breaks to save 850 jobs.[12]

That $10 million is now unavailable to Danville's schools and other community services.

Perhaps because of its public image as benefactor to public schools, Reich singles out General Motors as "among the most relentless pursuers of local tax abatements."[13] Although manufacturers like GM and Hyster have well-deserved reputations for gaining tax relief, financial services, high tech, and biotech companies which demand educated workforces have pressed cities just as hard. Notable among these are Morgan Stanley (New York), Lotus Development (Cambridge, Massachusetts), and Genzyme (Boston).

Oliver Wendell Holmes, Jr., once said that a citizen is justified in seeking to pay as little in taxes as the law requires, but Reich makes it clear that corporations cannot have it both ways. They cannot be both patrons of education and local tax misers.

Still, there is good news on the corporate front as far as school and education are concerned. Many companies participate in adopt-a-school programs that create a partnership between a school and a corporation with the goal of upgrading the education offered by the school. The relationship may be as minimal as providing supplies or computer equipment, or it may go much deeper. On a larger scale, General Electric recently announced a $20 million, ten-year commitment to improve public high schools; the Minneapolis public school system received $200,000 from Cray Research, Medtronic, and Honeywell to help establish an experimental school; in 1988 American Bankers Insurance Company built the nation's first on-premises K–2 school at its Miami headquarters, which will be run by the local school district.[14]

Procter & Gamble has made education an important priority. P&G has spent upward of $9 million per year on schools near its Cincinnati headquarters. In addition, it has sponsored "mentor" programs and SAT prep courses for the college-bound.[15] Westinghouse spent $4.3 million on education programs in Baltimore and Pittsburgh in 1990. Its partnership with a largely black high school in Pittsburgh offers a special science and math enrichment program to bring students up to standards for college enrollment.[16] Rohm & Haas, a major chemical producer, brings local science teachers into its laboratories at seven hundred dollars per week to upgrade their science skills and develop lab experiments they can take back into their classrooms.[17]

An interesting experimental program at a Textron plant in Williamsport, Pennsylvania, has revived the tradition of apprenticeship for students who have lost interest in their classes. The program appears to be succeeding in both teaching real-world skills and reviving the students' interest in school work.[18]

Without a trained and educated work force coming out of community schools, corporations will have to do the training themselves. In addition if the public schools in their areas of operations are of poor quality, they will be unable to recruit or transfer in managers with school-age children, particularly those in the middle ranks who cannot afford private school tuition.

TRAINING WORKERS

Many, if not most, businesses find that they must teach their employees specific job-related skills. In some cases, these skills relate to a current job; in others, they are required for advancement. The attention a company pays to training—learning activities designed to improve job performance—is an excellent bellwether for its attitude toward its employees and their communities because it is an investment in the future.

Some firms provide for the "continual improvement" of their work force. Motorola, for example, requires forty hours per year of training for each of its employees, and in 1987 started its own "university" near its Schaumberg, Illinois, headquarters with 410 full- and part-time staff members.

In 1987, Ingersoll-Rand spent $24 million to modernize its Athens, Pennsylvania, plant. It realized that half of the plant's three hundred employees—13 percent of whom were functionally illiterate—would need higher-level skills to manage the plant's more sophisticated equipment. So it spent an additional $1 million on a long-term training program.[19]

Ætna, the insurance giant, found itself with an even bigger problem: It could not find enough job applicants to fill its entry-level, low-skilled positions. In response, it began its much praised "Hire and Train" program, in which severely underqualified but motivated individuals are hired and trained—often in the skills they should have acquired in school. In 1990 Aetna expected "Hire and Train" recruits to fill one-quarter of its entry-level positions in Hartford.[20]

A corporation depends on an educated work force and a stable community. Enlightened self-interest has led to the Business Round Table calling on corporations to address this rapidly deteriorating aspect of American life. Many large corporations have made education their top charitable priority. Social investors tracking a corporation's citizenship record now must track both the positive and the negative impacts on local community educational systems.

DISPLACING WORKERS

A corporation's response to its need to reduce labor costs gives a strong indication of its sense of responsibility to its communities. Companies that fled high labor costs in the north thirty years ago are now leaving the Piedmont for the Maquiladoras in Mexico just over the U.S. border. Few socially responsible investors will find this behavior acceptable in companies they consider for investment. Table 7-3 lists some of the U.S. companies in the Maquiladoras.

The books we wrote in the 1980s praised companies like Polaroid and Digital Equipment (DEC) for their two or three decade old "no-layoff" policies that kept people working during lean times. In the early 1990s, many of these policies were abandoned as the Reagan-Bush recession deepened. Polaroid was offering aggressive early retirement programs to avoid layoffs. DEC began shrinking by encouraging early retirements, but the inducements it offered became progressively less generous. Then it began laying off thousands.

Forced retirements and layoffs leave deep wounds, even when companies offer generous severance benefits. Somehow, "The Godfather's" rationale for termination rings a bit hollow: It isn't personal; it's strictly

TABLE 7-3. COMPANIES RECEIVING MAQUILADORA RESOLUTIONS 1991–1992

Allied-Signal Inc.	General Motors Corp.
American Telephone & Telegraph Co.	ITT Corp.
Asarco Inc. (1992 only)	Johnson & Johnson
Baxter International, Inc. (1991 only)	Parker Hannifin Corp. (1991 only)
Chrysler Corp.	PepsiCo Inc. (1991 only)
Du Pont Co.	Waste Management Inc. (1992 only)
Ford Motor Co. (1991 only)	Zenith Electronics Corp. (1992 only)

Source: Coalition for Justice in the Maquiladoras, *Annual Report 1990–1991.*

business. Losing one's job is an intensely personal matter. Both individually and collectively, the pain is magnified when workers and their communities made sacrifices to keep the company prosperous.

For instance, many corporations have benefited from industrial revenue bonds (IRBs). Communities float IRBs using their tax-exempt status to obtain funds at lower interest rates, for the direct benefit of corporations, who use the funds to build or expand local facilities. It sounds nice: The corporation gets lower cost capital; the locality gets more jobs. Some corporations are now being charged with breaching the covenant underlying these arrangements. In 1982, the city of Duluth floated an IRB for Diamond Tool, a subsidiary of Triangle Corporation of Connecticut. According to the city and union officials, Diamond gradually transferred the toolmaking equipment purchased with the bond issue—and half the jobs—to a plant in South Carolina.[21]

A *Wall Street Journal* article has commented, "Leaving town after partaking of public largess is becoming more than rude. It may be actionable. Outfits that accept loans or other incentives and don't stick around are increasingly being sued for breach of contract."[22] West Virginia brought a $614 million suit against Newell Company when it closed a plant it had acquired in Clarksburg, thereby eliminating 942 jobs. Over the previous decade the plant had received $3.5 million in low-interest state funds.

Similar actions have been brought against General Electric and General Motors, involving the closing of plants partly financed by IRBs. In 1987 when GM announced that its Norwood, Ohio, plant was closing, the city had just spent $750,000 on street and railroad alterations to accommodate the auto maker.[23] In early 1992 General Motors announced another round of plant closings. Twenty-one communities—including Tarrytown, New York, which had made tax concessions to keep its plant in an earlier downsizing—learned their plants were to be shut.

Communities like Tarrytown will take no comfort from the prominent economists who think that periodic dislocations are good for our free-market economy. However, Clemson professor Richard McKenzie has argued that companies should be free to open and close plants as their interests dictate. Allowing government to control those decisions would concentrate too much power in the hands of politicians and bureaucrats. "Private rights to move, to invest, to buy, to sell," says McKenzie, "are social devices for the dispersion of economic power."[24]

Even Lester Thurow, a liberal economist and dean of MIT's Sloan School of business, complains that government is too quick to shield the nation's inefficient industries from the chilling winds of economic reality. "Instead of adopting public policies to speed up the process of disinvest-

ment," he wrote in *The Zero Sum Society*, "we act to slow it down with
protection and subsidies for the inefficient. . . . If we cannot learn to
disinvest, we cannot compete in the modern growth race."[25] The economists may be correct, but one doubts United Auto Workers members
took comfort from them as they sat in cafes and taverns watching then
GM chairman Robert Stempel announce their fate.

Like the tidal waves that follow undersea earthquakes, the later
effects of plant closings are often worse than the earlier ones. In *The
Deindustrialization of America*, Barry Bluestone and Bennett Harrison
followed the wave caused by one layoff of eight thousand auto workers.
They identified an additional twelve thousand lost jobs as a result.[26] Not
surprisingly, local taxing authorities are also hit. The Massachusetts
Executive Office of Economic Affairs indicated that in the late 1980s the
loss of a $10,000 job cost some $1,336 in state and local taxes.[27]

In 1989 the SEC reversed its long-standing policy of excluding shareholder proposals on plant closings from proxy statements saying that
"broad plant closings resolutions go beyond ordinary business and are
therefore suitable subjects for shareholders review through the proxy
process."[28] (However, in a 1992 decision involving a shareholder resolution presented to Cracker Barrel on its policy against employing homosexuals, the SEC staff indicated that all personnel decisions were
"ordinary business" and therefore immune from shareholder review.)

Social investors cannot stop plant closings. But companies can miti-
gate their ill effects. There are no limits on how generous corporations
can be in cases of plant closings, and how they deal with these situations
is a fair indication of a corporation's commitment to its employees and
their communities.

BANKS: A SPECIAL CASE

Investment opportunities almost always outstrip the supply of capital.
Banks and mortgage companies allocate that limited supply, so they are
in a unique position of creating either good or ill in their communities.

"Redlining"—accepting deposits from poorer neighborhoods but not
making loans to them—has been a persistent problem. Without financing, neighborhood merchants cannot carry inventory and must close
down. Jobs disappear. Residents cannot find home-improvement loans.
Housing and property values deteriorate. Home buyers cannot find mortgage loans. The neighborhood enters a spiral of decline as a result of a
self-fulfilling prophecy by lenders. In 1992, Fleet Financial found itself
at the center of a redlining controversy in Atlanta.

Partly to address the redlining problem, in 1977 Congress passed the Community Reinvestment Act (CRA). The Act requires banks and savings and loan institutions (S&Ls) to meet the credit needs of their entire communities and authorizes the Federal Reserve and other federal regulatory agencies to determine compliance through periodic examinations and reports filed by financial institutions. CRA ratings are a matter of public record, and an institution's statement is open to examination during business hours. Banking regulators also must consider how well an institution complies when it applies to open a new branch or to merge with or acquire another bank. It is usually at the time of one of these applications that a CRA compliance record gets into the news.

Banks and community activists often present opposed versions of the adequacy of local lending services. Bankers say that they can lend money only to qualified borrowers and that few applicants in poor neighborhoods meet even relaxed credit standards. Activists charge that racism underlies lending decisions.

A 1990 report by Harvard's Joint Center for Housing Studies found evidence to support *both* views with regard to home loans. It found that discrimination and low incomes, and even lower savings, have kept blacks out of home ownership for decades.[29] Not long ago, Nationsbank (once NCNB, née North Carolina National Bank), one of the country's most acquisitive banks, found itself in a controversy over adequacy of what it has done in Charlotte and elsewhere.

The problem with CRA is that it does not address a fundamental question: Is consolidation of banking and the consequent elimination of local control a good thing? Do bankers at Banc One headquarters in Columbus know more about lending to small borrowers than local bankers in rural Ohio, Indiana, and Texas? Is the draining of money from the hinterlands into central banks good social policy? It is ironic that from John Adams's administration through Franklin Roosevelt's, consolidation of banking was fiercely resisted on these grounds. Deregulation and the banking crisis accomplished what the banks and their allies failed to do—with hardly a whisper about what consolidation meant as social and political policy.

COMMUNITY INVESTMENTS

Without question, the best way for social investors to improve the economic life of their communities is to invest locally and to act like an owner.

COMMUNITY DEVELOPMENT BANKS AND BANK PROGRAMS

One community in Chicago has greatly benefited from local bankers committed to meeting local needs. Profiled in chapter 1, South Shore Bank was taken over more than twenty years ago by self-described "do-gooders" who wanted to conduct a social experiment: Could a bank stem the tide of extremely rapid deterioration of a neighborhood? The experiment has succeeded.

Banks creating community development subsidiaries or programs meld the financial stability of the existing infrastructure with new lending for specific need. Sadly only a handful of banks have committed themselves to a community development focus. However, they have been key to economic development in their areas. Community Capital Bank in Brooklyn, New York, deals with a high proportion of homelessness, abandoned property, and unemployment. Blackfeet National finances small industry and health care on the Blackfeet reservation in Montana. Elk Horn Bank serves rural Arkansas where small farms, craft cooperatives, and women-owned business are frequent borrowers.

Social investors can do two things to partcipate. They can buy the stock or they can make a deposit in the development bank. Vermont Financial Services is the holding company for the Vermont National Bank whose Socially Responsible Banking Fund is profiled in the Introduction. Its stock is in the Domini Social Index. Making a deposit in a community development banking program is the more proactive course because community banks or banking programs use deposits for loans.

Banks ought to be particularly interested in creating vibrant, economically robust communities. The few development bank programs that have emerged have done so in particularly hard-hit areas: Sunshine Bank in Wheeling, West Virginia; Flagship Bank in Worcester, Massachusetts; First Trade Union in Boston. As this mechanism becomes better understood, more banks will follow.

WOMEN- AND MINORITY-OWNED BANKS

Blackfeet National is owned by and serves a Native American population. Many other banks owned by women and minorities make a special effort to meet the particular needs of their constituencies. *Minority Bank Monitor,* a newsletter, reports that about 125 such banks exist and that about thirty do a good job.

Perhaps the oldest and best known of these is Mechanics Southern of Raleigh-Durham, North Carolina. Its CEO, Julia W. Taylor, is an African-American. The bank's lending has sustained the needs of Raleigh-

Durham's minority community, from which other banks had withdrawn.

A recent Federal Reserve Bank study indicates that as a group, minority-owned banks turn down a higher percentage of loan applications from minority businesses than do regular banks. William M. Cunningham, an adviser on minority-bank deposit programs and editor of *Minority Bank Monitor,* explained that many minority businesses are very small and struggling. Their owners do not even approach conventional banks. Mr. Cunningham points to the minority-owned savings and loan associations as proof. While banks tend to lend to businesses, S&Ls lend for mortgages. The minority-owned S&Ls have a much higher acceptance rate of mortgages applied for by minorities than do conventional S&Ls.

The release of CRA data on conventional banks will make minority- and women-owned banks and community development banking programs more attractive to socially responsible investors. As Fleet Financial learned in Boston and Atlanta in 1991–92, both businesses and the community at large have begun to focus on what banks are doing in their service areas, and they do not like what they are seeing. Unfortunately, it will be a long time before depositors have access to locally oriented banks and programs in every locale.

COMMUNITY DEVELOPMENT LOAN FUNDS

Community investments either create housing or foster business development. Most social investors concur with the National Association of Community Development Loan Funds (NACDLF) that lending should address the structural issues of inequity. Its approach is different from that of LISC, LIMAC, and NEF (all of which we discussed earlier) in that its members fund housing in such a way as to create permanent affordability. The jobs they create are in cooperatively owned businesses. This fundamental philosophical distinction has been NACDLF's great strength.

About thirty loan funds are members of the NACDLF. These share three traits:

- They borrow from many sources (not, for instance, one diocese).
- They loan for many needs (not just housing or business).
- They lend in such a way as to create economic justice for all.

The loan funds have stepped in to take the high-risk first step toward empowering the disenfranchised. Take the cause of three unemployed women and their dependents who "liberated" a building in lower Manhattan. They broke in and squatted. Then, with the guidance of grass-roots advocacy groups, they formed a cooperative and convinced the city to sell them the building for one dollar. But the city demanded that the building be brought up to code—an expensive project. These people were not a charity and therefore could not get a grant. None of them could cosign—much less obtain—a loan because the cooperative lacked a financial track record. Without a loan, their chance to get off the streets would vanish.

Those three women and their dependents fit the borrower profile of NACDLF's member funds. And the Lower East Side Credit Union made the loan and serviced it. With the lender's technical assistance, they began to function as a limited equity cooperative—and to build a credit history. Eventually they, and the loan, will be sufficiently seasoned (i.e., the borrowers will have made several on time payments) to convince a conventional bank to take it over, thereby freeing the loan fund's capital for the another borrower.

Socially responsible investors lend money to NACDLF member funds or to NACDLF itself. Lenders to these funds have some comfort in knowing the track record of the individual loan fund, its capital, and also in knowing that the members of NACDLF audit and train one another.

Large investors have found NACDLF to be a good loan recipient. (To avoid competing with its members, NACDLF solicits only very large loans.) For example, the national Episcopal church endowment lent NACDLF $1.6 million to reloan to members who could leverage local Episcopal church funds. NACDLF challenged several local funds successfully. The Vermont Community Loan Fund (VCLF) before the challenge had only one loan from the Episcopal parishes in its area. When NACDLF made available $70,000 in matching loans, the local diocese got the word out and fourteen parishes responded. By melding mission and money, the national church put its credibility and dollars behind relatively sophisticated and proven development channels, thus reassuring risk-averse parish finance committees of the soundness of the investment.

COMMUNITY DEVELOPMENT CREDIT UNIONS

All credit unions are nonprofit organizations owned by their members. Each member has one vote, regardless of the amount of his or her deposit. Most of a credit union's assets are invested in loans to its members. The vast majority are consumer loans, though credit unions may hold some mortgages and make some commercial loans.[30]

Community development credit unions offer investors an opportunity to lend to the nation's neediest, and yet realize a financial return. These credit unions are federally regulated financial intermediaries whose deposits are insured up to $100,000 by the National Credit Union Association (NCUA). Most credit unions cannot accept deposits of any meaningful size from outside of their membership. But by federal law, community development credit unions can. Social investors get market or near-market rates of interest on their federally insured deposits at these credit unions.

The Lower East Side Credit Union lends for back-to-school clothing, for groceries until the next pay day, or for Christmas expenses. A big loan might be $3,000 to renovate a barbershop. The nation's poorest do not borrow large sums. Community development credit unions meet many needs. Womens' craft cooperatives in North Carolina receive loans from the Self-Help Credit Union; Navajos from First American; farmers in upstate New York using appropriate farming techniques from First Alternative; and Chinese immigrants in San Francisco from Quitman.

The National Federation of Community Development Credit Unions (NFCDCU) is an umbrella organization like NACDLF. Indeed, NFCDCU is a member of NACDLF. Through a combination of loans to NACDLF members and deposits in NFCDCU members, social investors can either target an area of need or diversify among several. Individuals and foundations have lent to the network in order to strengthen the infrastructure of community development credit unions. For instance, a MacArthur Foundation loan to NFCDCU has been used as a source of funds to create "challenge deposits" at several emerging credit unions. The local credit union must meet a membership drive goal or a deposit goal to get the additional sums.

COMMUNITY DEVELOPMENT IN THE FUTURE

Community development banks and banking programs, minority banks, credit unions, and loan funds combine to give investors a chance to allocate a portion of their assets to high-impact, social-change opportunities. But they comprise a very small sector of the financial services industry. They lack the capacity to affect much of the problem.

In contrast many corporations, either individually or in concert, have the capacity to initiate positive social change in their communities. So it is ironic that one of the social issues to which corporations historically have paid the most attention is an issue to which social investors historically have paid little heed: corporate involvement in the community. Commonly, the CEO's level of interest determines the quality of a corporation's involvement in its communities. In the early years of this century, Milton Hershey, founder of Hershey's chocolate, turned his hometown into a model community. After giving his company to an orphanage before the Depression, he spent millions during the thirties keeping his neighbors working on jobs that would benefit their town. Today, CEOs such as Arnold Hiatt, who recently retired from Stride Rite, bring childcare and eldercare onto their work sites and devote hundreds of hours each year quietly shoring up the social services in their communities.

Sometimes even the best intentioned corporations lose a critical benefit of their contributions to the community. Some corporations have separated their charitable giving from their day-to-day operations by turning it over to a professional foundation staff, rather than a committee of employees. Without question, professionally administered programs are usually less traditional and more innovative. But employee-run programs have the virtue of stronger ties to a broader constituency within the organization, while professional givers are less integrated into the corporate culture. Corporations lose a valuable point of dialogue with their communities when those who deal directly with giving do not have a connection to operations. Such employees lack authority to speak for the corporation on matters other than giving, and the community knows it.

In the future, corporations are likely to integrate their community activities more fully and to take a more systematic approach to them. Affordable housing, education, and infrastructure issues will take on new meaning for corporations as they are called on to act in the public good in the face of government's abdication of its duties.

As we will see in chapter 11, the assumption of government's tasks by corporations is not novel. Indeed, corporations receive quasi-governmental powers, such as limited liability, so that the body politic can achieve some benefit. For now, however, we will look at the end result of corporate involvement in the community.

8

Employees and Their Corporations: Learning to Work Together

IN FEBRUARY 1990, United Mine Workers of America (UMWA) employees at the Pittston Company voted to accept a contract that ended a forty-six-week strike involving fifty thousand miners in nine states. The strike was one of the most violent in recent years. Over three thousand people were arrested.

Pittston, the nation's largest exporter of coal,* believed it had to cut costs to meet competition from foreign metallurgical coal in the world markets. Some of its competitors are subsidized by their governments.[1] The company incited the strike when it moved to cut health benefits to 1,500 retired and disabled miners and to make current employees pick up a substantial share of their health-insurance costs. Pittston had already pulled out of a long-standing arrangement with the UMWA whereby coal operators paid into a pool to fund health and retirement benefits for miners industry-wide. Pittston's withdrawal potentially threatened the benefits of 130,000 retired miners, if it set a precedent for other companies.

During the strike the union tried several new tactics, with some support from social investors.[2] It approached companies like Philip Morris, where Pittston's chairman, Paul Douglas, was an outside director, asking management and shareholders to remove him from its board. It

---

*Pittston also owns Brink's security services and Burlington Air Express.

also approached companies whose officers were outside directors of Pittston. Institutional investors who owned the company's stock received calls from UMWA representatives, who attacked Pittston's management.

Public opinion eventually turned against the company. Even *Business Week* complained in an editorial, "Rather than turn its back on retirees, [Pittston] should seek to secure efficient work practices and other cost savings from labor."[3] Pittston was cited by the National Labor Relations Board, which complained that the strike "was caused by Pittston's unfair labor practices."[4]

The war between Pittston and the union put a spotlight on the political and economic currents that have upset decades of relative calm in union-management relations: foreign competition, skyrocketing health costs, and the fading power of unions. It highlights the important employment issues for the years ahead: What level of health care can workers and their families expect now and after retirement? What retirement benefits should workers have? How much control should workers have over their workplaces? Do unions serve a useful function in today's world?

These issues affect social investors both as individuals and employees or retirees. Questions of social justice always mingle with critical questions of self-protection. It is just such situations that yield the best opportunities for advocacy.

RELATIONS WITH EMPLOYEES IN THE '90s

The dynamics of business competition have changed dramatically in just two decades. Assembly lines with mindless machines and minimally skilled tenders have given way to processes that require workers with computer and scheduling skills and the ability to make decisions on the spot. Audrey Freedman, executive director of the Human-Resources group at the Conference Board, has said that to succeed, companies must enlist the minds—as well as the hands—of their workers. "Workers can no longer be just appendages of machinery. Business will have to let workers use their judgment."[5]

Health and safety problems, compensation squabbles, and labor grievances keep minds off business and on self-interest. These issues never disappear. But some firms handle them much better than others. These firms tend to attract social investors for other reasons as well.

Despite the need for good employee relations, many companies, such as Caterpillar, have assigned employee relations de facto to corporate cost-cutters. Greater competition has put pressure on firms to reduce their costs: employee benefits, union agreements, staffing levels, and manufacturing capacity. At the same time, the demographics of the workplace and of the American health care system dictate that pension and medical programs will continue to be under great financial pressure. Indeed, these issues will probably dominate the 1990s and the first half of the next century.

RELATIONS WITH UNIONS

While most socially responsible investors do not buy only union companies, they do monitor how corporations deal with their unions.

The 1960s and early 1970s were the glory days of trade unionism in the United States. At labor's peak, close to 25 percent of the nonfarm American work force held union cards, and new groups—such as municipal and white-collar workers—were organizing. But at the moment of its greatest success, global economic forces were undercutting unionism's areas of strength—mining, steel, automobiles, and heavy manufacturing generally. Today only about 12 percent of the work force in America's private business sector is organized.

Not the least important reason for labor's misfortunes in the 1980s is management's discovery that they could beat the unions. With the Republicans in control of the federal executive and judicial branches for twenty-eight of the forty years since 1953, labor has had few friends where it needed them, on the National Labor Relations Board and in the lower courts. As a result, organizing efforts have often failed.

Pittston, as we've noted, tried to bust the United Mine Workers but lost. Phelps Dodge, which started this unhappy phenomenon, broke the Steel Workers in 1985 by bringing in replacement workers willing to take much lower wages. It successfully "decertified" the union at its El Paso copper refinery and Arizona mines. Replacement employees voted against union representation. Striking employees who had been on the picket lines for twenty-one months were kept from voting by a National Labor Relations Board (NLRB) rule that workers unemployed for a year are ineligible to vote.[6] Besides Pittston, several other companies, such as those listed in Table 8-1, followed Phelps Dodge's example.[7]

It is worth noting that Pittston's president, Paul Douglas, sat on Phelps Dodge's board during the strike. Conventional wisdom has it that corporate boards just collect their checks (see chapter 11). Whatever the truth of that argument, the people who serve on a corporate board are afforded a rare insight into the minds of senior management. Strong corporate managers are willing to deal with strong board members. Also, tracing connections among boards and their members often leads to interesting groupings—as it does on union busting.

TABLE 8-1. SUCCESSFUL USERS OF REPLACEMENT WORKERS

Phelps Dodge Corp. (1983)	International Paper Co. (1987)
Greyhound (1983 and 1990)	Eastern Airlines (1989)
Continental Airlines (1983)	*New York Daily News* (1991)
The Chicago Tribune (1985)	Caterpillar Inc. (1992)
Hormel Co. (1985)	

Source: J. Rosenblum, "The Dismal Precedent That Gave Us Caterpillar," *Wall Street Journal,* April 16, 1992, p. A25.

Unions and management must rethink the role of organized labor in a free society. Former secretary of state George Shultz started his career as an economist and labor-management arbitrator. Not long ago he remarked that a healthy workplace requires "some system of checks and balances" between those who supply the jobs and those who provide the labor, and a "system of industrial jurisprudence." Reduced circumstances within labor lead him to fear for checks and balances and justice in the workplace of the 1990s.[8]

Their weakness and global competition are forcing unions to cooperate with corporations. MIT's Thomas Kochan told *Financial World,* "The future of labor-management relations lies in unions winning a greater role in the longer-term decisions about the products they make."[9] Unions are having to drop outmoded work rules and pay demands that exceed increases in productivity. Corporations are having to share decision making on the factory floor with workers.[10] Ideally, corporations and unions will recognize and act in their mutual interests. When they do, the greater interests of the public will be served. But it would be naive to count on this. Many corporations are using the current weakness of organized labor to take advantage of workers on pay, benefits, and safety issues.

No doubt, in some industries union leaders shielded their power by perpetuating outmoded work rules and rebuffing invitations to involve line workers in decision making. But the demise of the union and the disappearance of well-compensated blue-collar workers are political and social disasters. Unions are a necessary counterbalance to corporate power. Until something like them emerges again, social investors must look to enlightened management.

WORKPLACE SAFETY

The decreasing political and social power of unions has affected workplace safety. Workplace safety is an issue that goes to the essence of employment relationships for most social investors. It tends to arise in the context of other employment issues, as it did in the long battle in the mid-1980s between the George A. Hormel Company and its union workers.

The creation of the Occupational Safety and Health Administration (OSHA) in 1970 was one of organized labor's last triumphs. That it has done next to nothing through three Republican administrations is well known. Less well known but probably of greater impact on workers is the states' withdrawal from the field, too. Since an estimated 78,000 Americans die each year from workplace accidents or work-related diseases and a similar number become permanently disabled,[11] one can assume better enforcement would improve these dismal statistics.

Experts disagree as to whether the situation is getting worse or better. An OSHA official told the *Los Angeles Times*, "I think workplaces are generally safer." But citing business pressures to produce more with lower staffing, Joseph Kinney, director of the National Safe Workplace Institute, disagrees: "People are getting hurt more than they ever were. They're under more pressure to produce than they ever were. A lot of companies that once were using seven workers to do a job are now asking five to do it."[12]

What is beyond debate is that the postindustrial age has changed the way many work, but it has done little to protect meat packers like those at Hormel from disabling muscular disorders[13] and lacerations. Nor has it done much for today's farm workers, who endure not only backbreaking labor but also the dangers of modern agricultural chemicals. White-collar workers at banks, newspapers, and other nonindustrial firms face uncertain dangers from the sick building syndrome, radiation from computer terminals,[14] and repetitive stress injuries from computer keyboards.[15]

Shareholder activists have long questioned corporations on workplace safety. In 1992 Martin Marietta was asked to "take the steps necessary to effect programs and policies which address the human and environmental risks inherent in the processing of uranium." The supporting statement says, "As investors, we are concerned that safety has been overlooked for so long and that health studies which show higher levels of radiation-related illnesses among workers are only now being published. Thus, we are asking for procedures which enhance and hasten care for the human community."

From the perspective of modern office buildings with corporate cafeterias and, perhaps, employee fitness centers, it is easy to believe that the quality of working life has entered a golden age. "Dark satanic mills" and stoop labor have faded from our experience. But many Americans do labor in shops, factories, and even gleaming office buildings where matters of health and physical safety are unresolved. Asian immigrants now slave in newly revived sweatshops.

Three generations ago when he developed his "hierarchy of human needs," the great industrial psychologist Abraham Maslow put security and safety at its base. Without a sense of safety from physical dangers, he reasoned, the working person has no interest in high levels of human psychic achievement and well-being. Employers have the ultimate control of their workplace. For that reason, social investors should take a keen interest in how corporations deal with this fundamental responsibility.

Whatever the economic pros and cons are of the downsizing and consolidation of American industry, a principal result has been that the workers who have kept their jobs are required to work harder in more stressful conditions. Ma Bell and Ma Exxon are long gone, and so are hundreds of thousands of jobs. Social investors have only limited means for influencing working conditions. Supporting employee groups, lobbying, and withholding votes for directors and management proxy resolutions are the main avenues. Because they relate to "ordinary business," the SEC rarely approves shareholder resolutions in this area.

The assembly-line conditions satirized in Charlie Chaplin's *Modern Times* may be no more, replaced in our service society with something equally bad. President Bush, in closing a brief meeting with the press, may have epitomized today's working conditions when he said, "I've got to run now and relax. The doctor told me to relax. The doctor told me. He was the one. He said, 'Relax.' "[16] Table 8-2 shows why for most employees the doctor's advice may be impossible to carry out. In any case, social investors should be paying much closer attention to working conditions both here and abroad.

LAYOFF POLICIES

On February 24, 1992, General Motors announced that it would lay off up to 74,000 employees at some twenty-one locations around North America. These would not be the usual auto-industry layoffs, caused by a mismatch of supply and demand. These layoffs would be permanent. Another industrial giant, IBM, announced plans to reduce its work force by 17,000 during 1992—in addition to the 50,000 positions it had eliminated over the previous six years. These reductions have less to do with conditions in the broader economy than with specific economies relating to these firms.

Since 1989, layoff announcements have come so regularly that we

TABLE 8-2. VACATION DEFICIT

Country	Vacation Days	Country	Vacation Days
Spain	32.0	Belgium	24.6
Netherlands	31.9	Italy	24.6
Norway	31.4	United Kingdom	24.5
Germany	29.9	Japan	24.0
Finland	28.6	Switzerland	23.4
Sweden	27.8	Ireland	22.9
France	27.0	Australia	22.4
Austria	26.8	Canada	14.7
Denmark	25.0	United States	10.8

If we Americans are as lazy and unproductive as we are told, we are certainly putting in long weeks at it. Perhaps the message of these figures—paid vacation days per year for 1991—is "work less and be more productive." Or perhaps there is something fundamentally wrong with a system where so many work so hard for so long for so little.
Source: Union Bank of Switzerland, *Prices and Earnings Around the Globe,* 1991 (Zurich: UBS, 1991), p. 8, as reprinted in A. L. Shapiro, *We're Number One!* Copyright © 1992 by A. L. Shapiro. Reprinted by permission of Vintage Books, a Division of Random House, Inc.

are numbed by them. But why and how a corporation lays off workers are significant concerns to socially responsible investors. Are the jobs going to the maquiladoras or Taiwan? What will happen to the community affected by the layoffs? (We looked at that question in the last chapter.) What kind of severance benefits do workers receive? What about their health care? How corporations deal with employees during periods of adversity—especially those upon whom the greatest burden will fall—tells a great deal.

Business cycles—from prosperity to recession and back again—are a fact of life. Since 1933, the country has experienced eleven complete cycles, roughly one every five years.[17] The costs of recession are reported in the aggregate but experienced in the specific. Instead of all of us being 8 percent unemployed—a small disaster for the many, 8 percent of us are 100 percent unemployed—a great disaster for the few. Regions and communities are likewise affected disproportionately during recession.

As we've seen, few corporations have "no layoff" policies. At best, they have "traditions" of maintaining employment through thick and thin. Since many of these firms are in high-growth industries, not many have had their traditions tested by adversity. Digital Equipment (DEC) had never laid off anyone until 1990. When it began experiencing severe difficulties in the late 1980s, it responded with a generous "voluntary separation" program, which reduced employment by some 5,500. Business worsened. DEC began "involuntary" layoffs of workers, who received less generous separation terms.[18] Of the major corporations with no layoff policies or traditions, only DEC had to end its policy. Others responded to the 1990s recession by spreading the pain. Nucor, a mini-mill steel company, reduced plant operations to three to four days per week. Hallmark Cards, which has never had a layoff since it opened in 1910, reassigned workers—even to community work. Hewlett Packard resorted to holiday closures and days off without pay.[19]

PARTICIPATION IN MANAGEMENT AND OWNERSHIP

One solution to the working-conditions problem is to bring employees into the decision-making process, to give them more say in how they work. Another is to make employees owners so that they can have a direct voice in management. Social investors tend to favor companies adopting these strategies. But here, too, there can be a considerable gap between corporate descriptions of employee involvement and reality.

A New Workplace

Some time ago it was said that the factory of the future would be filled with robotic machines and staffed by a man and a dog. The machines would do the work; the man would feed the dog; and the dog would make sure that the man did not touch the machines. The future turned out to be quite different. Our machines are much "smarter," but the people who work with them must be highly skilled. The modern workplace calls for workers with the ability to handle several different jobs and the discretion needed for on-the-spot decision making. They need the capacity to deal with statistical process control, material scheduling, and machine maintenance.

And they must be allowed to participate in decisions on matters that directly affect them. For example, line workers in Ford Motor Company plants now participate in product and process improvements that continue to reduce the time needed to assemble the typical Ford product. This is something new since 1980. But as Table 8-3 shows, the sheer numbers of managers may inhibit worker participation in decision making.

Japan's new manufacturing methods are now our models. American industry is adopting flexible manufacturing, quality control, and just-in-time inventory control—techniques that have proven their worth in Japan over the past forty years. These changes have important implications for employee training and development, the boundaries between

TABLE 8-3. MANAGERS AND PRODUCTIVITY GROWTH

Country	Managers (%)	Productivity Growth (%)
United States	12.1	0.7
Australia	11.9	0.9
Canada	11.9	1.2
Austria	4.7	1.9
Japan	3.7	3.0
Netherlands	3.3	1.5
Denmark	3.0	2.1
Finland	3.0	3.6
Ireland	2.2	—
Spain	1.3	3.0

If England was until recently "a nation of shopkeepers," America is a nation of managers. But what are our managers managing? This table compares the percentage of the working population who are managers or administrative workers in 1989 with the average annual growth of labor productivity in terms of output per employee for 1979 through 1990.
Source: International Labor Organization, *Yearbook of Labor Statistics 1989–90* (Geneva: ILO, 1990), pp. 120–186; Organization for Economic Cooperation and Development, *OECD Economic Outlook 50* (Paris: OECD, 1991), p. 136, as reprinted in A. L. Shapiro, *We're Number One!* Copyright © 1992 by A. L. Shapiro. Reprinted by permission of Vintage Books, a Division of Random House, Inc.

workers and managers, and the role of labor unions. Above all, however, they have challenged corporations to invest in the skills of their employees. Efforts to rearrange the workplace without upgrading the skills of labor have been costly failures.

Perhaps the best example can be found among firms that are developing a system of "mass customization," such as IBM, Bell Atlantic, Nissan, and Swatch. They are delivering higher product variety at mass-production prices. But rapid changeovers in production require that people close to the action do both the thinking and the doing.

SHARING THE PROFITS AND THE GAINS

Corporations have a number of ways by which they can give employees a sense of ownership in their work. No one can scientifically establish a causal link between the success of a company and its incentive plans. But many believe the link exists.

At Nucor, a company we noted has a no-layoff policy, employees receive roughly half of their pay from cash incentive programs. It produces high-quality steel with the best tonnage-per-employee record in America—twice that of Bethlehem Steel and USX. F. Kenneth Iverson, Nucor's longtime CEO, ascribes half of his firm's success to its system of worker incentives. The principle behind it is quite simple: The more quality steel you and your work team produce, the more you get paid.[20]

Incentives work for Nucor. And they work for Japanese corporations, where workers typically receive up to 25 percent of their annual earnings from plans that link their pay with the rising or falling fortunes of the company. Yet according to a study by MIT economist Martin Weitzman, as of 1988 U.S. workers received only 1 percent of their pay from such arrangements.[21]

Production incentives can be abused. In a piecework arrangement, management can manipulate goals to minimize payouts. Base pay can be held very low with the promise of illusory bonuses. Thus, it is the quality of the incentive program that is important, not the fact of its existence.

Profit sharing is another important incentive. Again, management's commitment to sharing determines the plan's quality. The advantage to the firm of a profit-sharing plan is that its expense is variable: If there are no profits, it makes no payments. A few firms give employees their share in cash. Others contribute either cash or company stock to the employees' individual tax-deferred retirement savings plans (401(k) plans).*

From the standpoint of the employees who earn a share of the profits, direct cash payments are preferable. Then they have the freedom to decide what to do with the money. Cash contributions—as opposed to stock—to a 401(k) plan are second best, since most such plans give the employee a range of choices of investment vehicles. Many companies such as AT&T make 401(k) contributions in the form of company stock. This is a good deal for the company—they do not pay cash out—but it is not so good for the employees. The plans suffer from a lack of diversification.[22] And naturally, employees are reluctant to appear disloyal by selling this stock. (These plans are discussed below.)

Gain sharing is an idea related to profit sharing, but it usually focuses on a division, a department, or a still smaller unit. Therefore, rewards do not depend on overall corporate profits—something few employees have any control over. Gain-sharing programs set levels of performance. The extent to which the unit exceeds that level determines the gain to be shared. Herman Miller, a Michigan furniture manufacturer, has used gain-sharing incentives since 1950. Its "Earned Share" system is based on a number of key measurements: service quality, product quality, growth, asset use, and cost savings. Workers are awarded points in each of these areas, and bonus payments are awarded accordingly.[23]

---

*These plans are discussed in detail at the end of this chapter.

REAL OWNERSHIP

Performance incentives are valuable. Profit sharing makes employees feel that they are getting their due. But nothing has greater potential for involving employees in the life of their companies than real ownership.

ESOPs. In the 1950s a San Francisco lawyer, Louis Kelso, decided that the trouble with capitalism was that there were too few capitalists. Just 1 percent of the population held half of the privately held stock in the United States. Few workers had an ownership stake in their firms—or any firm, for that matter.

Kelso set out to create a "people's capitalism" through a device called the Employee Stock Ownership Plan (ESOP). An ESOP is a defined-contribution plan* that invests primarily in the stock of the company sponsoring the plan. Typically, the employing firm contributes funds to the plan. The plan uses the money to purchase company stock to be held in tax-exempt trust for the benefit of employees covered by the plan. Special tax benefits make these plans appealing to corporations, which can deduct their contributions (within generous limitations).

By 1990, close to 11 million employees had become shareholders in their companies this way. ESOPs held stocks valued at the time at about $120 billion (roughly 3 percent of the outstanding stock of U.S. corporations).[24] A number of firms, principally in the steel industry, became wholly or partially owned by their ESOPs: Republic Engineered Steels, Oregon Steel Mills, CF&I Steel, Continental Steel, Crucible Specialty Steel, Texas Foundries, American Cast Iron Pipe, Worthington Industries, and others.

During the takeover frenzy of the 1980s, many firms—Polaroid being the prime example—either started ESOPs or picked up the pace of contributions. A large block of company stock in the hands of current employees deterred hostile takeovers, because employees usually vote their shares for people they know rather than for outsiders whose intentions they fear. While favoring employee ownership, social investors have taken a skeptical view of antitakeover ESOPs.

Employee ownership tends to increase democracy in the workplace by including workers in decision making. In 1990 the Michigan Center for Employee Ownership and Gainsharing studied seventy-two Michigan firms. It found that employee ownership programs resulted in measura-

---

*A defined-contribution plan is an employee benefit plan in which the employee's pay-in is specified but his or her payout usually is not.

bly increased employee participation. As Table 8-4 indicates, employee participation in quality circles, ad-hoc work groups, business education programs, and training programs all increased after ESOP plans were instituted. The same study indicated improvements in the critical performance measures: sales, profitability, and level of employment.[25]

Evidence from other studies and casual inquiries confirms the effect of employee ownership on economic performance. Speaking with *Business Week* six years after his firm set up an ESOP, Brunswick Corporation vice president for finance, William R. McManaman, remarked, "The ESOP has improved the morale of our employees by creating a sense of ownership and has had a definite impact on productivity." Sales per Brunswick employee jumped by 50 percent during the first five years of the ESOP.[26]

But neither greater worker participation nor improved business performance *necessarily* follow from an ESOP. Management has to be willing to share decision making. Without this, the benefits do not follow. And many ESOP shares do not carry voting rights, so the workers have no real voice as owners. Socially responsible investors count the existence of an ESOP as a plus, but they look beneath the surface for real participation—at every level—before giving a company full marks.

COOPs. The ultimate form of employee ownership is the cooperative. One investment advisory firm which specializes in socially responsible investing is 100 percent employee-owned. Franklin Research & Development Corp. was founded ten years ago in Boston by Joan Bavaria. She carried her values into the structure of her firm right from the start. Now managing over $200 million and employing over thirty persons, the firm is cooperatively owned and managed. The firm runs portfolios, sponsors shareholder actions, and gives to charities with the full input from its employees.

Community development investors have opportunities to support

TABLE 8-4. INCREASED PARTICIPATION WITH EMPLOYEE OWNERSHIP

	Before ESOP	After ESOP
Quality Circles	13%	22%
Employee Task Forces	23%	28%
Ad-Hoc Work Groups	9%	19%
Business Education Programs	37%	61%
Participative Management Training	19%	36%

Source: Michigan Center for Employee Ownership and Gainsharing as discussed in *Employee Ownership Report,* vol. X, no. 6, November/December 1990, pp. 1, 4.

cooperatively owned businesses as well. Perhaps the best known example is offered by the Industrial Cooperative Association (ICA) of Somerville, Massachusetts. ICA's program, which is national, provides technical assistance, loans, and equity for employee buyouts and community-based businesses that are employee-owned. Borrowing from the ICA Revolving Loan Fund allows coops to form without being overly burdened with debt.

A socially responsible investor can help ICA through its community jobs deposit program. It works like this. You buy a certificate of deposit at an ICA-selected bank—currently South Shore Bank in Chicago or the Boston Bank of Commerce. When you buy the CD, you specify a rate of interest you wish to receive that is below the prevailing rate. The difference goes into ICA's revolving loan fund. (Since the two banks involved are leading community development banks, your principal will also be put to good use.) ICA's projects include four home health care cooperatives form and the union-led employee buy-out of John Roberts Clothing, Inc.

REACHING OUT

Roughly 12 percent of the U.S. population is black; 9 percent is Hispanic. About 51 percent is female. Approximately 10 percent is homosexual. Perhaps 17 percent is physically or mentally disabled to some degree. And, a growing percentage is afflicted with AIDS. Historically, employers have discriminated against people in these categories. The extent to which a corporation draws on these groups says much about its values. In chapter 10, we will explore issues relating to ethnic minorities and women in the workplace. Here, we will take a brief look at how corporations treat the disabled, AIDS sufferers, and gays and lesbians.

THE MENTALLY OR PHYSICALLY CHALLENGED

Given the right training and jobs that recognize their impairments, disabled workers are overwhelmingly successful. The disabled are among the most reliable and diligent workers. Hiring them is both good business and the right thing to do.

Marriott Corporation, the hotel and catering firm, employs over 6,000 disabled workers (3 percent of its total staffing). It helps mentally challenged individuals adjust to working life through programs that teach social and job-readiness skills. Marriott pairs the challenged worker with a manager/mentor. While annual employee turnover at Marriott is 105 percent, the turnover of disabled workers is just 8 percent. McDonald's and Pizza Hut are also large employers of individuals with challenges.[27] Box 8-1 describes a model policy for employing the disabled.

Many socially responsible investors view positively those firms that seek out mentally or physically challenged workers. It follows that they view negatively companies recently cited for violations of the federal Americans with Disabilities Act or state laws that guarantee equal opportunities in employment.

WORKERS WITH AIDS

Unless a cure or vaccine is found sometime soon, Acquired Immune Deficiency Syndrome (AIDS) may become the plague of the twenty-first century. Already it has swept through large sections of sub-Saharan Africa.

In the United States, it has grown from a handful of cases to an

---

BOX 8-1. A MODEL POLICY FOR EMPLOYMENT OF THE DISABLED

The International Association of Machinists and Aerospace Workers (IAM) has been a leader in bringing disabled people into the workplace. Between 1981 and 1989, it placed 5,395 individuals in wage-paying positions. Its own model labor agreement contains provisions that are useful practices social investors can look for when evaluating the practices of corporations. In condensed form, the IAM policy requires:

Nondiscrimination: on the basis of disability, race, gender, religion, sexual preference, or national origin.

Job Retention: retain workers who become disabled on or off the job, and bring them back to work as soon as possible.

Reasonable Accommodation: accommodate the working situation to the known limitations of the disabled worker.

Retrain and/or Transfer: as needed due to disability.

Promotion: based upon ability and merit. Disability alone shall not be grounds for nonpromotion.

Labor-Management Committee: to find ways to enhance the productivity and opportunities of disabled workers.

Source: IAM Suggested Contract Language, as discussed in Gopal Pati and G. Stubblefield, "The Disabled Are Able to Work," *Personnel Journal,* December 1990, pp. 31, 33.

epidemic. By early 1992, one in 250 Americans either had the disease or its precursor, HIV. Perhaps because they have been largely from groups outside the mainstream of society—Hispanics, blacks, intravenous drug users, prostitutes, and homosexual men—AIDS victims are treated as modern-day lepers. But as AIDS makes inroads into the larger population, that attitude is changing slowly.

AIDS sufferers face catastrophic economic impacts—loss of earnings and horrendous medical costs. In 1992 the cost of care for an AIDS patient from diagnosis to death averaged $145,000. That figure will escalate as new treatments prolong life.

Few companies have programs that support the AIDS-afflicted as a special category of employee. However, a growing number do recognize AIDS as an important social concern by supporting education and research, community care systems, and technical assistance.[28] The leaders are firms with major facilities in the San Francisco Bay area, including AT&T, Bank of America, Chevron, Pacific Telesis, Transamerica, and Wells Fargo.

One of the worst aspects of the disease is the ostracism AIDS victims often suffer. Lack of education on the means by which the disease is transmitted leads coworkers to fear contact or even proximity. In the early 1980s, this was the case at Levi Strauss. The company met the problem head-on. It made information available in the workplace and adopted a policy statement: Employees with AIDS or any other life-threatening disease would be treated with dignity and respect. At about the same time, Wells Fargo had an employee with AIDS who wished to return to work after medical treatment. The bank defused employees' fears by providing seminars with a medical expert. Beyond that, the employee's coworkers were given the opportunity to make more specific, private inquiries on company time.[29]

GAY AND LESBIAN WORKERS

No publicly traded corporation currently has a reputation for reaching out to gay and lesbian workers. But there are a few glimmers of light. Lotus Development Corporation, which is based in Cambridge, Massachusetts, recently announced that its health care benefits would now extend to the spousal equivalents and families of gay and lesbian workers. While other corporations had cried that the "proving" of a relationship would be too difficult and that the benefits would be abused, Lotus simply asked its employees to elect the coverage. Lotus's fine example led Ben & Jerry's Homemade, another company with an extraordinary commitment to its extended community, to take the same step.

Surrounding these points of light is darkness. We mentioned Cracker Barrel Old Country Store, Inc., in the last chapter. Its policy had been to fire any homosexuals who find their way onto the Cracker Barrel payroll. The firm's policy came under national attack. As a result, the company rescinded it, but reports persisted of firings which seemed linked to sexual orientation. The company heard from shareholder activists. The New York City Employee Retirement System asked the company to "implement nondiscriminatory policies relating to sexual orientation and to add explicit prohibitions against such discrimination to their corporate employment policy statement." Unfortunately, the SEC staff chose the challenge to this resolution to announce its new "ordinary business" standard for resolutions relating to employment.

BENEFITS

"Enlightened self-interest" sounds like an oxymoron. Yet this very human combination of wanting to protect yourself while advancing the welfare of others is at the heart of many movements for social justice. In no area is this relationship clearer for socially responsible investors than in employee benefits—pensions, health care plans, educational programs, day care, and the like provided by or through employers.

Employee benefits consist of services or noncash compensation to an employee that the employer either pays for or facilitates. Some benefits are required by law—Social Security, worker's compensation, and unemployment compensation. Others—private retirement plans, health care insurance, and the like—are either negotiated with management by unions or created by management because it is in the company's best interests, or both. Table 8-5 outlines benefits commonly offered.

Social investors have an interest in protecting their own rights to these services, but they also recognize the need for them across society. They are uniquely positioned to press for positive change. As shareholders, they can lobby the corporation; as plan participants, they can influence their pension plans; and as employees or managers, they can work for internal change and increased charitable contributions.

The availability and adequacy of benefits will become an increasingly important issue as the baby boom generation starts to require more health care and to draw on their retirement programs. As that clamor grows, it will be important to remember that since 1981 similar services to the poor have declined year by year and that the Reagan/Bush–era funding cuts affected the young and the voteless much more than they did other population segments.

TABLE 8-5. THE BROAD RANGE OF MODERN EMPLOYEE BENEFITS

REQUIRED BY LAW

Social Security (FICA)
Worker's Compensation
Unemployment Compensation

PROTECTIVE BENEFITS

Medical and Hospitalization Insurance
Dental and Vision Care
Life Insurance
Disability Insurance

EQUITY BENEFITS

Pension Plans (defined-contribution, defined-benefit)
Profit sharing
Thrift savings plans (some employers "match" employee contributions)
Cash-deferred plans (401(k))
Stock Plans (stock-purchase options; ESOPs)

ENTITLEMENTS

Vacations
Holidays
Educational Assistance
Other

Source: Adapted from William R. Tracey, ed., *Human Resources Management and Development Handbook* (New York: AMACOM, 1985), pp. 646–53.

Until recently social investors were only concerned with how management dealt with benefits not required by law. The emergence of health care as a national issue and the looming—albeit somewhat quieter—issue of retirement benefits has put in the spotlight the interplay between government and corporations on the entire benefits question. The debate about health care and the care of the elderly and poor is irrational and intemperate, because the issues are intertwined with the two dominant themes of our time: race and intergenerational transfers of wealth.

Businesses are caught in the middle. Many have tried to meet needs they defined as individual but that are in reality societal. The United States has rejected "socialized medicine" and direct taxes to support living standards of the "truly needy." So it is both easy and wrong to blame corporations for taking their case to Congress and the legislatures for removing at least part of the burden from them.

HEALTH CARE

Like most crises that seem to burst unheralded onto the front pages, the benefits controversy has been with us for a long time. In the early 1980s, companies such as Navistar (née International Harvester) and Chrysler tried various strategies to hold down their health care costs. They largely failed.

The U.S. Chamber of Commerce estimated in 1987 that benefits comprised 39 percent of payroll, up from 24.7 percent in 1959. That percentage has grown further in the wake of skyrocketing health care costs. In the Boston area in 1992 families not covered under group plans paid between $4,700 and $5,300 in annual health insurance premiums.[30] In 1987, GM estimated that it was paying more for just one class of benefits—medical—than it was for the steel from which its vehicles are made. Many employers see increasing benefits costs as a major, if not a prohibitive, cost of doing business when foreign firms may not incur them.

Not surprisingly, the most active shareholders on this issue have been pension funds. In 1992, New York City Employees Retirement System (NYCERS) asked Brunswick, Albertson's, Dole, 3M, and GTE to study the effect of health care reform proposals on their balance sheets and publish the results. According to NYCERS' supporting statement, "Roughly 50 million Americans have inadequate health care coverage and another 37 million have no protection at all." Yet at Brunswick, NYCERS noted, "We are concerned that the costs and inadequate quality of health care in the United States threaten to undermine the company's competitive advantage in the international market place."

Few studies have confirmed the value of health care benefits to firms in terms of attracting and retaining desirable employees.[31] However, anecdotal evidence indicates that people are keeping jobs they would otherwise leave because of them. The aging U.S. work force is becoming more and more concerned about health care and pensions, and regularly ranks them in that order as the most desirable benefits.[32]

RETIREMENT PLANS

One of the most memorable "Doonesbury" sequences from the 1970s featured Uncle Duke as the Redskins's general manager. Under gentle questioning, the rascal admitted how he had acquired the services of Lava Lava Lenny, the Slingin' Samoan; "Besides, the pension fund was just sitting there. . . ."[33]

By the mid-1980s, life had imitated art with such regularity that the joke was lost on many people. Corporate raiders and leveraged-buyout kings had discovered "overfunded" pension plans as sources of free capital to finance their ventures. Financial piranhas were not the only people who recognized the value of pension-fund assets.[34] For example, in early 1992 General Motors planned to put $500 million of its stock in its pension funds, thereby retaining $500 million in cash it would otherwise have had to contribute.[35] Funds could be terminated, their beneficiaries paid off, and the "surplus" could be used to "increase shareholder value." Even public-sector pension funds, such as the California Public Employees' Retirement System (CalPERS), have made "voluntary" contributions toward their states' deficits.[36]

Not surprisingly, underfunded pensions are now common. Social investors can identify companies with such pensions by looking at the pension-liabilities notes to a company's financial statements in the annual report.

Pension plans are classified as either "defined-benefit" or "defined-contribution" plans. Typically, the employer makes contributions to a plan on the employee's behalf. In a defined-benefits plan, the fund bears the investment risk because it promises to pay a specific amount after retirement. It must manage contributions so as to meet the promised payments. In a defined-contribution plan, the employee bears the investment risk. Benefits paid after retirement are determined by how well those contributions were invested.

After the '80s bash, few employers were adding benefits that cost them much, and pension plans are expensive. Instead, they opted for "retirement savings plans" to which they need contribute little or nothing. These programs are called "401(k) plans"* because of the section of the Internal Revenue Code that authorizes them. In a 401(k) plan, employees may put aside a portion of their annual pay (within specific limits). Income taxes are deferred until after retirement on their contributions and on the interest and profits they earn. Employers sometimes match employee contributions up to a certain dollar amount or a percentage of annual income. A 401(k) plan appeals to some because it removes some of the feeling of responsibility management may have for employees' postretirement well-being. However, the level of benefits an employee will derive from a 401(k) are relatively meager.

A critical element in the retirement plan controversies is the ignorance of plan beneficiaries. Many employees are unwilling or unable to assume the level of control required. Most are ill-equipped to make

---

*Not-for-profits offer a similar vehicle, the 403(b) plan. Some of the criticisms of the 401(k) plans apply to them as well.

BOX 8-2. INDISPENSABLE RESOURCE: *PENSIONS & INVESTMENTS*

Pensions & Investments bills itself as "the newspaper of corporate and institutional investing." Unlike other newspaper slogans, for example, "all the news that's fit to print," this one is accurate. Anyone concerned with employee-benefits issues, corporate-governance questions, and the role of financial institutions in our society must read this biweekly. *P&I* illuminates issues that the mainstream financial press often misses. For instance, it highlighted Caterpillar's efforts to alter its benefits plans during its lockout of employees represented by the United Auto Workers.

P&I takes an uncharitable view of socially responsible investing generally, but it has given substantial coverage—much of it favorable—to shareholder actions.

Pensions & Investments, 965 Jefferson Street, Detroit, MI 48207-3185; (313) 446-0474; $150 per year.

---

investment decisions. A large financial institution found that its relatively sophisticated work force was not putting money into its 401(k) plan because they could not understand the concepts used in the plan literature. And the literature had been dumbed down! *Pensions & Investments* has editorialized, "Employees need help in investing their 401(k) plan assets, and companies ought to provide it."[37] Amen!

Economically Targeted Investments. The large sums committed to pension funds have also proven attractive to advocates of community-based economic development or, as it is sometimes called, "economically targeted investment" (ETI).[38] Pension funds that are not subject to the Employee Retirement Income Security Act (ERISA)—that is, all pension funds except those sponsored by private-sector corporations—have some latitude to invest in vehicles that will both provide a financial return and serve a public purpose.*

In 1991, the Pennsylvania state treasurer, Catherine Baker Knoll, set up low-income mortgage programs using a tiny portion of assets from the pension funds under her control.[39] In June 1992, the Board of Pensions of the Evangelical Lutheran Church in America put $300,000 in the

---

*To what extent, if at all, ERISA funds can invest in ETIs is a matter of debate. In a letter issued on April 7, 1992, the Internal Revenue Service's general counsel indicated that permitting a trustee to consider nonfinancial criteria in investment decisions or to invest in projects providing community and social benefits but at a lower-than-market rate of return jeopardized a fund's tax status.

Community Reinvestment Fund, a secondary market for loans made by community-based organizations.[40] These are just two of many examples. However, there are some failures, too. The Connecticut state treasurer, Frank Borges, has allocated up to 3 percent of the state's pension fund's assets for ETIs. In 1990, the state put up $25 million in exchange for a 47 percent interest in CF Holdings, a company organized to take over the bankrupt Colt Firearms, an important employer in Connecticut. In 1992, Colt reentered bankruptcy, and it was unclear how much, in terms of money or jobs, the state would salvage.[41]

Obviously, where retirees' futures are concerned, caution must be the watchword in investing. However, there is room for innovation in pension-fund investment. We may never see the level of ETIs that Jeremy Rifkin and Randy Barber argued for in their brilliant and prophetic book, *The North Shall Rise Again* (1978). But pension funds should be putting a prudent amount into ETIs that benefit the communities they serve. Social investors can put pressure on their pension funds and their state treasurers to do just that.

WHAT ABOUT TOMORROW?

You don't have to be Jeanne Dixon to predict that benefits—broadly defined—will dominate the issues concerning social investors for the foreseeable future. The environment will continue to be a critically important item on their agenda. But the impact of health care and pension issues on them personally will put benefits at the top of their list.

It would be easy to paint benefits as a baby boom issue. But it isn't. Baby boomers will begin retiring in fifteen years or so. Much sooner they will reach the stage in life when the demand for health care increases. The inadequacy of these benefits is already apparent to anyone who has seen retirees in their seventies working alongside disabled adults and minority teenagers in fast food restaurants.

Business will play a critical role in determining how the costs of pensions and health care are allocated across society. For that is what is coming. The structure cobbled together in the great New Deal compromise that saved capitalism has collapsed. That it lasted sixty years was miraculous, but now the assumptions underlying it are invalid. Factory workers and unionized workers in general were to be taken care of by industry health and pension plans such as that of the United Mine Workers. Management was to receive company-sponsored health and pension benefits. All these were to be supplemented by Social Security. Today, the unions are largely broken. The great industries are downsized or gone. The prosperity of 1945 to 1965 led to a baby boom. The economic crisis of 1971 to 1982 produced a baby bust. Improvements in health care have greatly increased costs while at the same time lengthening life.

Beginning in the second decade of the twenty-first century, the burden of supporting a large and increasingly unproductive generation will fall on much narrower generations. Those generations, unless matters change dramatically, will have beneath them a safety net with a very broad mesh. Their working conditions and benefits will look poor compared to their grandparents'.

The debate over how we will take care of our citizens is one in which social investors can play a major role. It is an issue ideally suited to shareholder resolutions and other forms of lobbying corporations. How we resolve these issues will say much about us as a people.

9

Product Quality and Attitude Toward Consumers

THE CONSUMER MOVEMENT OF THE 1960s was one of modern social investing's parents, as we have seen. And it was the quality of a particular Chevrolet model—the Corvair—that put the movement in the spotlight. The notion that whatever Americans manufactured was the best was so ingrained that a large segment of the public regarded Ralph Nader's *Unsafe at Any Speed* as an attack not simply on GM, but on the national character. They were right, but so was Nader.

Today among individual social investors, questions of product quality and suitability rank near or at the top of their concerns. In this, they and corporate America agree. We know companies by their products* and by the mix of service, customer responsiveness, promotional imagery, and marketing tactics that surround them. Our consideration of companies is not much different from our response to the people we meet: What do they say and do; what is their demeanor toward us and others; and what is their general reputation for integrity?

Social investors think about "product" in terms of its inherent quality and of how it either enhances or diminishes the well-being of its purchasers and society. The oldest product screens excluded companies whose businesses are based upon products or services deemed damaging to individuals and society. Alcohol, tobacco, and gambling—the odious

---

*We use the term *product* broadly. It includes not only tangible goods but services as well. For example, Federal Express's on-time, hassle-free deliveries are its "product."

"sin stocks"—as well as firearms and war-materials companies have been targets of these screens. Despite mottos like "responsible drinking," "low tar," and "Guns don't kill, people do," social investors avoid companies that trade in these products. (We discussed these product screens in chapter 4.) Since the 1970s, the negative product screen has expanded with highly publicized controversies over the Dalkon Shield intrauterine device, the marketing of infant formula in the Third World, and the like.

In recent years, social investors have expanded their product screens to include positive aspects as well. They consider a product's physical qualities and their value to the consumer. The physical quality of a product is the sum of the processes that go into its design, engineering, materials, and manufacture. Thus when socially responsible investors consider investment opportunities, they tend to give high marks to companies whose products are well-designed and hold up under heavy use.

Since the late 1970s, both the public and many American corporations have begun to think more deeply about these issues. That thinking is paying off today in products with better design integrity, measurably improved fitness for use, greater durability, and often—paradoxically— no greater cost.

QUALITY PRODUCTS, QUALITY COMPANIES

"Quality" is a much used, but largely undefined, term. The "quality movement" in American businesses, David Levine has noted, has been variously defined as:

- a set of techniques to reduce the defect rates in manufactured products;
- a way of simultaneously increasing customer and worker satisfaction while increasing profits; and
- a management speed-up technique that makes workers work harder, but is unlikely to improve the quality of American products.[1]

Thus, "quality" is much like pornography: You know it when you see it—to borrow Justice Potter Stewart's immortal observation. Nonetheless, various writers and the federal government spent much of the 1980s trying to define the undefinable. Fortunately, a number of businesses ignored the talk and kept their attention on their products. Some of these are listed in Table 9-1.

Box 9-1. Indispensable Resource: *The Ethical Consumer*

A British consumer magazine would seem an unlikely resource—much less an indispensable one—for U.S. social investors. But *The Ethical Consumer* puts much more emphasis on the second word of its title than the third. According to its masthead, the magazine is published by "the Ethical Consumer Research Association (ECRA) which exists to research and publish information behind brand names, and to promote the ethical use of consumer power."

The bimonthly is filled with information on both U.S. companies and companies whose stock is traded here. Unlike *Consumer Reports, The Ethical Consumer* does not compare individual products. Instead, it offers an overview of a product area, say, kitchen appliances, and then briefly describes the social performance of the principal companies that sell them in the United Kingdom. ECRA uses fifteen screens: South Africa; oppressive regimes; employee relations (three screens); environment (two screens); irresponsible marketing; nuclear power; armaments; animals (three screens); political contributions; and boycotts. Each comment is sourced.

In addition to product surveys, *The Ethical Consumer* contains news on U.K. social investment and extensive coverage of boycotts. It also gives extended treatment to the development and application of its screens. Its description of oppressive regimes (Issue 18) as a screen is superb, though some of ECRA's ratings will come as a shock to Americans.

The Ethical Consumer, ECRA Publishing Ltd., 100 Gretney Walk, Manchester M15 5DA, United Kingdom. Bimonthly. £23 per year.

One outstanding example of a company more concerned with products than theory is Rubbermaid.

Rubbermaid makes plastic and rubber products for home, office, and industrial use. In 1992 it was among *Fortune*'s "most admired" corporations—for the seventh consecutive year. It also placed first in product quality. Why? Here's just one example. In 1991 Rubbermaid introduced the first "litter-free" lunch box for kids. Called the "Sidekick," it is an insulated cooler with integrated containers for a sandwich, a drink, and other items. Stylish and durable, the new product eliminated the daily stream of plastic wrap, lunch bags, and small drink cartons its owner would otherwise send to the trash bin every school day.[2]

**TABLE 9-1. SOME PUBLICLY TRADED COMPANIES KNOWN
FOR QUALITY PRODUCTS**

Alaska Air Group, Inc.	Federal Express Corp.
American Express Co.	FPL Group, Inc.
AMP, Inc.	Home Depot, Inc.
A.T. Cross Co.	Marriott Corp.
Carolina Freight Corp.	Maytag Corp.
Caterpillar Inc.	Motorola, Inc.
Deere & Co.	Rouse Co.
Delta Air Lines, Inc.	Super Valu Stores, Inc.
Deluxe Corp.	Tennant Co.
Fastenal Co.	Wachovia Co.

These companies show a reputation for quality goods and services.
About a third would fail other commonly applied screens.
Source: Kinder, Lydenberg, Domini & Co., Inc., the KLD Social
Investment Database.

REWARDING QUALITY

In the late 1970s, Japanese consumer goods—as well as office products—of exceptional quality at reasonable prices hit American markets.
U.S. consumer-electronics manufacturers were the first to feel the heat.
Producers of autos, machine tools, semiconductors, and other industrial
goods came next.

The American manufacturers found themselves on the wrong end of
the quality movement—an approach to production and, more broadly,
to business management that had developed in postwar Japan. The chief
missionary of this movement was a statistician, W. Edwards Deming.
Rebuffed by his American compatriots, Deming took his methods of
statistical quality control to Japan in 1950, where his ideas took hold.[3]
His contribution to the postwar economy of Japan was such that the
Japanese Union of Scientists and Engineers now gives out the "Deming
Prize" to companies that most thoroughly integrate quality-control principles in the workplace and that produce the best-quality products.
(Only one American company, Florida Power & Light (FPL) has won this
award. In a curious turn, however, a new management team, installed
shortly after FPL won the Deming Award, scrapped many of the initiatives that won it.)

By 1980 American industry was getting so beaten up by its Asian
rivals that many companies hired Deming, and a host of other quality
gurus, to give them a dose of the new smelling salts. The principles of
quality control, which had originated in the United States, had finally
begun to attract a following.

During the early 1980s Xerox experienced a sharp drop in market share and profits. Japanese companies offering more reliable copiers at lower prices began to displace the firm that had developed and commercialized the plain-paper copier. Xerox's share of the U.S. market went from 18.5 percent in 1979 to just 10 percent in 1984.[4] Stunned by these developments, then-CEO David Kearns and his management team mapped out a renaissance of Xerox's products and customer services. Their program reached into design, manufacturing, and distribution. It required training the firm's 100,000-person work force in quality management principles. Estimates of the training costs alone run to $125 million.[5] These investments paid off. Xerox has returned to prominence in its industry. In 1989, its Business Products and Systems unit, its flagship operation, received a Malcolm Baldrige National Quality Award.

The Baldrige Awards are America's own quality prizes. They are made on the basis of a "process incorporating rigorous and objective evaluation of the applicant's total quality system underlying its products and services."[6] The Baldrige criteria that matter most to social investors are:

Customer-driven Quality.   Quality is judged by the customer. "This includes the relationship between the company and customers—the trust and confidence in products and services—that leads to loyalty and preference."

The success of Ford's Taurus and Sable models, introduced in 1985, stands upon four years of consumer research that led to creation of a customer "want list" of 1,401 features. Ford was able to incorporate half of them on the Taurus/Sable.[7] Ford also listened to drivers and engineers in determining which of its competitors was considered "best in class" across a range of auto characteristics—seats, dashboard configurations, transmissions, door latches, et cetera—and set out to match or exceed them. Ford's efforts in this area bore fruit in terms of high sales and lower production costs. Ford reduced by 50 percent the number of labor hours required for auto assembly relative to its domestic competitors. Before the end of the 1980s, its profits exceeded those of its much larger archrival, General Motors.

Continuous Improvement.   Quality-conscious companies can never be satisfied with their products, processes, or services. Some firms, such as Motorola, have an obsession with quality. From six thousand defects per million components in 1987, Motorola drove its defect rate down to forty per million in 1992 and plans to cut the current defect rate in half by 1995.[8] The goal of continuous improvement extends beyond the narrow issue of product defects to the broader problems of product design and the time it takes to bring a new product from R&D into full production. For example, Japan's auto manufacturers can design, engineer, and bring a new model to market in three years, versus almost five years for a U.S. manufacturer.[9]

Full Participation.   Meeting quality and performance objectives requires a fully committed, well-trained, and involved work force. "Factors bearing upon the safety, health, well-being, and morale of employees need to be part of the continuous improvement objectives." We looked at those issues in chapter 8.

Partnership Development.   "Companies should . . . build internal and external partnerships serving mutual and larger community interest." That partnership spirit must prevail with unions, suppliers, and customers. Adoption of quality principles by a corporation eventually results in suppliers having to adopt them as well. This is how the quality movement is being diffused throughout industry. Large manufacturers like Ford, IBM, and Motorola usually require that their suppliers have quality programs and in most cases work with them in setting them up.

Public Responsibility.   "A company's requirements and quality system objectives should address areas of corporate citizenship and responsibility. These include business ethics, public health and safety, [and] environment." And that is what this book is about.

THE BALDERDASH FACTOR

A lot of flackery surrounds the quality movement in America. Thomas Hout of Boston Consulting Group told *Business Week,* "The majority of quality efforts fizzle out early, or give some improvements but never fulfill their initial promise."[10]

According to a Gallup survey of 1,237 corporate employees conducted for the American Society of Quality, company representations on this issue are often superficial. Over one-half of the respondents said that their companies assign quality as a top priority, but only one-third said that their companies had followed through with effective programs. A mere 14 percent said that the companies involved employees in decisions affecting quality.[11] *Fortune* has reported a significant "gap" between top management's pontifications on making quality a priority, employee participation, and the like, and what is observed within the company.[12]

Thus, the social investor must be wary of official pronouncements and look for hard evidence that quality is taken seriously. You should look for:

- a company-wide quality program
- a track record of at least three years
- the commitment of top management
- established programs for training of employees in quality management principles
- a rewards structure that recognizes quality improvements
- awards for the program by independent, accredited third parties.

And you should satisfy yourself that even if all these factors are present, the program is not simply a device to extract more work from employees.[13]

Is Quality Its Own Reward?

Forty years ago Deming said quality was its own reward. He was wrong. As we have seen, there is plenty of evidence that time and money spent on implementing quality control programs pay off.

Armand V. Feigenbaum, one of the pioneers in the field, contends that companies with successful quality programs have a 10 percent cost advantage over their competitors "because fewer defects mean less rework and wasted management time, lower costs, and higher customer-retention rates."[14] Motorola estimates that progress on product quality saved it $700 million in manufacturing costs alone between 1987 and 1992. Carbon-black producer Cabot Corporation cites $1 million savings over just two years at its Franklin, Louisiana, plant because it was able to cut defects by 90 percent.[15]

Measuring quality in manufacturing is significantly easier than measuring it in service industries. Carolina Freight, a much-praised regional trucking firm, has made great progress in measurement. In 1989, the company developed a computer model for customer satisfaction. It quantifies on-time delivery, invoice accuracy, and problem resolution. Each of those areas is in turn divided into subareas, and points are assigned in each. Carolina Freight tracks every account and every shipment using this index.

If you are looking for a precise correlation between success in quality programs and corporate profits, stop. It does not exist. Baldrige winners like Motorola, Xerox, GM, IBM, and Federal Express have experienced declines in earnings and share prices.[16] Many forces, including business cycles, are at work here. Competitors may be improving quality at nearly the same rate. And other factors may intervene. For instance, Motorola's ills were related to delays in the delivery of a new semiconductor.

QUALITY MARKETING AND ATTITUDE TOWARD CONSUMERS

Quality products go hand in hand with quality marketing and an attitude of respect toward—if not partnership with—customers. When companies have durable, well-designed products that address the real needs of their customers, there is little reason to resort to false or deceptive advertising. Informational advertising that addresses specifications and performance becomes the dominant mode of communication with the customer. Companies that have not earned bragging rights on the quality of their products appeal to some other interest of the customer. Auto manufacturers wrapped their machines in American flags and hometown scenes, while remaining silent on repair records, miles per gallon, and other performance values. GM's "Heartbeat of America" and "Apple Pie and Chevrolet" campaigns were merely the worst of these.

Quality products imply quality relationships with customers. Quality-oriented companies are not interested in pushing the product and moving on; they rely on feedback—good and bad—from the customer. They want to hear from customers who have a problem with their products; this is how they learn and improve. Several years ago, Dryden Press published a finance textbook that offered a cash reward for any error the reader could find. Given the number of formulae and problems in finance books, this offer expressed both confidence in the current edition and a commitment to make future editions better.

Recent research by Louis Harris & Associates on behalf of John Hancock Financial Services indicates that American consumers believe service quality in industries like banking, health care, entertainment, insurance, and telecommunications leaves much to be desired. While 50 to 58 percent thought that many areas (commitment to quality, handling complaints, and the competence of service employees) had improved over the past ten years, almost 40 percent disagreed. Fully 60 percent felt that customers were getting less value for their money than a decade ago.[17]

Companies that listen to unhappy customers and resolve their complaints have a higher rate of repeat sales to these customers—54 percent versus 19 percent of those whose complaints went unresolved.[18]

PRODUCT LIABILITY ACTIONS

Major product-liability problems at least raise questions about the quality of a company's products and its commitment to customers. The Pfizer heart valve and the Dow Corning breast implant are recent examples of products that had to be recalled due not only to lack of quality, but the potentially lethal side effect of that lack.[19]

Legal liabilities and regulatory problems can plague a product despite the best intentions of its manufacturer. Consider the Gillette Company's Liquid Paper, a popular correction fluid used by typists. In 1982 evidence mounted that it was being used in ways Gillette had not anticipated, and people were getting hurt. Disreputable dentists used the fluid to paint discolored teeth, causing inflamed gums and lips. Worse, teenagers were sniffing Liquid Paper and other correction fluids to get high. Gillette had to take action to avoid injuries—and possibly deaths—due to its misuse. Gillette reformulated Liquid Paper to include an essence that eliminated the sniffing problem.[20] Another widely respected company, H.B. Fuller, ran into a similar problem with one of its glues marketed in Honduras. Fuller could not reformulate the product, but it could repackage the glue in larger, industrial sizes to keep it out of children's hands. The repackaging failed to halt the abuse, so Fuller stopped manufacturing this profitable product.

LEADERSHIP IN RESEARCH AND DEVELOPMENT

Many social investors—and investors generally—pay close attention to a company's investment in research and development (R&D)—the process of creating and bringing out new products or of improving existing products. Other things being equal, companies that consistently lead their industries in R&D as a percentage of sales are able to develop innovative products. Table 9-2 lists some R&D leaders.

Perhaps no better example exists than Merck & Company, a major pharmaceutical firm. For several years, *Fortune* named Merck the "most admired" U.S. corporation. In 1990 the magazine ranked it first in four categories, including "quality of product."[21] Merck put 10 percent of sales—$1 billion—into R&D in 1991. That has been the pattern since now-chairman Roy Vagelos became research chief in 1976. Vagelos has sought the best minds in bioscience and given them laboratories, budgets, and a creative atmosphere rarely matched in academia or industry. Merck has rolled out ten major drugs since 1981.[22] Furthermore, in the risky pharmaceuticals business, Merck's products have enjoyed an enviable safety record.

Tandem Computers, a leading designer and manufacturer of fault-tolerant computer systems and networking products, spent $267 million on R&D in 1991 (14 percent of revenues). In its fast-paced field, average increases in R&D expenditures run at a rate of about 5 percent per year.

TABLE 9-2. SELECTED LEADERS IN R&D SPENDING

Advanced Micro Devices, Inc.	Merck & Co., Inc.
Amdahl Corp.	Microsoft Corp.
American Cyanamid Co.	Minnesota Mining and Manufacturing Co.
Apple Computer, Inc.	Nucor Corp.
Bergen Brunswig Corp.	Polaroid Corp.
Borland International, Inc.	Raychem Corp.
Cognex Corp.	Safety-Kleen Corp.
Cray Research, Inc.	Tandem Computers Inc.
Groundwater Technology, Inc.	Tellabs, Inc.
Hewlett-Packard Co.	Thermo Electron Corp.
Lotus Development Corp.	

These companies invest significantly more of their income in research and development (R&D) than other U.S. companies do. Many of these companies would fail other commonly applied screens. Data are current as of August 1, 1992.
Source: Kinder, Lydenberg, Domini & Co., Inc., the KLD Social Investment Database.

One of the most debatable arguments for trade restrictions is that they keep prices up so companies can invest in R&D. Not open to debate is how the auto industry used the money it made as a result of the "voluntary" quotas on Japanese cars in the 1980s. Led by GM, they passed on the $10 billion they gained to their shareholders through stock buybacks[23]—a corporation's repurchase of its outstanding stock, often for the purpose of maintaining the stock's market price. No doubt, this pleased Wall Street in the short run. But one has to wonder what the U.S. auto industry would be like today had the Big Three put that money to work. The answer seems self-evident. In 1992 GM was saddling itself with expensive debt and trying to sell stock to bolster its restructuring. If you saw the film *Roger and Me* or reviewed GM's board's actions in 1991–1992, one could argue GM would not have spent its windfall well.

SERVING THE ECONOMICALLY DISADVANTAGED

As we observed in chapter 7, the economically disadvantaged are sent to the back of the line when it comes to obtaining the financing necessary for buying or improving their homes. They are also isolated from most of the retail services that the rest of us take for granted within our neighborhoods.

Many companies have moved their offices and retail outlets out of the nation's inner city neighborhoods over the past twenty years or so, with disastrous affects on the life of those communities. Not only have residents been cut off from employment opportunities, but the absence of large and efficient merchandisers means that low-income people have nowhere to purchase food and clothing except at the few higher-priced, low-quality outlets that remain. Fortunately, there are exceptions to this dreary picture. Dollar General Corporation sites its discount stores in low-income neighborhoods and hires its clerks and store managers from these neighborhoods. This type of business strategy is considered a strong positive by socially responsible investors.

Two other examples of companies serving the needs of low-income people are the Federal National Mortgage Association (FANNIE MAE) and the Student Loan Marketing Association (SALLIE MAE). Both are government-chartered corporations, though their stock is in private hands. Table 9-3 lists companies that specially serve the economically disadvantaged.

ADVERTISING, MARKETING, OR CONSUMER VIOLATIONS

Consumer fraud and deceptive marketing practices are now important bases on which social investors screen companies. The first of these, consumer fraud, is a statutory violation and is publicly reported. The area of deceptive marketing is not as clearly defined or as rigorously policed by regulatory agencies.

A number of companies have been involved in recent controversies over exploitation of the economically disadvantaged. Perhaps the most egregious examples involve companies that social investors would screen out on other grounds:

- liquor companies that target minority youth with "high-test" malt liquors;
- cigarette manufacturers that develop brands strictly for blacks, who already have the highest incidence of lung disease in the nation; and
- makers of handguns.

TABLE 9-3. COMPANIES SERVING THE ECONOMICALLY DISADVANTAGED

Baxter International, Inc.	Federal Home Loan Mortgage
DeVry Inc.	Federal National Mortgage Association
Dollar General Corp.	Medeo Containment Services, Inc.
Family Dollar Stores, Inc.	

As a matter of corporate policy, these companies have committed themselves to aid the economically disadvantaged. Data are current as of August 1, 1992.
Source: Kinder, Lydenberg, Domini & Co., Inc., the KLD Social Investment Database.

Cigarette makers who comply with advertising restrictions here continue to recruit new customers abroad. And companies like RJR Nabisco with its "Old Joe Camel" campaign have found ways around the advertising restrictions to reach the market they need—the young.

Sometimes shareholder activists step in. Food irradiation was heralded as a means of controlling parasites, bacteria, and insects that cause food to spoil. Under this treatment, food is exposed to ionizing radiation, sometimes from gamma rays from radioactive isotopes. This process has been approved by the Food and Drug Administration (FDA) for many types of food.

In 1992 the Sisters of St. Francis of Philadelphia asked Kroger, a large supermarket chain, to report on the sale of any irradiated foods. In their supporting statement, the sisters point out that A&P, Marks & Spencer, and Albertson's have stated that they do not sell irradiated food. And the states of Maine, New York, and New Jersey have banned its sale. It is ironic that a corporation's owners must remind it of the virtues of selling only safe products.

Firms in "clean" industries can practice exploitation, too. When selecting the stocks of financial institutions, for example, look closely at how they service the economically disadvantaged. With higher mortgage rates? "Redlining"? Some U.S. pharmaceutical firms such as Upjohn continue to market drugs in the Third World that are deemed unsafe at home, such as Depo-provera. Cigarette makers who comply with advertising restrictions here continue to recruit new customers abroad.

In the United Kingdom, the Advertising Standards Authority—an industry-funded group—enforces the British Code of Advertising Practices to which the advertising industry subscribes. Some U.K. social investors screen on violations of the Code.

A GLANCE AT THE FUTURE

Never again will attention to product quality be treated as un-American, as it was when Ralph Nader began criticizing GM. GM has also established the link between the character of the employer and quality of the product. As this is written in the fall of 1992, GM has just fired its CEO after earlier removing its president. Blood in the executive suite has flowed as swiftly as the red ink in GM's financials.

If anything good can be said for the economic transformation of the last two decades, it is that the businesses that survived are much more attuned to customer needs. Many public companies in the United States are providing products and services that meet the high standards of social investors. There is no shortage of companies here. And the most satisfying part of this abundance is the growing evidence that these companies not only serve their customers well, but they also reward their shareholders.

So long as we pay no heed to calls for protectionism and insulation of product manufacturers from liability for shoddy products, we can look forward to an era when "American" will once again be a synonym for high quality.

10

Diversity:
Employing Women and Minorities

> I have done a great deal of work; as much as a man, but did not
> get so much pay. I used to work in the field and bind grain,
> keeping up with the cradler; but men doing no more, got twice as
> much pay. . . . We do as much, we eat as much, we want as much.
>
> —Sojourner Truth (1867)[1]

> Please just don't look at part of the glass, the part that is only less
> than half full.
>
> —George Bush[2]

DIVERSITY IN THE WORKPLACE has been an issue on the social investment agenda since Project GM in the early 1970s.[3] Nonetheless, it is still
a frontier in terms of implementation and sophistication. More anger
lurks just below the surface in this area than in any other of social
investing. Occasionally an event such as the Clarence Thomas–Anita Hill
hearings or Rodney King's videotaped beating by the Los Angeles police
force will reveal the canyon of perceptions that exists between the sexes
and between the races.

Women account for at least 60 percent of all socially responsible
investors. And as Box 10-1 indicates, women also lead the social investment movement. Probably for these reasons, social investors regard
issues around women, minorities, sexual orientation, and physical challenges as important lenses to apply to corporations. Most look for companies with good records. Even those who do not explicitly screen in these

areas tend to avoid companies with poor reputations. Because of the nation's changing demographics, these issues—as both positive and negative screens—will become increasingly important.

THE CHANGING AMERICAN WORKPLACE

Americans love success stories. An Wang, a Chinese immigrant, started a computer firm that grew to employ thousands. Barbara Jordan became the first black female U.S. representative from the South and after retiring began a distinguished teaching career. Roberto Goizueta, a Cuban émigré, rose to the top of Coca-Cola Corporation, a company that symbolizes America throughout the world. George Soros, one of many Hungarians to flee his country in the 1950s, became a successful money manager. The United States has benefited from its relative lack of barriers to advancement and its tradition of attracting talented individuals from around the world.

Perhaps nowhere in the world are success stories—pluck and luck—so much a part of the cultural heritage. But reviewing the success of the few in rising to the top or in building large corporations gives us a false sense that such paths are accessible to all.

FACTS OF THE GAME

The American workplace has unwritten rules based on race, gender, and class that play a big part in who gets hired, fired, trained, promoted, or well paid. Some facts speak for themselves:

- In 1990, *Fortune* surveyed 799 large public corporations to determine the number of women among their highest-paid directors and officers. Of 4,012 key individuals, 19 were women.[4] See Table 10-1.
- Across all occupations, women receive on average 71 percent of what men earn and just 57 percent in sales jobs.[5]
- While blacks make up about 14 percent of the U.S. population, about 3 percent of corporate managers are black and only one company among the *Fortune* 1,000 was run by an African-American.[6]
- Blacks earn from 10 to 26 percent less than whites with similar educational backgrounds.[7]

Historical and social phenomenon explain, in part, these disparities in status and earnings. For instance, as a career path business management has opened to women only in the past twenty years. However,

BOX 10-1. WOMEN IN SOCIAL INVESTING

Women have been leaders in socially responsible investing almost since the beginning. They include:

- Joan Shapiro, senior vice president of Chicago's South Shore Bank, the nation's leading community-development bank. A founding board member of the Social Investment Forum (SIF), our trade group, she also served as its second president.
- Joan Bavaria, a founder—and first president—of the SIF. She is cochair of the Coalition for Environmentally Responsible Economies which produced the CERES Principles. She is also a founder and President of Franklin Research & Development Corporation where she manages social portfolios.
- Amy Domini, coauthor of this book also coauthored *Ethical Investing* (1984), *The Challenges of Wealth* (1987), and *The Social Investment Almanac* (1992). She is the founder of the Domini Social Index (see chapter 2), a member of ICCR's governing board and an advocate of social investing for the past decade. Today, she is a trustee with Loring, Wolcott & Coolidge in Boston.
- Elizabeth Glenshaw, first head of the Vermont National Bank Socially Responsible Banking Fund, is now an associate trustee with Loring, Wolcott & Coolidge managing social portfolios in Boston.

Among the other women in social investing are: Diane Coffey, president of Dreyfus Third Century Fund; Alisa Gravitz, executive director of Co-op America; and Sophia Collier, president of Working Assets.

Chuck Matthei, a founder of the Institute for Community Economics, is the Johnny Appleseed of community-development lending. To whom would he turn first for funding new types of projects? "The nuns, go to the nuns. They put their values on the line." Shareholder activists include Sister Susan Mika, who helped develop the Maquiladora Principals, is a longtime fighter for better working conditions in American-owned plants in Mexico.

TABLE 10-1. BOARD REPRESENTATION

American Water Works, Inc.	Nordstrom, Inc.
Beneficial Corp.	Ogden Corp.
BET Holdings, Inc.	Pacific Telesis Group
Federal National Mortgage Association	People's Energy Corp.
Gannett Co., Inc.	Petrie Stores Corp.
New York Times Company	Spec's Music Inc.

In these companies, women and minorities hold either four board seats in aggregate or one-third of the board seats if the board numbers less than twelve (with no allowance for double counting). Data are current as of August 1, 1992.
Source: Kinder, Lydenberg, Domini & Co., Inc., the KLD Social Investment Database.

women continue to assume the greater burden of child-rearing responsibilities—often during their thirties, critical years in any manager's career development. This combination of newness and child-care responsibilities has limited the pool of experienced female candidates for moves into the higher ranks in corporations.

Blacks and Hispanics have matriculated from undergraduate and graduate programs at much lower rates than other groups, slowing their progress in the workplace. Their near-absence from the ranks of graduating scientists and engineers, in particular, has limited their representation within the professional and managerial ranks of manufacturing, chemical, and high-technology firms.

Even these factors do not entirely explain the discrepancies in employment for women and minorities. Nor do they relieve corporations of their obligation to create a workplace that is fair and equitable, and that reflects the diversity of the broader society. Shareholder activists such as the Capuchin-Franciscan Friars and the Redemptorist Fathers have filed resolutions with Dayton-Hudson, K Mart, May Department Stores, and Wal-Mart asking for reports on their equal employment opportunity (EEO) records.

In *Workforce 2000: Work and Workers for the 21st Century* (1987) the Hudson Institute suggested that immigration and birth rates would increase the percentages of nonwhites joining the labor force. Nonwhites and white women would represent the most significant number of new workers available to U.S. corporations—indeed, 85 percent of them.[8]

In a better world, the subject of women and minorities in the workplace would not be a separate book chapter. In a still more perfect world, the subject would not merit any special mention. The world is far from perfect, but it is changing.

WOMEN IN THE WORKPLACE

"Why can't a woman be more like a man?" Henry Higgins complained in *My Fair Lady*. Historically, American employers have done more than bemoan the differences between women and men: They have penalized women for them. Today, because of legislation and changes in the work force, employers are having to adapt their workplaces to accommodate those differences. While there are many success stories here—which we will highlight—the country still has a long way to go before the workplace becomes equally hospitable to men and women.

The Mommy Track

For twenty-five years most articles on women in the workplace have concentrated on fast-track professionals. However, the vast majority of women getting a paycheck have important interests outside the workplace and are less than single-minded about careers. Many of them covet jobs at corporations with programs that allow them to contribute and advance while fulfilling other roles as mothers and care-givers.

In a 1989 article in the *Harvard Business Review,* Felice N. Schwartz articulated a concept that later came to be called (by others) the "mommy track." She has continued to spell out its benefits to companies and women ever since. "Denying that women have babies leads to a self-fulfilling prophecy of failure for women and their employers," she has written.[9] Employers must take account of the facts about women and families and babies. Failure to do so, she warns, causes women to either drop out or reduce their productivity. Schwartz suggests that women be allowed to follow a career path that includes some laps on a slower track.

Not everyone agrees with Schwartz. Many fear that the "mommy track" is a path to second-class corporate citizenship. But several forward-thinking companies had recognized what Schwartz described and were already acting on it. Polaroid and Procter & Gamble were early standouts. Programs lumped into the "mommy track" category include flexible scheduling of work hours, job sharing, and pregnancy leaves. Some companies actually offer alternative career paths that allow fast-track women to slow the pace while they are raising young children.

In its *Corporate Reference Guide to Work-Family Programs*[10] the Families and Work Institute has catalogued the programs in corporate America that make the balancing of work and family more achievable. It identifies four companies—Johnson & Johnson, IBM, Ætna Life & Casualty, and Corning—as exemplary. At Ætna 70 percent of the work force is female. The programs the insurer offers include: flextime, flexplace, part-time work and job sharing, and a formal family-leave policy that accommodates childbirths and care of sick dependents (including elderly relatives).

Many companies now provide on-premises child-care facilities. In fact, more than half of the firms listed in *Working Mother's* 6th Annual Survey of "The 85 Best Companies for Working Mothers" have them.[11] Hewitt Associates has found that 56 percent of 259 major U.S. employers it surveyed offered some kind of child care to their employees, though not necessarily on premises.[12]

Russell Corporation, the maker of leisure clothing and athletic uniforms, is in an industry not noted for high-quality employee-management relations. That makes the presence of child-care facilities at three of its plants and a kindergarten at its headquarters all the more impressive. Russell even provides time off for parent-teacher conferences.

The recent recession was not kind to some companies that had offered innovative programs to their female employees. Over the years, Digital Equipment Company received considerable praise for its flexible hours, job sharing, and part-time programs.[13] *Savvy* and *New Woman* cited DEC as among the best places for women to work. But as we noted in chapters 8 and 9, in 1991 the company had to abandon its no-layoff policy. Will DEC's much-praised accommodations to the needs of working women go, too? It is too early to tell.

TABLE 10-2. SOME PUBLICLY TRADED COMPANIES WITH EXCEPTIONAL BENEFITS PROGRAMS SUPPORTING FAMILY ISSUES

Aetna Life & Casualty Co.	NationsBank Corp.
Apple Computer, Inc.	Polaroid Corp.
Corning Inc.	Procter & Gamble Co.
Digital Equipment Corp.	Southern New England Telecom
General Mills Inc.	Stride Rite Corp.
Hechinger Co.	Travelers Corp.
International Business Machines Corp.	UNUM Corp.
Johnson & Johnson	US West Inc.
Lotus Development Corp.	Warner-Lambert Co.
Merck & Company, Inc.	

These companies have outstanding employee benefits programs or programs addressing work/family concerns, *e.g.*, child care, elder care, and flextime. Groups advocating such programs have recognized these companies' efforts. Data are current as of August 1, 1992.
Source: Kinder, Lydenberg, Domini & Co., Inc., the KLD Social Investment Database.

On the Way Up

Few women are at the top in the business world (see Table 10-3). However, the influx of women into middle management over the past ten years will result in more of them breaking through the "glass ceiling," the invisible barrier of subtle discrimination that separates women and minorities from senior management positions and corporate directorships.[14] Shareholder activists, such as the Methodist Church's General Board of Pensions and the Disciples of Christ, have challenged "glass ceilings" in resolutions filed with Cablevision Systems, Capital Cities/ CBS, GE, and the Tribune Company.

With women taking upward of one-third of the MBAs at top-tier schools, we should expect progress in the years ahead. Among public companies, Gannett, the publishing giant, is a leader in giving authority to its female employees. It boasts 40 percent women employees. In top managerial and professional positions, women fill from 27 percent to 44 percent of slots, depending on the job. Twenty of its eighty-two daily newspapers have women as publishers. In 1992, the company's directors included three women, an extraordinarily high number. In 1991 the firm got the top marks from *Working Woman* in the category of "opportunities for women to advance." Naturally, this progress did not just happen. Support for the promotion of women (and minorities) has come from the top, and up to 10 percent of a manager's bonus can come from following through on this policy. US West, Avon, CBS, Dayton-Hudson, American Express, and Kelly Services are also frequently mentioned as pacesetting companies in the promoting of women to the top ranks.

Female directors are considerably more common than female senior executives (see Table 10-3), primarily because they serve as window dressing for management. Graef Crystal, an expert on executive and

TABLE 10-3. COMPANIES WHOSE CHIEF EXECUTIVES ARE WOMEN OR MINORITIES

ASK Computer Systems	Lillian Vernon Corp.
BET Holdings, Inc.	Quarterdeck Office Systems
Dime Savings Bank, NY	Spec's Music Inc.
Golden West Financial	Tootsie Roll Industries, Inc.
Johnson Products Co., Inc.	Value Line, Inc.

The chief executive officers or presidents of these companies are women or members of a minority group. Data are current as of August 1, 1992.
Source: Kinder, Lydenberg, Domini & Co., Inc., the KLD Social Investment Database.

directoral compensation, describes boards as consisting of "ten friends of management, a woman and a black."[15] His cynicism is well-founded.

A few companies, such as Ford, Sara Lee, and Sears have published in their annual reports the percentage of women and minorities in all job categories. Companies generally do this because of shareholder actions some years ago. Others, such as Bristol-Myers Squibb and General Motors, publish these figures separately. Although difficult to evaluate in themselves, these figures can be compared with industry averages (as published by the U.S. Equal Employment Opportunity Commission [EEOC]) to provide some perspective.

MINORITIES IN THE WORKPLACE

Shareholder activists have begun to focus again on equal employment issues. In 1992 several companies received resolutions asking for an equal employment report. Resolutions at Cablevision Systems, CBS, and General Electric (NBC) took a somewhat different tack. These addressed the images of females and minorities in television programming. The supporting documents read, "We agree that it is vitally important in the television industry to end all vestiges of discrimination and take initiatives to overcome barriers to full equality particularly since the media has such a strong impact on public attitudes."

African-Americans comprise 10.1 percent of the nation's 112.4 mil-

TABLE 10-4. SOME PUBLICLY TRADED COMPANIES WITH NOTABLE RECORDS ON PROMOTING WOMEN OR MINORITIES

ALZA Corp.	Federal Express Corp.
American Express Co.	Federal National Mortgage Association
Apple Computer, Inc.	Gannett Company, Inc.
Autodesk, Inc.	Kelley Services, Inc.
Avon Products, Inc.	Petrie Stores Corp.
Baxter International, Inc.	Spec's Music Inc.
Beneficial Corp.	Stride Rite Corp.
Claire's Stores, Inc.	The Limited, Inc.
CoreStates Financial Corporation	US West Inc.
Dime Savings Bank, NY	Xerox Corp.

These companies have made notable progress in promoting women and minorities, particularly to line and operating positions. Some of these companies have received recognition for their progress in hiring women and minorities from group advocating fair hiring policies. Data are current as of August 1, 1992.

Source: Kinder, Lydenberg, Domini & Co., Inc., the KLD Social Investment Database.

lion civilian workers; of these, only 6.2 percent are managers or professionals and 8.5 percent hold technical positions.[16] For Hispanics, the
percentages are even lower. In addition, many minorities who do climb
the corporate ladder are "ghettoized" into support functions, such as
personnel. The vice president for Affirmative Action may count on EEOC
filings as a black officer but is on a pay and influence rung far below, say,
the VP of Manufacturing.

Affirmative Action led to increases in hiring and promoting minorities throughout the 1980s. During the latter part of the decade, the
economy was expanding—at least in terms of the number of jobs. The
1990s present different challenges. The downsizing of America's corporations and the impact of the 1990–1992 recession have resulted in the
wholesale elimination of management and staff positions across American business. Well over half of currently seated federal judges are Reagan
or Bush appointees, including Clarence Thomas, and many are enemies
of affirmative action. Whether the gains made through affirmative action
will survive is anyone's guess. Arguing in the negative are decisions such
as the one holding that under collective bargaining agreements the
principles of "last hired, first fired" applies to minority workers, although
the impact on them is disproportionate. Even apart from the effects
of the recession, there are signs of a backlash against affirmative action programs. White managers have begun to complain loudly of re-
verse discrimination and the promotion of individuals perceived as less
qualified.

THE BEST COMPANIES

Many companies have made commitments to hire and promote minorities. Each year *Black Enterprise* picks the twenty-five large companies
that provide the best work atmosphere for African-Americans. The 1992
list appears in Table 10-5. While the specifics of each program and the
achievements of each firm on the list are different, they share a number
of characteristics: hiring goals, making managers responsible for the
success of minority management candidates, diversity training for non-
minority employees, a commitment to buy from minority-owned suppliers, and minorities in the ranks of top management.[17]

UAL, the parent of United Airlines, relies on multicultural training,
minority-employee focus groups, and groups like United's Black Professional Organization to build a diverse work force. Of the company's
72,491 employees, 9.5 percent are African-Americans. Among them are
144 pilots, the most among U.S. airlines. African-Americans also account
for 7.3 percent of all managers and 4.5 percent of senior executives.[18] Of

TABLE 10-5. 1992 *BLACK ENTERPRISE* 25 BEST PLACES FOR BLACKS TO WORK

Ameritech Corp.	International Business Machines Corp.
American Telephone & Telegraph Co.	Johnson & Johnson
Avon Products, Inc.	Kellogg Co.
Chrysler Corp.	Marriott Corp.
Coca-Cola Co.	McDonald's Corp.
Corning, Inc.	Merck & Co. Inc.
E. I. du Pont de Nemours & Co.	NYNEX Corp.
Equitable Financial Cos.	PepsiCo Inc.
Federal Express Corp.	Philip Morris Cos. Inc.
Ford Motor Co.	TIAA-CREF
Gannett Company, Inc.	United Airlines
General Mills Inc.	Xerox Corp.
General Motors Corp.	

Each year *Black Enterprise* picks the large companies that offer African-Americans the most opportunities. Of these, only TIAA-CREF—the nation's largest pension plan—is not a publicly traded company.
Source: "25 Best Places for Blacks to Work," *Black Enterprise,* February 1992, pp. 72–96.

the managers in its executive-development program, 25 percent are minorities.*

Phillip Morris's minority banking and minority purchasing programs are among the nation's largest. The firm buys over $180 million in goods and services from minority vendors. Ryder System, a diversified transportation company, appeared on *Black Enterprise*'s 1989 list. Ryder can boast that 6.5 percent of its managers are African-Americans. It subcontracts 5 percent of its purchases to companies that are woman- or minority-owned. The company has also appeared on *Hispanic*'s list of the one hundred best places for Hispanics to work.

THE FAIR SHARE CONCEPT

Starting in the 1970s, minority advocacy groups—the NAACP, Fair Share, Operation PUSH, and more recently, the HACR (Hispanic Association of Corporate Responsibility)—revived a tactic developed in the mid-1930s by Harlem's longtime congressman Adam Clayton Powell: "Don't buy where you can't work."

Using the power of the boycott, these organizations negotiated agreements to give minorities a fair share of the employment, franchises, and

*UAL's record is not entirely good. The company settled a 1976 EEOC suit by agreeing to hire minorities and women at a rate double its other hires. In 1988, the EEOC sought to have UAL held in contempt for violating that decree.

supplier contracts that their patronage of the companies' products would warrant. Thus, if minority customers provided 25 percent of the revenues for a particular company, logic would dictate that the company should provide an equivalent amount of jobs. Among those who signed fair-share agreements were: Adolph Coors, McDonald's, Chrysler, Pacific Bell, Ford, US West, and General Motors—all of whom are leaders in minority hiring today.[19] Each agreement is different. In Ford's, for example, the auto maker pledged to increase its Hispanic-owned dealerships, increase its use of Hispanic-owned banks, and establish scholarship and literacy programs.[20]

THE HIGH COST OF THE UNFRIENDLY WORKPLACE

Social investors—even those who do not have a formal women-and-minorities screen—tend to be extremely sensitive to employment issues. Companies sued more than very occasionally for employment discrimination fall off social investors' buy lists. Discrimination disputes are very costly to firms, not just in terms of fines or penalties or civil judgments, but also in terms of company morale, and therefore employee retention. It is good business to hire and fire justly.

THE COST TO A COMPANY

Hiring, keeping, and training employees represents a major expense for a business of any complexity. Anytime an employee leaves, the business loses an investment and incurs the costs of finding and training a replacement. Companies that have made a commitment to increase the hiring of women and minorities find that their job is not finished when new personnel report for duty. An unfriendly atmosphere—one of sexual or racial harassment, artificial impediments to advancement, and even the unintended isolation that a woman or a black feels in certain working situations—leads to many resignations.

In the late 1980s, Corning, Inc. spent about $4 million per year to recruit and train women and minorities. The attrition rate among women managers was 13.1 percent for women versus 7.8 percent for white males.[21] Black professionals were leaving the firm at slightly more than twice the rate that the firm's white professionals left. Part of the problem was the Upstate New York glassmaker's small-town location—undesirable to many blacks and single women. But exit interviews identified "lack of career opportunities" as the primary cause. Chairman James R. Houghton complained, "We do a good job at hiring but a lousy job at retention and promotion. And it's not good enough just to bring them through the front door."[22]

Corning committed itself to actively advance women and minorities. That commitment, expressed in required seminars on race and gender, has helped Corning increase its retention rate and cut its $4 million recruiting bill in half. Corning appeared on *Black Enterprise*'s 1992 list (see Table 10-5), *Working Mother*'s 1991 best companies for working mothers list, and on *Business Week*'s 1990 list of the best companies for women.

Some corporations have not shown the same solicitude as Corning. Some have done what they thought was right and went wrong. Many chemical and high-technology manufacturing companies have had "fetal protection" policies. These prohibited women from holding jobs at which they might expose their unborn to harmful chemicals. In March 1991, the U.S. Supreme Court ruled unconstitutional such a policy at Johnson Controls Inc. Other policies have lacked an element of altruism. For instance, women have fought dress, weight, and appearance requirements by airlines. In May 1991, after the highly publicized firing of a flight attendant for refusing to use make-up, Continental Airlines revoked its policy requiring women in customer-service positions to wear cosmetics.

THE COST TO THE NATION

As the United States moves toward the twenty-first century, it is essential that it does so with all of its human resources fully engaged. The world has become too competitive for any country to think that its future can be assured if only one segment of its population is earmarked for the best training, the best jobs, and the greatest responsibility.

The riots in Los Angeles in the spring of 1992 provided dramatic proof of how America has shortchanged some of its citizens. Politicians pontificated on the failings of the justice system, gangs, the increase in single-parent families, and hopeless inner-city schools. But it seemed clear to many that lack of employment—meaningful employment—was at the heart of the hopelessness and rage that provoked the riots.*

Minorities, especially blacks, have made tremendous strides since the

---

*Very few commentators linked the drug war to the riots. The $25 billion spent annually on drug control has done little but make the rewards of dealing almost irresistible—both financially and socially—to the poor, and put upwards of 56 percent (in cities like Baltimore) of black males between 18 and 35 into the direct control of the criminal justice system. This two-decade-long distortion of reward and risk by a highly visible hand dooms all efforts to address the problems of urban poverty.

riots of the mid-1960s. Blacks now have real power in city halls, planning boards, police departments, and schools in some of the large cities. And yet the plight of the average black citizen has worsened. The reason seems clear: Political empowerment counts for less than economic empowerment. Only when women and minorities have equal access to the economic resources of the country will these problems be solved. Corporations have the greater part in determining that outcome. Social investors can help them find the way.

THE SOCIAL INVESTOR'S CHALLENGE

Many of America's best companies have embraced the concept of workforce diversity and the promotion of talented women and minority workers. A growing number of social investors are taking women and minority employment issues seriously. No doubt this phenomenon stems from our society's rising general concern for fairness. It also reflects the increasing control women have over investable funds—a control they no longer hesitate to exercise.

The challenge to investors is to identify committed companies. As a conclusion, here are six bellwethers for evaluating a company's claims of support for workplace diversity.

CEO

Is the company's chief executive officer a woman or minority member?

The firm's public documents—its annual report, Form 10-K, and the proxy statement—will tell you. Among large companies you will find almost none. You will have better luck finding one as you move away from the *Fortune* 1000. Among those with minority or female CEOs are: Value Line, Johnson Products, BET Holdings, Golden West, and Lillian Vernon.

PROMOTION

Has the company made notable progress in the promotion of women or minorities, particularly to line and operating positions? Has the company received recognition for its efforts from organizations that represent these groups?

Usually companies want the world to know what they have achieved. So they will tell you quite willingly, if you ask. But you must beware of hype.

Perhaps the best large firm with respect to the hiring and promotion of African-Americans is Xerox. In 1992 the firm had twenty-six black vice presidents, more than any U.S. industrial company. Two occupy top-tier positions: A. Barry Rand is president of the U.S. Marketing Group; another African-American is president of Xerox Canada. Xerox attained its leadership role in this area by designing and implementing what it called its Balanced Work Force Strategy, which has numeric goals at all levels of the organization. Blacks currently represent approximately 13.5 percent of the firm's total work force and hold 10 percent of its management positions.[23]

BOARD REPRESENTATION

Does the company have a strong representation of women and minorities on its board of directors?

The proxy statement and the annual report—which often include pictures of the board—are your best bet here. But finding corporations that meet these criteria will be a challenge. Korn/Ferry International's 1990 survey of U.S. corporate boards reveals that 59.1 percent of the companies surveyed had one or more women on their boards and 31.6 percent had one or more ethnic minorities.[24] If data from Heidrick & Struggles's survey of California corporations is an indication of the country as a whole, the percentage of women and minorities on corporate boards is very small. They found that 82.2 percent of board members of California firms in 1989 were white men.[25] A glance through the annual report will make clear in most cases the number of women members. Representation by minorities is harder to determine, unless they are known celebrities.

In 1992 shareholder activists filed resolutions at four companies— Illinois Tool Works, Ralston Purina, Safety-Kleen, and U.S. Tobacco— that lacked female or minority representation on their boards. Those filing resolutions included: the Sisters of St. Joseph (Chestnut Hill), the National Benevolent Association, the Disciples of Christ, and the New York State Common Retirement Fund. Their resolutions did not demand tokenism. Rather they asked that the boards direct their nominating committees to make greater efforts to consider women and persons from minority groups. As Box 10-2 reveals, other shareholders took a somewhat different approach to the problem.

BENEFITS

Does the company have outstanding benefits relating to child care, elder care, flexible work schedules, and other programs that address work/

Box 10-2. Voting Against Unrepresentative Boards

Shareholder activists, particularly from the churches, have long pressed corporations on their hiring policies and on the inclusion of women and minorities on the board. Some institutional shareholders, such as the Domini Social Index Trust and the Calvert Group, support these initiatives by withholding its proxies or by voting against management's slate of directors or its resolutions—often on executive compensation schemes. Shareholders let management know by letter why they took the action.

As in every other area of social investing, the key here is to let management know what you expect of them and why. Then back it up with your vote. The authors use the following letter.

Dear Sir/Madam:

As you can see from the enclosed photocopy of your recent proxy solicitation, I have voted not to affirm your slate for your board of directors. Investors in the Domini Social Index Trust cannot support a board that has no women or minorities on it. It is time for American corporations to hear voices that reflect the population at large. I urge you to move toward a Board which is at least 50 percent female and at least 15 percent minority in its composition.

Very truly yours,

---

family concerns? Has the company received substantial recognition for its progress in these areas from women's groups?

Again, the best source is the company. The largest companies might receive publicity for their programs. For instance, *Working Mother's* annual article describing the 85 best companies for women discusses their benefits programs. The "Ten Best Companies" for 1991 were Beth Israel Hospital (Boston), Du Pont, Fel-Pro, Hewitt, HBO, IBM, Merck, Patagonia, SAS, and UNUM.[26]

COMMUNITY INVESTMENTS

Does the company have a record of investments in community economic development?

Community economic development, particularly that geared toward housing, targets the disenfranchised. Increasingly corporations, such as

Amoco and BP America, are joining with community groups to help build a new infrastructure to society, particularly in areas tied to the corporation, such as Chicago and Cleveland. Finding and keeping a job is nearly impossible if you do not have a roof over your head.

One area where there is a desperate need for investment is small business development. The press has hailed the growing number of women and minorities who have started their own businesses, featuring many success stories. But for each success, there are hundreds of failures. For this reason, corporations that want to support the advancement of women and minorities should consider community development investments.

Vehicles of this type make loans available to those who would otherwise go without. They lend their funds to meet the needs of the nation's poor—women and minorities. For instance, a loan to the Lakota Fund goes into a pool of funds available for the creation of cottage industries. It serves Native Americans in the nation's poorest county, where unemployment is 80 percent in summer and almost 100 percent in the winter. A deposit in Community Capital Bank in Brooklyn helps make available community development loans in one of the most desperately poor inner city areas. The bank offers services like check cashing for the homeless and loans to not-for-profits building shelters.

THE RECORD

Does the company have a long and consistent record of exceptional support for women- and minority-owned businesses?

Support for women- and minority-owned ventures can take a number of forms: maintaining payroll accounts with banks owned by minorities; developing supplier relationships; or allocating pension-management work to such companies. Again, your best source here is the company, though larger companies often receive press coverage.

Keep the pressure on!

11

Changing the Definition of Ownership: Institutional Control of Corporations

> **corporation,** *n.* An ingenious device for obtaining individual profit without individual responsibility.
>
> —AMBROSE BIERCE (1906)[1]

BUSINESS CORPORATIONS are so much a part of our lives that we take their existance for granted. We assume that they have always been a part of our social fabric. But that is not the case. Until well after the Civil War, they were relatively uncommon. Their structure and characteristics, too, have changed. John D. Rockefeller and his peers created "trusts" to hold the stock of their corporations because until the 1890s, the law limited the ability of persons in one state to own the stock of corporations chartered in another.

Since the early part of the twentieth century, how publicly traded corporations were structured and who owned them remained essentially unchanged—until the 1980s. The profound restructuring of American assets exceeds both the scope of this book and the grasp of most observers. We have touched on many of its symptoms in the preceding chapters. But the change in who owns American businesses and how that ownership is exercised directly affects socially responsible investors.

Over a very brief time, institutions have come to control more than 50 percent of publicly traded stocks, and the percentage is increasing.

Without being aware of it, social investors participate in this transformation when they, say, buy life insurance. The concentration of ownership in institutional hands has not resulted from a conspiracy of capitalists.* On the contrary, much of the impetus has come indirectly from government initiatives (in response to voter outcries) to protect savers and investors.

There is no precedent to guide either investors or the institutions themselves in defining the proper exercise of this concentration of immense economic and political power. In situations like this, one must look to history for a sense of the underlying principles that should guide policy. This chapter is a modest first step in that direction.

THE INSTITUTION: A BRIEF LOOK

"Institutions" comprise an amorphous category of corporate entities that gather funds from many sources and invest them. They are fiduciaries, persons or institutions who undertake to act for another person's benefit and on whom the law imposes a duty of trust. (We discussed fiduciaries in chapter 2.) They are also financial intermediaries, entities that have the power to make investment decisions on another's behalf. As a class, institutions include: mutual funds, banks, insurance companies, pension funds, brokerages, endowments, foundations, and charitable trusts.

The characteristic institutions share is that they hold money that others have some claim on. Mutual fund shareholders have the right to cash their interests. Pension-fund beneficiaries are entitled to the benefits promised them. The body politic has a right to the benefits for which endowments and charitable trusts are established.† The Pax World Fund, South Shore Bank, The Dreyfus Third Century Fund, U.S. Trust Company (Boston), the Methodist and Lutheran church pension funds, Teachers Insurance & Annuity Association—College Retirement Equities Fund (TIAA-CREF), and the Calvert Group are institutions that have played leading roles in socially responsible investing since the early 1980s—and before.

---

*Only "a conspiracy so huge . . ." in Senator Joe McCarthy's immortal phrase could accomplish this concentration, and only a mind like his could conjure it up. As James Grant ably documents in *Money of the Mind,* we are looking at an unintended consequence of six generations of economic policy decisions.

†State attorneys general (and in some rare instances, country prosecutors) acting in their capacities as the legal representatives of the state are the only people who can enforce the purposes of charitable trusts and endowments in court. The federal government, through the Internal Revenue Code, has a limited role in forcing certain types of charitable trusts (i.e., foundations) to put their money to work.

WHO ARE "THE INSTITUTIONS"?

When *Pensions & Investments* and *Business Week* refer to "shareholder activists," they are no longer referring to gadflies, such as the Brothers Gilbert, or church groups. The phrase now refers to certain large holders of stock in publicly traded corporations that vote their proxies aggressively. In terms of size, the most notable of these organizations are public-employee pension funds, such as the New York City Employee Retirement System (NYCERS) and the Wisconsin State Investment Board.

Some institutions have joined with the traditional shareholder activists to protect their rights as shareholders. In no small part, judicial and regulatory holdings have spurred institutions to pay attention to proxy issues as they did not a decade ago. Formerly, most trustees believed that their fiduciary duties to their beneficiaries did not extend to whether or how they voted their proxies. The corporate governance battles (see Table 11-1) that dominated the financial pages in 1990 through 1992, revealed that these institutions at least recognize the need to have the power to hold management accountable, though they rarely form such alliances on social justice issues.

The different degrees of institutional investors' participation in shareholder activism makes a rough classification necessary. There is considerable overlap between the categories, especially the first and second.

- *SRI institutions*—institutions that screen their investments and take an active role on social-issue proxy resolutions.
- *Governance activists*—institutions that do not screen their investments or take an active role on social-issue resolutions (other than South Africa) but do participate in governance issues.
- *Nonparticipants*—institutions that vote their proxies only because the law requires it but otherwise do not participate.

The vast majority of institutions fall into the third class. But the whopping votes against management at Sears[2] in 1992 shows that the nonparticipants are not asleep. It is a very hopeful sign for socially responsible investors.

CONCENTRATION AND INSTABILITY

At no time since the era of the great trusts (1890–1910)—and probably not even then—has so much power to shape the economy been so concentrated in the private financial sector. And as General Motors

TABLE 11-1. SELECTED 1992 CORPORATE GOVERNANCE VOTES

TO REQUIRE SHAREHOLDER VOTE ON OR TO REDEEM POISON PILL

Browning-Ferris	45.0% (for)
Caterpillar	48.5
EG&G	38.6
First Bank System	41.0
Grumman	39.3
Hartmarx	64.1
Union Carbide	43.1
Whirlpool	48.8

TO REQUIRE SHAREHOLDER VOTE ON GOLDEN PARACHUTE

Lubrizol	24.0% (for)
Union Carbide	27.6

TO ADOPT CONFIDENTIAL VOTING

Allied-Signal	38.2% (for)
American Cyanamid	33.1
Caterpillar	45.3
EG&G	44.5
First Bank System	29.0
Foster Wheeler	47.0
Lubrizol	24.0
Union Carbide	35.3

The votes in favor of these three types of corporate governance resolutions makes clear how dramatically shareholders have begun to assert their interests.
Source: Institutional Shareholder Services, *ISSue Alert,* May 1992, p. 5. Data derived by United Shareholders Association from company reports.

learned in April 1992, institutions are prepared to use that power. On that, more in a moment.

Money is being drawn—in the form of savings and investments—from investors of many types and concentrated in intermediaries. Increasingly, there is no connection between individual investors and publicly traded corporations. The public has little say about who manages several types of institutions, for example, endowments and charitable trusts, but institutions have much to say about who manages the corporation and how. Politically and socially, this concentration of wealth and power may be unstable and destabilizing.

One hundred years ago a very wise—though not prophetic—judge had before him plaintiffs seeking to break up an institution that had

grown very rich: the charitable trust created under the will of Benjamin
Franklin. The judge observed that concentrations of capital create

> a menace to the community, by placing in the hands of a few individu-
> als so vast a power as money insures, and putting the people in danger
> of having their government undermined and their liberties taken away
> by the power and corrupt use of large amounts of money. . . .
>
> [The] remedy of the people when the wealth of individuals or
> corporations . . . becomes so great as to threaten their liberties, is in
> statutes of Mortmain* and confiscation, and happy will the people be
> when they can save themselves from resorting to these extreme mea-
> sures, and are able to preserve their liberties through peaceful means
> instead of violent revolution. As yet, we in this country have had no
> danger from that source, but England had, and England applied the
> remedy, perhaps not wisely, but certainly with great effect.[3]

Twenty years later, in 1911, the Supreme Court affirmed the breakup of
the Standard Oil Trust under the antitrust laws. So America, too, has
applied "extreme measures" to concentrations of capital.

In the years ahead, the concentration of economic—and therefore
political—power in financial institutions may prove as large an issue as
trusts and monopolies did in the first half of the century. It is far too early
to predict how institutional ownership will evolve or what the political
response to it will be. For now, it is being shaped by a battle over
corporate governance. It is a mistake to interpret this as simply a battle
over power at several large corporations. Rather, we are witnessing a
redefinition of the corporate form and the social contract between corporations and society. Institutions will shape this change, both in the
positive sense of initiating change and in the negative sense of being
reacted to. And the institutions—themselves corporations of one form or
another—will be transformed, too.

CORPORATE GOVERNANCE

Corporate governance is a phrase that applies to the ways a corporation
runs at the highest levels, to the relationships among the shareholders,

---

*Mortmain statutes, the earliest of which was the Magna Carta, prevented religious institutions
from acquiring feudal estates that would remove them from control by the crown. They were
expressly designed to limit the church's secular power. If economics has become our religion, as
some argue, the institutions are our church. People turn over property to institutions for protection
and salvation. Civil government is in a struggle with institutions for both tax monies (institutions
oppose taxes as drags on the investments from which they profit) and control of domestic affairs
(institutions play a major role in shaping economic policies and budgets).

senior management, and the board of directors. But like many bloodless phrases, "corporate governance" means something quite real: control.

Control can take many forms. When raiders like Robert Campeau and T. Boone Pickens stalk the markets, it can mean a takeover. Look back at Table 11-1. The votes reported there were on antitakeover devices (poison pills and golden parachutes) and confidential voting of proxies, a system that would keep management from knowing who voted against it. These issues concern institutional investors because they affect the investors' abilities to fulfill their fiduciary responsibilities to their bene-ficiaries. Selling the company's stock to a hostile bidder may benefit their

---

BOX 11-1. INDISPENSABLE RESOURCE: *INSTITUTIONAL INVESTOR*

In the early spring 1992, part of the press hounded the leading Democratic candidate for president, seeking minor moral lapses as if they were high crimes and misdemeanors. Meanwhile, another part of the press, led by *Forbes,* prostrated themselves before Michael Milken, who deigned to grant interviews from his picnic table at Club Fed.

Someone who didn't know better might have thought when pick-ing up the April issue of *Institutional Investor* that the cover story on *Den of Thieves* author James B. Stewart was part of the same plan to canonize Milken. Instead, what *Institutional Investor* staff writer Ida Picker produced was a long contemplation of the relationship be-tween the reporter and his subject, the way in which works of nonfic-tion come to be published in this era, and the relationship between publications and their reporters. But most importantly, it probed the way in which business reporting has developed in the last twenty years. It is this level of reporting that makes *Institutional Investor* a must-read.

For a magazine to do stories like the one on Stewart while in the same issue it explains concisely the joys of market-neutral manage-ment and the difficulties of nondiscrimination-testing requirements on small pension funds is no minor feat.

For social-investment managers looking for nuggets of informa-tion about S&P 100 companies, *Institutional Investor* will regularly reward them. Best of all, *II* has a knack for presenting the people who make investing the great indoor sport that it is.

Institutional Investor, 488 Madison Avenue, New York, NY 10022. Monthly. $325 per year.

beneficiaries more than retaining stock in the corporation under its current management. And the institutions do not want anything to inhibit their freedom to make that choice.

Thus, control refers to a line of responsibility between management and the publicly traded corporation's shareholders. But aren't managers always responsible to shareholders? Yes, in theory. What marks the rise of the institution is that, probably for the first time, the answer to that question may also be "yes" in practice.

THE SHAREHOLDER'S INTEREST

To appreciate the magnitude of this change, consider the historic role of shareholders in the publicly traded corporation and its ancestors. The modern corporation has two direct ancestors. Entities we will call "protocorporations" appeared in the late Middle Ages, and business organizations called joint stock companies flourished first in the sixteenth century.

Protocorporations and Joint Stock Companies. The protocorporation consisted of people in the same trade to whom the crown granted a charter to regulate all aspects of the trade in a given locality. A charter specified the powers, rights, and privileges of the corporation.* As with the medieval guild, the protocorporation was supposed to protect tradesmen while stabilizing supply and demand. When Adam Smith railed against monopolies and the control of labor and prices, protocorporations and the laws that allowed them to exist were his targets.[4] By the time Smith wrote, in the last quarter of the eighteenth century, the protocorporations had received their death blow from capitalism. In the meantime, the joint stock company had risen, fallen, and was about to rise again.

In the seventeenth and eighteenth centuries, a joint stock company consisted of a group of people who agreed to pool their funds in a single "stock."[5] In organization it looked and functioned remarkably like a present-day corporation. The crown granted charters that often carried with them monopoly powers, as with the Hudson's Bay Company. While these ventures were commercial—including paper makers, a saltpeter company, and several mining companies—they often had a national purpose. The Hudson's Bay Company saw to the exploitation and settlement of British Canada; the saltpeter company manufactured a crucial element of gunpowder.[6]

---

*For simplicity's sake, we will refer throughout this discussion to corporate "charters." The term is now obsolete, replaced by *articles of incorporation*.

Henry Carter Adams, writing at the beginning of the century, was surely correct that "A corporation . . . may be defined in the light of history as a body created by law for the purpose of attaining public ends through an appeal to private interests."

Other People's Money.   Not surprisingly, Adam Smith disapproved of joint stock companies, too. He disliked the idea that shareholders could transfer their shares to others without permission from the company. He did not like limited liability. Unlike a partnership, where each partner is bound for the debts contracted by the company to the whole extent of his fortune, in a joint stock company each stockholder is bound only to the extent of what he or she paid for the shares.

To Smith, limited liability meant a limited sense of responsibility. And the way joint stock companies were run proved his point. Its directors were subject to the control of the shareholders, but most of the latter

> seldom pretend to understand any thing of the business of the company; and when the spirit of faction happens not to prevail among them, give themselves no trouble about it. . . . This total exemption from trouble and risk, beyond a limited sum, encourages many people to become [shareholders] in joint stock companies, who would, upon no account, hazard their fortunes in any [partnership].[7]

As for the directors, because they managed "other people's money"* rather than their own, they could not be expected to watch over it as a partner would in a partnership.

> Like the stewards of a rich man, they are apt to consider attention to small matters as not for their master's honour, and very easily give themselves a dispensation from having it. Negligence and profusion, therefore, must always prevail, more or less, in the management of such a company.[8]

Given Adam Smith's reputation as the Nostradamus of economics, it is astonishing how seldom cited are his comments on joint stock companies, especially since he identified the central problem of modern corporate governance: the lack of responsibility among shareholders and their representatives—the directors—for corporate actions.

But *The Wealth of Nations* makes no pretense of prophecy. Smith describes the world as it existed in the late eighteenth century. The

---

*This phrase—"other people's money"—has a fascinating history. In 1913 future Supreme Court justice Louis Brandeis took it as the title of his assault on the banking industry. Franklin Roosevelt used it derisively when he spoke of the banks' failures in his first inaugural address in 1933. One of the more sensational frauds of the early 1980s—before Milken et al.—involved O.P.M. Leasing, which exchanged forged equipment leases for "other people's money."

crown had virtually halted chartering joint stock companies in 1723 with
the collapse of the South Sea Company. He was describing a remnant,
historical relics. He saw the rising businesses taking the forms of partnerships and unchartered joint stock associations (which lacked limited
liability). Indeed, in Britain's North American colonies the crown had
issued only seven charters by the time *The Wealth of Nations* was first
published in 1776. By 1800, only 335 charters had been issued in the
United States.[9] Until about 1850, the partnership was the standard legal
form of business. Even the great enterprises of the early to mid-
nineteenth century, such as the ones owned by the Astors and the
Lawrences, were partnerships.[10]

THE LURE OF LIQUIDITY

Adam Smith's "invisible hand" worked because self-interest was wedded
to responsibility. The eighteenth-century entrepreneur lived with the
real possibility not only of losing *all* one's money because of a bad
investment, but also of going to debtor's prison until the creditors were
satisfied. Bankruptcy was not the relatively free and easy process it is
today.

Smith recognized that two aspects of the joint stock company uncou-
pled self-interest and responsibility: limited liability and the ability to
freely sell one's shares.[11] Even so, the ability to transfer is one thing when
seller and buyer must meet and negotiate the sale, and the buyer must
assume the seller's unlimited liability. It is quite another when a market
exists to transfer shares between people who may never have seen the
marketplace—much less the person on the other side of the transaction—and the buyer's liability extends only to the price paid for the
shares. Then the shares are liquid, a characteristic Smith did not foresee.
When shares are liquid, it is only the conscience of the stockholder that
imposes a sense of responsibility.

The rise of corporations with liquid shares was not rapid. Public
trading of shares and bonds formally began in London in 1773 and New
York in 1792. The total number of issues traded in New York was 5 in
1792; 117 in 1840.[12]

General Incorporation.   By the middle of the nineteenth century,
corporations had become less uncommon in the United States. Relatively
few charters went to ventures that lacked at least some arguable further-
ance of state policy. Pennsylvania, for instance, issued 2,333 charters to
businesses between 1790 and 1860, of which approximately 1,500 went
to transportation companies—not just to transporters of people and

goods, but also to owners of bridges, canals, and so forth—and fewer than 200 to manufacturing companies.[13]

Charters required an act of the state legislature, and serious money could change hands to obtain them. The scent of corruption coupled with the American dislike of privilege led to general incorporation laws, which began to appear in the mid-1840s. These laws made incorporation a matter of right. When they were fully articulated early in the twentieth century, incorporation only required filling out forms properly, paying a small fee, and making appropriate filings. All of the general incorporation statutes limited a shareholder's liability for the obligations of the corporation to the amount of his or her investment.

By 1920, what Adam Smith reviled had become the dominant business form for large business organizations.

Social Darwinism.   Smith could not have foreseen the rise of a world view that would, in practice, not just separate investments from responsibility but assert that there was no connection. This perspective, social Darwinism, was a bastard application of Charles Darwin's evolutionary principles to the social sphere.

Entranced with Darwin's unfortunate phrase "survival of the fittest," its advocates argued against any interventions by government that prevented the "best-adapted" economic entities to survive. The courts in the United States embraced social Darwinism in what one writer has called "the jurisprudence of industrialism."[14] Based on the concept of the freedom to contract and the sanctity of the executed contract, it held, "Any general law which deprived parties of vested rights . . . must be held obnoxious; any denial of freedom of action to the entrepreneur was by definition a denial of due process."[15]

In practice, this meant the courts looked at contracts without reference to the parties' relative bargaining positions. The courts indulged the fiction, for instance, that individual employees and corporate employers negotiated as equals. Many attempts to adjust legislatively for such often-gross disparities were stricken down. For fifty years, until Franklin Roosevelt's second term, the courts regularly voided wage and hour laws, pure-food and drug laws, and restraints on predatory business practices, while upholding racial segregation and restrictions on labor unions.

This focus on the contract had an important effect on the emerging corporate form. In 1880s and 1890s, the Supreme Court took the view that a corporation was a person whose contracts were entitled to constitutional protections.[16] The concept of corporate personhood was

new.* It emphasized again the separation of investors—and even management—from responsibility for actions by this abstraction.

Furthering the separation between investors and responsibility was
the perpetual life of corporations. State courts in the early twentieth
century were holding that since a charter was a contract between the
corporate person and the state, the state could not take it away or alter
it substantially unless the state could prove that the incorporators had
obtained the charter with the intent to use it fraudulently—a near-
impossible burden of proof. This line of cases keeps states from revoking
a charter and thereby imposing a death penalty on a corporation. These
cases protect "innocent" investors in corporations.[17]

The Managerial Corporation.   The stock market crash of 1929 and
the Great Depression whose beginning it marked put the relationship
between corporations and the public on the front pages for years. After
Roosevelt's election, Congress and the newly formed Securities and
Exchange Commission (1934) attempted to control corporations by
regulating how they sold their securities to the public.

Two academics, Adolf Berle and Gardiner Means, framed this discussion. Public trading of stocks gave shares liquidity—they would be converted into cash easily. Liquidity, Berle and Means argued, had turned a
share into a token whose value had little or nothing to do with the assets
of the company whose name was on the certificate, much less with the
responsibility for the company's actions. In their influential book, *The
Modern Corporation and Private Property* (1932),† they argued that
the shareholder of a publicly traded corporation exchanged "control for
liquidity."[18]

Publicly traded corporations had once operated as they believed
corporations were supposed to, with shareholders taking a direct responsibility for their operation. But as the number of shares and shareholders
increased, the incentives to manage disappeared, and the shareholders'
rights to control eroded away. These changes produced the modern
corporation in which ownership and control were divorced—to the benefit of management.[19]

> The surrender of control over their wealth by investors has effectively
> broken the old property relationships [in which ownership and con-

---

*The concept of the corporation as a sole person may also be an oxymoron, since a corporation
is a body—a corpus—of persons.

†*Influential* is a grossly inadequate adjective for this now-unread book. Berle and Means
permanently stamped their romantic vision of the corporation's history on American scholars.
However, their greatest contribution lay in outlining the reform of the securities markets implemented by the New Deal.

trol were united] and has raised the problem of defining these relationships anew. The direction of industry by persons other than those who have ventured their wealth has raised the question of the motive force back of such direction and the effective distribution of the returns from business enterprise.[20]

Today it seems clear that Berle and Means had the first concept backward.[21] Ownership and control never were united in publicly traded corporations. And if it happened, unification would require a redefinition of property relationships. But their question about distribution of returns remains valid. And it is that question that several institutional shareholders have begun putting to corporate boards and management.

Box 11-2. CalPERS as Corporate Reformer

With $68 billion in assets, the California Public Employees Retirement System (CalPERS) has plenty of weight to throw around. Historically, America's big institutional investors, which today hold nearly 50 percent of the publicly traded stock in the United States, have been passive bystanders in matters of corporate governance, preferring to "walk," that is, sell their shares, when a company's investment performance or ethical practices are substandard. But with so much to spread over a limited number of sizable investment opportunities, big funds like CalPERS have few places left to walk to. In 1992, CalPERS decided not to walk but to "act like an owner"— to complain to corporate boards that it was displeased with their performance on CalPERS' behalf. On March 20, 1992, CalPERS' chief executive, Dale Hanson, already considered troublesome by many in the corporate establishment, threatened to vote against the reelection of directors of ten major firms. Citing excessive pay for executives, boards stacked with insiders, and corporate strategies that did not reflect the interests of shareholders, Hanson remarked, "It's no wonder these companies are such poor performers, given their attitudes towards shareholders."

The ten companies on CalPERS' list were: American Express, Dial, IBM, Time Warner, Salomon Brothers, Hercules, Chrysler, Control Data, Polaroid, and US Air Group.

Sources: R. W. Stevenson, "Huge Fund Turns Up Proxy Heat," *New York Times,* March 21, 1992, pp. 37, 43; J. Chernoff, "GM Fallout: Who Will Be Next?," *Pensions & Investments,* April 27, 1992, p. 1.

UNITING OWNERSHIP AND CONTROL

Forty years ago pension funds, mutual funds, charitable trusts, insurance companies, and the like owned less than 15 percent of the publicly traded common stock in U.S. corporations. But today, two hundred years after shares began to trade publicly, ownership and control of publicly held companies is being united in institutions. In 1992, as we've seen, institutions held more than 50 percent.[22] Under our system of "one share, one vote," in terms of the power to elect directors, control is passing from individuals to institutions.

It is one thing to have power and quite another to exercise it. But the SEC, ERISA, and the law of trusts now require institutions to take an active role in the companies they own—at least with respect to voting their proxies. They can no longer avail themselves of the Wall Street rule: If you don't like management, sell the stock.[23] Their sheer size coupled with fiduciary restrictions on what they can own limits their ability to increase their return on their assets through trading—by buying and selling stock.

How, then, will institutions improve their financial performance and protect their stakeholders' interests? By exercising the power they now have to force the companies whose stock they own to improve *their* performance. The institutions' role as the guardians of other people's money and interests imposes on them a high degree of accountability. If institutional shareholders impose that level of accountability on corporations, they will have removed Adam Smith's largest objections to the form.

IN WHOSE INTEREST?

Robert Monks* and Nell Minow are, respectively, the founder and president of Institutional Shareholder Services, Inc., a firm that advises institutions how to vote their proxies. Monks is perhaps best known for his (thus far, unsuccessful) campaign for a seat on Sears's board and to force Sears to increase outside representation on its board, separate the offices of board chair and chief executive officer, and study the value of the company if it were to be broken up and sold, among other things.[24]

Monks and Minow have written a book, *Power and Accountability*, which is, in their words,

*Mr. Monks served as head of ERISA for a time during the first Reagan administration.

about how changes in the composition of the shareholder community over the past decade have made it possible to restore corporate organization to its original design. And this will revive the management accountability that is the best guarantee not just of corporate performance in the public interest, but of competitiveness and productivity as well.[25]

Monks and Minow equate the public interest with the shareholders' interest. Since the biggest shareholders in publicly traded companies are institutions, their interests define the public interest.

Chain of Representation.   Monks and Minow argue that U.S. managers have failed to act in their shareholders' interest. Management's inattention to the environment, for instance, is a result of shareholders' failure to exercise control.[26] The authors also recite the examples of director and manager abuses—at Time Warner, General Motors, and Lockheed (their examples were chosen only from publicly traded companies). They demand strict accountability to shareholders through boards that take their responsibilities seriously.[27] Indeed, Monks and Minow suggest applying to corporate directors the strictest standard of fiduciary responsibility which now applies only to partners and trustees.[28]

The same kinds of abuses cited by Monks and Minow and Adam Smith exist across all economic entities—in government agencies, such as the Interior Department; in pension funds, such as that of the Teamsters; in charitable trusts and endowments run by Baptists, Pentecostals, Christian Scientists, and Catholics; and even in the United Way.[29] The problem is not what type of stakeholder controls, but remoteness from the corporation's success or failure on the one hand and the ultimate beneficiary's well-being on the other. There is also the problem of ethics—the managers' and the board members'. While the corporate form is inherently flawed, the people who manage and direct a particular company can either compensate for the flaws or make the situation worse. To borrow a phrase from *The Godfather,* it's not business, it's strictly personal.

The Monks and Minow construct raises troubling questions about who could serve on their reconstituted corporate boards. Under the fiduciary standard they have chosen, the directors would have only one constituency: the corporation's shareholders. They could not divide their loyalties, say with the institution that employed them, as well. Even assuming the dual loyalty issue could be resolved, as the proxy votes listed in Table 11-1 hint, institutions have widely different views even on governance issues. So, institutional representatives on a board would not necessarily have a united view of problems.

The problem here lies in the fundamental assumption that institutional directors on corporate boards will better represent the interests of the corporation's shareholders. But if they can, wouldn't these directors be in the position of violating their institutions' fiduciary duties to *their* beneficiaries and shareholders? In the end, one cannot expect a high level of accountability—much less of responsiveness to social issues— from a daisy chain of representatives increasingly remote from the person whose ultimate interests the institutional directors of publicly traded corporations should advance.

The daisy-chain problem is especially troublesome when an institution is not organized to give its beneficiaries an effective voice in its own deliberations. More than a generation ago, Cornell law professor David Ratner wrote of institutions:

> [Their] decisions—on investments, voting of shares, and everything else—are made by a small group of managers on behalf of scattered beneficiaries, the great majority of whom have no idea what shares their institution owns, let alone how those shares are being or should be voted.[30]*

For the most part, trustees of public pension funds are appointed, not elected. Endowments and charitable foundations sometimes seek service outside representation. It must be noted that some of these organizations—the Ford Foundation, for example—have brought the voices of their beneficiaries into the boardroom.

Accountability.   Adam Smith, of course, identified the problem with any type of a representation model for corporate boards: other people's money. And the structures suggested to reform publicly traded corporations hold no promise of addressing that fundamental flaw.

Edward Waitzer, a prominent corporations lawyer in Toronto, has argued that a major barrier to effective participation in corporate governance is the institutions' lack of accountability mechanisms. Apart from pension funds subject to ERISA, institutions are subject to "few meaningful requirements . . . to explain and account for their proxy voting, investment decisions or otherwise. Aristotle first observed that 'good intentions don't control power; only power does.' "[31]

---

*Thus, the beneficial owners have little power to determine how the shares are used. Not for this reason alone is "shareholder democracy" an oxymoron. Democracy assumes the equal value of citizens—"one person, one vote." Corporations operate on the principle of "one share, one vote." Given their sixteenth-century origins, it is not surprising that plutocracy—government by the richest—is the organizing principle of corporations.

The drafters of the U.S. Constitution took this lesson and built into it a system of checks and balances, legal mechanisms to keep one branch from taking power from another whatever the quality of its intentions. In this era of antigovernment sentiment, regulation hardly seems an option. Instead, as a byproduct of the takeover era, a body of law has developed holding that corporations may be accountable to constituencies beyond their shareholders. But the balancing of these interests depends on the directors, not some outside source of power. A 1990 Pennsylvania law, for example, grants directors the prerogative to subordinate the interests of shareholders to those of other groups.* Indiana has a similar law.[32] These statutes suggest that the interests of employees, creditors, customers, and the communities in which workplaces are located—corporate stakeholders—should be taken into account in corporate decision making.

Many oppose this view, however, believing that the subordination of shareholder interests to those of other groups will eventually diminish the economic viability of the corporation and, in the end, hurt the long-term interests of everyone. Evidence from Germany and Japan does not support this notion. In Germany, companies with more than five hundred employees must assign at least one-third of the seats on supervisory boards to worker representatives.[33] In Japan, the communitarian ideals that guide economic activity harmonize with the idea of broader accountability of corporations. In surveys of Japanese executives, the goal of "maximizing the wealth of the shareholders" places far down the list of corporate objectives.

For cultural and legal reasons, neither the German nor the Japanese model seems adaptable to the United States. But the lesson to be drawn from their experience does apply here: Business enterprises have constituencies beyond their shareholders to whom they must account. Thus the chain of accountability for directors representing institutional interests is a long one indeed.

A New World Order

The real moving force behind the assertion of institutional control is the size of their share of the financial market. Institutional managers may no longer be able to improve their performance by taking advantage of market liquidity through active portfolio management—buying and sell-

---

*"Stakeholders" laws were passed to ensure that other state courts would not apply Delaware precedents in actions brought to force management to sell to a raider. As the legislators—and others—read these cases, management could only consider who gave shareholders the best deal, once their companies were "put into play."

ing securities. Contemporary financial theories hold that institutions own so much of the market that it is futile for them to try to beat the indexes. Only improving the underlying investments' performance holds any promise of enhancing their shares' value.[34] In this problem, Monks and Minow see a great opportunity.

American *Keiretsu.* The institutions' holdings make "it possible to have . . . a key ingredient in Japanese and German competitiveness: a dominant class of corporate owners with a long-term orientation." The model here are *keiretsus*—the Japanese business combines that typically include "a bank, a trading company and a wide range of manufacturing and commercial companies" bound together by interlocking holdings in one another.[35] The new controlling shareholders should decide national economic policy—government having failed—by making strategic decisions for their companies.[36]

Socially responsible investors and their institutional allies have used their influence at corporations to affect national policy decisions in most of the areas we discuss in this book—from animal testing to South Africa. But there is a great difference between lobbying a corporation and running it. What Monks and Minow suggest poses enormous difficulties under U.S. securities and antitrust laws and perhaps still larger cultural problems. What limited historical precedent we have for cooperative ventures is not promising. Our businesses seem to work better alone.

Perhaps the most serious problem with Monks and Minow's notion lies in our deep-rooted fear of conflicts of interest. Today, an institution can own stock in competing companies. Indeed for the fiduciary, prudence may dictate diversification of just this sort. One of the very real advantages of shares that are liquid—and therefore of the separation of ownership and control—is that it makes diversification within industries acceptable. But what if the institution had a director on the board, say, of Chrysler and it began taking an active role at Ford? The conflict seems clear. The alternatives would seem to be to undiversify by eliminating the other auto makers or to elect truly independent directors—which would destroy Monks and Minow's concept of institutional guidance. There are, it would seem, worse options for institutions than remaining outside the corporations they own.

Caring Shareholders. In the end, however, Monks and Minow have set an admirable goal for institutional shareholders. It is best expressed in an anecdote about George Siemens, founder of Deutsche Bank and the inventor of the *hausbank,* the German holding company that probably served as a model for the *keiretsu.* When criticized for spending too much time on a troubled client, Siemans responded, "If one can't sell, one must care."[37] Institutions must work out how they will care.

The sign of a caring shareholder in this framework is precisely what Monks and Minow advocate: a long-term view. Many will watch institutional shareholders skeptically because they are regarded as caring only about the quarterly financials. This "show me" attitude runs very deep.[38] A key test will come in the area of research and development. We pointed out in chapter 9 that substantial ongoing investments in R&D is a sign of a forward-looking company with management committed to a long-term vision. But R&D money *will* be spent on dry holes or wild-goose chases. So an R&D budget is an easy target for someone maximizing short-term earnings. In the United Kingdom, the Institutional Shareholders Committee (sponsored by the Bank of England) responded to complaints of short-termism by issuing guidelines to corporations on how to justify their R&D expenditures to institutions. These guidelines were expressly designed to put "the onus" on the companies.[39]

Socially responsible investors will find much to cheer if institutional shareholders simply find ways to compel management to disclose more. Since the passage of the Securities Acts in 1933–1934, disclosure has been a "self-effectuating control; many things are not done by corporate managements which would be done if they could be done without disclosure."[40] And if the controversy over executive compensation is any guide, greater disclosure is the direction in which institutions are heading.

COMPENSATION OF TOP MANAGEMENT

Andrew C. Sigler is chair and CEO of Champion International, the paper giant. Howling about Sigler's pay was one way institutional investors protested Champion's performance. His cash compensation—that is, excluding perquisites, benefits, and noncash items—ranged from $1.37 million in 1988 down to $1.14 million in 1991.[41] (One source puts his total compensation as high as $2.1 million for 1989.)[42] During his first seventeen years as CEO, shareholders had received a compounded annualized return of 7.6 percent. Had they invested in ninety-day Treasury notes—considered the safest form of investment—they would have received 8.2 percent. So said Ralph Whitworth, president of United Shareholders Association. What is extraordinary is that Whitworth said it to Sigler at a session of the annual meeting of the Council of Institutional Investors to which Sigler had been invited to defend his performance.[43]

That the head of a $2.5 billion (by market capitalization) company was called on the carpet by some of its major shareholders 250 miles from headquarters was perhaps unprecedented. And Champion has paid a cash dividend each year since 1940.

The protests about compensation should not obscure the real issues here. The board of directors must approve senior management's compensation. So an attack on executive compensation is also on the board's administration. Once again, other people's money. In addition, there is a real social-justice issue here: What is top management worth in terms of dollars? Put somewhat differently, how much more are top management's efforts worth to a company than its lowest-paid employee? This issue has two aspects: one of pay for performance and the other of workplace equity.

PAY FOR PERFORMANCE

Pay for top managers might have much less to do with corporate performance than with the recommendations of the CEO's friends among his board's members and the executive headhunters' compensation consultants they employ. John Kenneth Galbraith once noted, "The salary of the chief executive of a large corporation is not a market award for achievement. It is frequently in the nature of a warm personal gesture by an individual to himself."[44] Table 11-2 lists some companies who appear to have indulged such gestures.

These gestures can be warm indeed. According to compensation specialist Graef Crystal's book, *In Search of Excess,*[45] CEOs of America's major firms receive almost 150 times more in compensation than the

TABLE 11-2. COMPANIES WITH EXCESSIVE BOARD OR MANAGEMENT
COMPENSATION

American Express Co.	McCaw Cellular Communications
Ameritech Corp.	Paramount Communications Inc.
Bally Manufacturing Corp.	PepsiCo Inc.
Blockbuster Entertainment Corp.	Ralston Purina Co.
Chrysler Corp.	Reebok International Ltd.
Coca-Cola Co.	Sara Lee Corp.
Dillard Department Stores, Inc.	Sears, Roebuck and Co.
H.J. Heinz Co.	Time Warner Inc.
May Department Stores Co.	Walt Disney Co.

These companies have records of compensating excessively their board members or top management. Data are current as of March 1, 1992.
Source: Kinder, Lydenberg, Domini & Co., Inc., the KLD Social Investment Database.

average U.S. worker. *Business Week* computed the figure at a mere eighty-five times more. CEO pay rose by 212 percent in the decade ending in 1990 as compared to 54 percent for workers.[46]

The Economist commissioned Mr. Crystal to study 348 large public firms in the United States. For 1987–1990, he determined that earnings per share at 223 increased and 125 decreased, both by an average of 10 percent. The top executive at companies that grew received a 13.3 percent compensation hike on average. At the 125 firms whose earnings dropped, the average raise was 3.2 percent.

Crystal and other critics of excessive executive pay focus on financial performance, not its ethical aspects. Many institutional investors do the same. It does not bother them that Disney's Michael Eisner earns almost $60 million over three years if his firm is making money.

The disparity between pay and performance and the extent to which it is tolerated by boards whose duty is to corporation's stakeholders concern some critics. In most cases, the CEO sits on the board. He may even be its chair. Of *Fortune* 1,000 board members, 63 percent are themselves CEOs of other firms.[47] And according to a 1990 survey by Korn Ferry International, most individuals considered for board membership are recommended by the chair.[48] Nonetheless, some companies, listed in Table 11-3, have imposed limits on compensation. James E. Preston, chairman and CEO of Avon Products Company, announced in late 1991 that he would freeze his base salary and link future pay increases to the performance of the company's stock.[49]

WORKPLACE EQUITY

Robert Levering, coauthor of *The 100 Best Companies to Work For,* has said, "There's something incompatible about astronomical salaries

TABLE 11-3. COMPANIES WITH LIMITATIONS ON COMPENSATION

Ben & Jerry's Homemade, Inc.	Herman Miller, Inc.
Dayton-Hudson Corp.	Petrie Stores Corp.
Egghead, Inc.	

These companies have exceptional policies on limiting the compensation of board members or senior managers. Data are current as of March 1, 1992.
Source: Kinder, Lydenberg, Domini & Co., Inc., the KLD Social Investment Database.

and a good workplace."[50] The idea of a vast pay gulf between automatons at the bottom and captains of industry at the top may have been accepted in the past, but when corporations ask employees to share the risks of modern enterprise, great differentials in compensation are insupportable.

Some CEOs recognize this fact. Chuck Denny, CEO of ADC Telecommunications, a $230 million Minnesota firm, has noted that overly generous executive pay packages damage the social contract between workers and managers.[51] Some firms have chosen to deal with the disparity head-on. Herman Miller, a furniture manufacturer that often shows up on lists of most admired companies, caps its CEO's cash compensation at twenty times that of the company's average factory worker. Ben & Jerry's, the Vermont ice cream maker that is also a leader on employee relations, caps salaries at six times that of its lowest-paid worker.[52]

A WORD FROM WALDEN

It is truly enough said that a corporation has no conscience; but a corporation of conscientious men is a corporation with a conscience.

—HENRY DAVID THOREAU (1854)

Quoting Henry David Thoreau to business people produces the same reaction as reciting Simone de Beauvoir to misogynists. But at the risk of losing some readers we must quote him since we cannot put better the standard which institutions—and socially responsible investors—must apply in judging their exercise of their powers as shareholders.

If institutional control leads to a new framework of corporate responsibility that emphasizes the exercise of individual consciences, we must hail it as a great success. If, however, institutional control insulates the individual still further from the consequences of a decision, it must be judged a cataclysm.

In pop talk, the rising generation of the Reagan years was the me generation, as in "give it to me." Socially responsible investors argue for an I generation, as in "I did it." They must carry that argument to both corporations and institutions.

Creating systems to make corporate management accountable via shareholder's initiatives, separation of CEO and board chairmanships, and providing means for outside directors to represent the interests of stakeholders will be an important challenge to investors of all persuasions during the coming years.

When the system that holds hired managers accountable to share-holders breaks down, it is not surprising that management builds a cushy fiefdom for itself and its friends. The SEC has generally gone along with management. Corporations routinely excluded shareholder proposals against lucrative management compensation from proxy ballots, and the SEC went along with them. In February 1992, with outrage growing at unconscionable executive pay, the SEC buckled and ordered several companies to entertain these proposals.[53] But that victory may well be temporary. In mid-1992, the SEC was considering regulations that would keep 95 percent of the shareholder resolutions now being filed off proxy ballots.

Executive compensation is an issue tied to the greater questions of corporate governance and institutional shareholder control. It is also tied to the questions of workplace equity we looked at in chapter 9. Social investors and institutional investors have common objectives in trying to rein in compensation, though their ultimate goals may be somewhat different.

Social investors have taught institutional investors a great deal about being effective shareholder activists. Fruitful partnerships have developed on issues such as the Valdez Principles and executive compensation. As the institutions assume a greater role in corporate affairs, social investors have every reason to expect that the partnership will ripen to the benefit of all stakeholders.

12

International Investing

The British and the Americans are two peoples separated by a common language.

—George Bernard Shaw

INTERNATIONAL INVESTING is really an exercise in cross-cultural communication. A friend of ours learned this when he visited London for a week. During his first three days in the city, he kept hearing about ethical bond funds. "Ah! Socially screened debt funds," he mentally translated.

Our friend is very interested in debt and found the idea exciting. On the fourth day in the course of a conversation with a bond specialist, he mentioned how excited he was by the profusion of socially screened bond funds. He rattled off the names of some. The bond specialist looked at him like he was out of his mind. Then he started laughing. A bond fund in the United Kingdom is like a variable annuity. A bond is a promise to pay. All the funds he had mentioned were equity or balanced funds that were in the "bond funds."

Determined not to look stupid again, our friend went to one of the many business bookstores that dot London's financial district. He looked at the four dictionaries of business and finance and a guide to reading the British financial pages. None of the dictionaries hinted at the existence of "bond funds." Only by working backward from where they were listed in the financial pages would he have been able to decode the phrase.

THE CHALLENGE OF GLOBAL INVESTING

The mood of the times is almost giddily international. Ideological barriers seem to be falling everywhere; trade barriers are much complained about, but are lower than they have ever been. One international social investment fund, the Calvert World Values Global Equity Fund, was launched in 1992. It will not be the last. Are there good reasons for socially responsible investors to consider foreign issuers? Yes, there are. But there are also some serious problems.

DIVERSIFICATION

Social investors and their advisers *must* begin preparing to screen foreign companies. Prudence probably demands an international component in very large portfolios, and it may someday soon require some exposure of this sort in all portfolios. The reason: diversification.

Most portfolio managers try to do two things simultaneously: reduce risk and enhance return. Perhaps the single most effective way to reduce risk is diversification, an investment strategy that spreads risk across a portfolio by owning several types of assets whose returns are not related to one another. National Widget Company may be completely safe, but putting all your investment dollars in its stock is imprudent. An earthquake could destroy its manufacturing facilities just when a plane crash removes top management. To diversify against specific company risks like these, most studies indicate that a portfolio should hold at least twenty stocks.

Diversification across companies removes only one kind of risk. Another remains. Most portfolios only hold American securities. The world economy is becoming increasingly interdependent, but that has not kept markets in one country from booming while those in other countries tumble. Just look at the Japanese market, which plummeted in 1992 while U.S. markets remained relatively strong. Diversification across national lines reduces the risk that one country's economic woes can harm overall return.* Most Americans fail to realize the significant risk that lack of international exposure has implied. American stocks account for less than half of the world's stock value. The largest corporations in banking, chemicals, drugs, food, and a dozen other industries are not domiciled in the United States.

---

*Of course, a portfolio should be diversified across classes of assets, too.

Reducing risk over time, studies show, enhances return. Institutions are increasingly placing assets with managers who specialize in foreign securities. Social investors demand the same high returns and low risks as other investors. But circumstances that uniquely affect socially responsible investors have caused them to avoid international issuers.

RESTRAINTS ON INTERNATIONAL SOCIAL INVESTING

Any American investor considering non-U.S. companies must ask three questions:

- Do the words in the reports mean the same thing to me as they do to the issuer?
- Do the accounting categories and conventions correspond to U.S. practice?
- Does the issuer's home country, its country of domicile, require it to report to securities holders at the same level that the United States does?

To those three questions, a socially responsible investor must add three more:

- Will the reports indicate whether the company passes my social screens?
- Do reliable external sources of information exist on the application of my screens to the company?
- Are the screens applied in the United States applied in the same way outside the United States?

With very few exceptions, the answers to all six questions will be "No."

Thus, for very good reasons socially responsible investors have avoided non-U.S. issuers. Information is not available. Worse, there is the problem of applying screens across cultural boundaries. For instance, the role of women in society is viewed quite differently in Japan and even Western Europe than it is in the United States. Would you apply the standard of the company's country of domicile? Or the standard you apply to U.S. companies? Or a different, culturally based standard for each country in which the company operates?

Nonetheless, social investors and their advisers *must* begin preparing to screen foreign companies. Three things have made this a necessity:

- Foreign debt already plays a significant role in U.S. portfolios.
- The SEC and the New York Stock Exchange (NYSE) are pushing us in this direction as hard and as fast as they possibly can.*
- Both at home and abroad, corporations are going to have to take a much more serious approach to questions of race, culture, and ethnicity than they have before.

Let's take a closer look at these issues.

CORPORATE DEBT'S ROLE

Debt—bonds and commercial paper fuels the engine of world finance. It comes as a shock to most Americans—fixated as they are on the stock markets—to learn that even in this country, the market for debt is far greater than the market for stocks—perhaps ten times greater. *The Economist* reported that publicly issued debt on the world's major exchange rose 15 percent in 1990 to $12 trillion. Of that, $4.32 trillion were corporate.

Non-U.S. corporate debt already figures large in insurance and bank portfolios. Individual investors led by baby boomers heading for retirement are likely to want more fixed income vehicles in their portfolios. They, too, will be looking at some of these foreign issues.

The SEC has always imposed far lower reporting requirements on debt issuers than on equity issuers. Widows and orphans, presumably, would not find their way into the higher-priced debt market. Since sophisticated investors made the market, they needed less information in public reports. Neither of the Securities Acts even hints at this distinction. However, the SEC has done this for fifty years.

PRESSURE FROM THE SEC

Perhaps in its own mind the SEC has relied on the precedent of its dereliction of duty as to bonds to justify limiting the reporting requirements applied to foreign issuers. The agency's stated motive is more seductive:

The SEC wants our capital markets to be "competitive" with other

---

*The SEC to date has spoken out of all sides of its mouth on this issue. Chairman Breeden has said he is opposed. However, policy papers the SEC has circulated for comment indicate a strong inclination to open our markets.

world markets.[1] In other words, they want more commissions and fees for seatholders on our exchanges. Foreign companies now make up about 9 percent of the ten thousand companies traded on U.S. exchanges.* They are large companies, and fairly well known, like Sony.[2] Until now, companies wishing to trade on our stock exchanges had to meet at least a somewhat stripped-down set of requirements. Soon they might not.

To achieve the noble objective of competitiveness, the SEC has proposed dismantling the regulatory structure built up since the Depression to protect investors. U.S. securities laws have relied much less on federal or state policing of securities transactions than on private lawsuits. The key element in these laws is full disclosure by publicly traded companies of all facts material to an investment decision. If you disclose, you can't be sued—that is the basic rule. And it has worked very well.

Reduced Reporting Requirements

The SEC now regards the reporting requirements it is charged with enforcing as a barrier keeping foreign companies out of our equity capital markets. Its solution: Open American markets to any company or mutual fund that meets the reporting requirements of its country of domicile.[3] No other country requires our level of reporting. Indeed, some countries—Spain and Singapore come immediately to mind—would make Joe Isuzu feel right at home.

If the reporting barriers drop, a flood of foreign companies will come into our equity markets. The debt markets—bonds and commercial paper—are already awash with foreign issues. The foreign companies will start showing up in mutual fund portfolios and private portfolios to a much greater degree than they do now. And social investors will have the devil's own time screening them.

Another ill effect of the SEC's proposals is that it may torpedo efforts in the European Community and elsewhere to move toward U.S.-style reporting. Even the Swiss have been considering abandoning their traditional secrecy. They want to attract foreign institutional investors and believe the key lies in improving the quantity and quality of information their companies provide.[4] But instead of encouraging this trend, the SEC has created an incentive for all countries to reduce their already-puny reporting requirements.

*As of October 1991, there were 964 actively traded issues representing 850 companies in forty-one countries. Most trade over the counter, but some do trade on the New York Stock Exchange.

The worst effect of the SEC's proposals, if they are implemented, will be demands by U.S. corporations for level reporting requirements. Why should U.S. companies have to meet more exacting standards than foreign companies on our exchanges? One ray of sunshine breaks this gloomy prospect: The largest transnationals are improving their public reports on their own to conform to the expectations of global investors. However, the areas they are improving—accounting, financial disclosure, and dividend policies—do not affect information needed for most social screens.[5]

We have had a taste of what reduced reporting requirements will be like. Following the SEC's revisions in its Form 10-K requirements in the early '80s, the volume of information in the 10-K's decreased in some cases as much as 90 percent, but more typically 40 percent. That is a lot of information about products, plants, litigation, and the like that we now do not get. The SEC claims it is working to improve the 10-Ks.

If these prospects were not bad enough, in October 1991 the SEC allowed the National Association of Securities Dealers Automated Quotation system (NASDAQ) to open at 3:30 A.M. so that it could handle European transactions. There's nothing wrong with that. But the SEC also said that the NASDAQ does not have to provide information on trades during the early-morning session and only a summary of the trades after these. Those are European rules. The *New York Times* editorialized that this was an open invitation to Salomon-type manipulations—or worse.[6] That is not an exaggeration.

ALTERNATIVE INFORMATION SOURCES

International social investing is in its earliest infancy. Little social research is being done in the United States on foreign securities or even American corporate behavior abroad. The companies on which reports are available, for example, Volvo and Rueters, tend to be squeaky clean. This is not surprising since a major factor inhibiting international social research is the law of libel.

In the United States, the constitutional guarantee of freedom of expression protects journalists even when they are wrong. The burden is on the plaintiff—the person claiming to have been harmed—to prove that a statement is false, that the publisher was at fault in giving the statement publicity, and that the statement caused an injury. Truth is virtually an absolute defense. In all other English-speaking countries, truth is not a defense if the plaintiff was held up to ridicule. In addition, the burden of proving truth is on the press. British publishing magnate Robert Maxwell avoided exposure for years because he regularly sued authors whose stories he did not like. By one count, he had filed twenty-one libel actions.[7]

Needless to say, journalists outside the United States are a good deal more restrained in their coverage of potentially embarrassing issues than they are here. Thus, a good deal more must be read between the lines than in the United States.* But that is not the only effect of the libel laws on social research. If social researchers around the globe do reach agreement on common reporting, libel laws will inhibit their coverage, too.

Social researchers around the globe do not apply common standards. Not long ago, we did a quick comparison of our screens and those of a leading European research house. We did not screen on 50 percent of the issues they did—or we did so in an altogether different manner—and vice versa. We suspect that a more thorough comparison would reveal even less overlap. Culture and history give different shapes even to screens that sound the same. We noted some of these differences in chapter 3.

Traditionally, social investors have looked to screened mutual fund holdings for guidance. British and German social-investment vehicles apply different standards from those common in the United States, and there are significant cross-cultural barriers in interpreting standards we seem to share. Canadian funds tend to be closer to U.S. funds in their screening, but they, too, have very limited foreign exposure. Among U.S. funds, only the Calvert World Values Global Equity Fund, which is managed by a Scottish firm, invests heavily in foreign securities.

Once again, shareholder activists are leading the way. Faith-based groups make effective activists because there are missionaries at work around the globe. For instance when the Oblates in Haiti became concerned about working conditions in a baseball factory, their American members traced the plant's ownership to Figgie International. They were able to convince other religious shareholders to open a dialogue with Figgie. This pattern has repeated itself in virtually every area American social investors need information.

Faith-based groups also made Americans aware of the devastating effects of infant formula sales in Third World nations. They have pointed out the damage caused by pushing tobacco products on the poor abroad. The sale of agricultural pesticides banned in America would have been a nonissue but for their diligence. Drugs, known to be unsafe for children, are sold to cure infant's diarrhea in Mexico, but faith-based groups are

---

*The perception of the English press as willing to say anything comes from their treatment of the royals, who consider it beneath their dignity to sue. Demigods like Maxwell sue, and coverage of them is much more restrained.

working to halt these sales. And these groups made us aware of the terrible human toll Third World debt burdens were taking.

Some international environmental groups are beginning to see the value of making available information about American corporate behavior overseas. Labor and human rights advocates and other constituencies are gaining in sophistication in their analyses of corporate performance. They are raising questions not only with American companies, but with foreign ones. Nestlé, the object of the infant formula boycott, is not an American company but a Swiss one.

Advocacy groups and social-investment researchers around the world are beginning to get to know one another. Very preliminary discussions have occurred about pooling research and standardizing screens. But off-the-shelf international social research products are years away. For now, American investors are on their own.

CROSS-CULTURAL EXCHANGE

The third factor compelling social investors to think globally also, and very importantly, applies locally. Just when corporations have learned to think globally on issues of finance and the environment, they must focus on the local problems of culture, race, ethnicity, and gender. The collapse of the Eastern Bloc has forced into our consciousness the differences between ethnic groups. The "American Dilemma" that Gunnar Myrdal identified forty years ago is not uniquely American. Almost every country—and even regions within countries—must devise ways for its peoples to live and work together.

Corporations, particularly the large transnationals, must also convince people of different cultures to work harmoniously. Remember the stories about Honda's Japanese management arriving in Marysville, Ohio, and the cultural misunderstandings that took place there. Or the stories on the sports pages about the problems of American baseball players in the Japanese leagues. Successfully working in foreign environments requires extreme sensitivity to cultural nuance.

These interactions between cultures have another dimension for socially responsible investors. Does one look with favor at the multinational that gave shoes to its Indonesian workforce or do we penalize it? Would your answer change if four workers had tripped and fallen to their deaths because they were not used to shoes? U.S. social investors have had the luxury of working with relatively clear lines. For example, a company makes liquor products or does not. But with global investing come questions of global dimensions in very local contexts.

All transnationals—whatever their home country—are subject to the dangers of ethnicity and cultural clash, both as actors in foreign lands and as micronations. *The Prize,* Daniel Yergin's Pulitzer Prize–winning book on the oil industry, should be read as a cautionary tale on the disasters of cross-cultural contacts, particularly when they involve relatively young, rapidly growing companies and ancient empires, such as British Petroleum and Iran. It is worth remembering that micronations such as Xerox, Sony, Honda, Hanson, and Microsoft came into existence after World War II. Indeed, the last two date to 1969 and 1975, respectively. Very few transnationals—GE, Mitsubishi, Nestlé, and Unilever, among them—are older than Yugoslavia and the U.S.S.R.[8]

AMERICAN TRANSNATIONALS

Many Americans invest internationally without being aware of it. That is because many U.S. corporations are in fact international. Johnson & Johnson, Gillette, Corning, Coca-Cola, Caterpillar, Colgate/Palmolive, Xerox, and Dow Chemical, among others, generate more than half of their revenues outside the United States. This success represents more than just good salesmanship; it indicates the extent to which these entities have embedded themselves into the fabric of other countries through joint ventures, subsidiaries, and local distributors. Some, like Whirlpool, employ more foreign nationals than Americans.

Can U.S. transnationals substitute for foreign issuers? The advantage of U.S. transnationals is that we know a lot more about them. However, we still run into very real problems in researching their activities, particularly in the Third World.

The extent to which firms have become global as opposed to national enterprises provoked Robert Reich to pose his now-famous question: *Who Is Us?* While scholars and policy makers in the United States busy themselves with ways to enhance the competitive capabilities of domestic corporations, many of them may not be domestic but rather free floaters without a real national allegiance. Companies like IBM, Hewlett-Packard, and Texas Instruments, Reich argued, are no longer American firms operating globally, but global firms operating in America.[9] Reich probably exaggerates, but his point is well taken.

Global operations make the application of social screens to U.S.-headquartered firms more difficult. Information on business activities is hard to come by. And there are significant cross-cultural problems in evaluating the information available. For example, with three dozen production facilities, General Motors is the largest employer in the maquiladoras.[10] We know more about these operations because they are so close. Labor and religious groups have focused on them because domestic operations have closed so GM could take advantage of lax Mexican labor and environmental standards—not to mention low pay scales and benefits. Even though we know much about maquiladoras, the Mexican government provides little information by comparison with the United States. The press is controlled—or worse.

Similarly, Motorola has a new plant outside Hong Kong. How capable are we of knowing about its employee relations, its advancement of women, or its relationship with the community near this important facility?

EFFECT ON INVESTMENTS

Cross-cultural problems affect even investors who do not apply social screens. In 1991 *Institutional Investor* compared the performance of the ten top U.S. mutual funds for the last five years with the ten top U.K. funds that invested in North America. Of the twenty funds, the first-ranked was a U.K. fund—Premium Life American. The next ten were U.S. funds. The number-ten U.S. fund (eleventh overall) was the Kemper Growth Fund, which rose 128.1 percent over the five-year period. The number-two U.K. fund—twelfth overall—rose 95.1 percent. The difference is rather staggering between number eleven and number twelve. *Institutional Investor* drew the logical conclusion: British investors wanting a North American play would have been better off with a fund run by U.S. managers.[11]

INTERNATIONAL SCREENING ISSUES

The standards to apply to either U.S. corporations' international behavior or foreign-based corporations have not been set. Indeed, American investors are just beginning to grasp the issues.

HUMAN RIGHTS

> All the great family of mankind are bound up in one bundle. When we aim a blow at our neighbor's rights our own are by the same blow destroyed. Can we look upon the wrongs of millions—can we see their flow of tears and grief and blood, and not feel our hearts drawn out in sympathy?

> —ABBY KELLEY, ANTISLAVERY AND FEMINIST ORATOR (1811–1886)[12]

Yes, he's an S.O.B., but he's our S.O.B.

—Franklin D. Roosevelt (attributed), about Nicaraguan
dictator Anastasio Somoza[13]

As a people, we Americans have always had a schizophrenic attitude toward the rights of our fellow humans. In our time, the S.O.B.s have included Somoza's son and namesake, the Shah of Iran, President Marcos, and General Pinochet. And we have lavished arms, gifts, and economists on their regimes. Not a few people have noted the inconsistencies between our Declaration of Independence from a dotty king and his ministers and our support of governments bent on suppressing just such urges among their own peoples.

These standards are Western, American. Social investors must confront the issue of whether they can impose their cultural/political ideals on other cultures. Are North Korea, Peru, Myanmar (née Burma), and Indonesia so different from us that another set of rules applies to them? Thus far, socially responsible investors have chosen a Western standard. As Eastern Europe and the Indian subcontinent fragment, social investors may have to revisit this choice. In two current instances, Northern Ireland and China, opinions are not likely to change.

Many British social investors eliminate companies that do business with oppressive regimes. *The Ethical Consumer* (discussed in chapter 10) defines an oppressive regime as one that has been criticized in the *Amnesty International Report 1991* for, (1) torture, (2) extrajudicial executions or disappearances, and (3) prisoners of conscience; *and* in *World Military and Social Expenditures 1991* for "frequent violence against the public."[14] An oppressive-regimes screen is a logical extension of South Africa screening for social investors who do not wish to invest in companies that support governments with bad human-rights records.

This screen is not common in the United States.* Only two funds, Working Assets and the Calvert Global Fund, have analogous screens. However, it is safe to predict that such screens will become common here as the pace of internationalization quickens.

Once social investors identify regimes that fall below their standards, they must confront a practical question: How should they treat companies doing business in those countries?†

---

*The explanation for this difference lies in Britain's imperial heritage, which gives it a global perspective. Companies traded on the London Exchange tend to be more international in their orientation than U.S. companies. In early 1992, over half of the seven-hundred-plus companies making up the *Financial Times* All-Share Index would not pass a strict South Africa screen. Fewer than one hundred of the companies on Standard & Poor's 500 failed.

†For the most part, such countries will not have companies with securities listed on major world exchanges. (South Korea is a notable exception.) So, the question of what to do about their companies will rarely arise.

Although South Africa brought this issue into the screening process, we lack a model for extending it to corporate contributions to other oppressive regimes. Screening by nation, as we did in South Africa, would certainly be the easiest approach. It could be implemented by examining the taxes paid to each host country. Perhaps the screen ought to be placed on a dollar level of taxes paid to repressive regimes world-wide. Perhaps it ought to be a percent of profits paid. Perhaps we ought to rank regimes by oppressiveness as *The Ethical Consumer* has.

The best answer would seem to be the "strategic goods or services" approach we described in chapter 5. Transnationals supplying goods or services that directly supported the government (e.g., military or police equipment) or the socioeconomic infrastructure (e.g., logging in Indonesia) would fail the screen.

There are indications that a strategic-assistance screen may not be rigorous enough. Shareholder activists connected with the National Council of Churches and the Interfaith Center on Corporate Responsibility have begun pressing Amoco and PepsiCo to suspend their operations in Myanmar until democracy is restored. PepsiCo owns 40 percent of a Rangoon bottler, and Amoco has a drilling contract with the state-owned oil company.[15] Canadian church groups are urging Petro-Canada to leave, too.[16] Most of the other issues—Third World marketing practices, maquiladoras, environmental protection, and the like—remain largely confined to discussion rather than implementation.

NORTHERN IRELAND

Continuing violence in Northern Ireland calls our attention to the fact that beneath the issues of British/Irish and Protestant/Catholic conflict

TABLE 12-1. SOME COMPANIES WITH OPERATIONS IN NORTHERN IRELAND

Digital Equipment Corp.	Mobil Corp.
DuPont Co.	NYNEX Corp.
Exxon Corp.	Oneida Ltd.
Federal Express Corp.	Pitney Bowes Inc.
Ford Motor Co.	Procter & Gamble Co.
Honeywell Inc.	Sara Lee Corp.
Illinois Tool Works Inc.	Texaco Inc.
International Business Machines Corp.	United Technologies Corp.
Marsh & McLennan Companies, Inc.	V.G. Corp.
McDonnell Douglas Corp.	Xerox Corp.
Minnesota Mining and Manufacturing Co.	

Data are current as of August 1, 1992.
Source: Kinder, Lydenberg, Domini & Co., Inc., the KLD Social Investment Database.

lie a number of important human-rights problems, often manifested in employment discrimination. Table 12-1 lists some companies with operations in northern Ireland.

At issue is employment discrimination on religious grounds. Some years church groups and several institutional investors have filed shareholder resolutions urging corporations to sign the MacBride Principles for fair labor practices in that part of the United Kingdom.

Many of the same objections to the Sullivan Principles are now heard about the MacBride Principles. TRW, Inc., the electronics and defense company, sold its Northern Ireland operation rather than go through a proxy battle. A senior TRW officer told *Pensions & Investments,* "We totally support equal opportunity but we could not legally support the MacBride Principles. We did not think they could be implemented."[17] Box 12-1 contains a summary of the Principles.

THE PEOPLE'S REPUBLIC OF CHINA

Not long after the massacre of peaceful demonstrators in Beijing's Tiananmen Square, California legislators began agitating to require the state's pension fund to divest itself of companies involved in China. Taking their cue from the South African experience, these legislators and many others in the United States thought it time to apply the economic pressure for reform that the Reagan and Bush administrations had not. "Now," said California legislator Tom Hayden, "the pressure will come to China."[18] Unfortunately, it did not.

The spotlight on China's human-rights abuses grew brighter in 1991, when it was revealed that prison laborers were turning out manufactured goods for export to the United States and other Western countries, often through Hong Kong middlemen who conceal the source of their products.[19] Investors have questioned the sources of imported goods. They should expand their inquiries to working conditions in Thailand and the archipelago as well.

CONCLUSION

The move toward commonwealths in North America, Europe, Eurasia, and South America means investors must shift their focus dramatically. For more than two centuries, the key factor in international investing

---

BOX 12-1. THE MACBRIDE PRINCIPLES—SUMMARY

1. Increasing the representation of individuals from underrepresented religious groups in the work force including managerial, supervisory, administrative, clerical, and technical jobs.
2. Adequate security for the protection of minority employees both at the workplace and while traveling to and from work.
3. The banning of provocative religious or political emblems from the workplace.
4. All job openings should be publicly advertised and special recruitment efforts should be made to attract applicants from underrepresented religious groups.
5. Layoff, recall, and termination procedures should not in practice favor particular religious groupings.
6. The abolition of job reservations, apprenticeship restrictions, and differential employment criteria, which discriminate on the basis of religion or ethnic origin.
7. The development of training programs that will prepare substantial numbers of current minority employees for skilled jobs, including the expansion of existing programs and the creation of new programs to train, upgrade, and improve the skills of minority employees.
8. The establishment of procedures to assess, identify, and actively recruit minority employees with potential for further advancement.
9. The appointment of a senior-management staff member to oversee the company's affirmative action efforts and the setting up of timetables to carry out affirmative action principles.

---

and in a business' overseas operation was host government policy. Investment analysts could watch government policies and make informed predictions. They still will, but power has shifted from the center in many parts of the globe. The shift from the center makes it more difficult for companies to know with whom they should deal.[20] What is crucial now is ethnic and local politics.

Notes

INTRODUCTION

1. Vermont Financial Services Corp., *1991 Annual Report,* pp. 1–5; Vermont Financial Services Corp., FY 1990 *Annual Report on* [Securities and Exchange Commission] *Form 10-K* (1991), p. 2.
2. Financial data derived from Vermont National Bank Socially Responsible Banking Fund, *Quarterly Progress Report,* December 31, 1991.
3. Nonfinancial information about Vermont National Bank and the SRB Fund provided by David Berge, director, Vermont National Bank Socially Responsible Banking Fund.

CHAPTER 1

1. "The Ethical Way to Invest," *Financial Times* (London), April 14, 1990, p. 6.
2. T. E. Deal and A. A. Kennedy, *Corporate Cultures* (Reading, Mass.: Addison-Wesley, 1982). This may be the only worthwhile pop-biz book published in the last twenty years. The title tells all. Anyone who does not look at corporations as cultures denies their humanness and their capacity to change.
3. Monsanto Corp., *Quarterly Report: Third Quarter, 1991,* October 1991.
4. Interfaith Center on Corporate Responsibility, *Church Proxy Resolutions 1992,* pamphlet (New York, 1992), p. i.
5. D. Vogel, *Lobbying the Corporation* (New York: Basic Books, 1978). This excellent book, now long out-of-print, describes the early shareholder movement. Professor Vogel demonstrated a sharp eye for what the future would bring and for the weaknesses of the movement.
6. Tim Smith, interview with the authors, June 17, 1992.
7. For the text of the resolution, see Interfaith Center on Corporate Responsibility, *Church Proxy Resolutions 1992,* January 1992, pp. 33–34.
8. *The Georgeson Report,* no. 361, as quoted in D. Bratcher, "Will the Social Responsibility Resolution Become an Endangered Species?," *The Corporate Examiner,* vol. 21, no. 1 (1992), p. 3A.
9. As quoted in S. MacNeille, "Architects Have Known Sin," *New York Times Book Review,* December 29, 1991, p. 26.
10. For a brief history of South Shore Bank and of community-development banks, see

D. Osborne, *Laboratories of Democracy* (Cambridge, Mass.: Harvard Business School Press, 1988), pp. 305–12.

11. Lord Macaulay, *The History of England* [1848–1861] (Harmondsworth, U.K.: Penguin Books, 1979), p. 93. Thomas Babington Macaulay, like Winston Churchill, was a politician who wrote great historical narratives to justify his contemporary positions.

12. Richard Hofstadter gave this term currency in *The Age of Reform* (New York: Vintage Books, 1955). He dated the end of the era to the beginning of World War II. The beginning of the ratification process for the XVIII Amendment to the U.S. Constitution (national prohibition)—1916—seems a more likely end.

13. T. Roosevelt, *Autobiography,* as quoted in S. E. Morison, *The Oxford History of the American People* (New York: Oxford University Press, 1964), p. 764.

14. G. G. Atkins, *Religion in Our Times* (New York, 1932), p. 156, as quoted in R. T. Handy, *The Social Gospel in America 1870–1920* (New York: Oxford University Press, 1966), p. 3.

15. As quoted in H. F. Ward, *The Social Creed of the Churches* (New York: Abington Press, 1914), p. 5.

16. J. Train, *Telephone* (New York: Harper & Row, 1976), p. 114.

17. See generally A. D. Chandler, Jr., *The Visible Hand* (Cambridge, Mass.: Belknap Press, 1977).

18. C. W. Powers, *Social Responsibility and Investments* (Nashville, Tenn.: Abington Press, 1971), p. 179.

19. D. Cutler, ed., *The Religious Situation: 1968* (Boston: Beacon Press, 1968).

20. R. W. Morano, *The Protestant Challenge to Corporate America* (Ann Arbor, Mich.: UMI Research Press, 1984), p. 12.

21. Vogel, *Lobbying the Corporation,* pp. 30–33; Powers, *Social Responsibility,* p. 16. The preceeding two paragraphs also rely on these sources.

22. A. Miller, president, Social Investment Forum United Kingdom, conversation with the authors, June 21, 1992; P. Meehau, presentation to the U.K. Social Investment Forum, October 7, 1992.

23. Joan Kanavich, acting executive director, Social Investment Forum, conversation with the authors, June 15, 1992.

CHAPTER 2

1. "The Weed of Liberation," *The Economist,* December 21, 1991, p. 116. James's example is more apt than it might seem, since he controlled import duties, which he used to fund his lavish court. See G. P. V. Akrigg, *The Jacobean Pageant* (New York: Atheneum, 1962), p. 86.

2. C. Silverman, Employee Benefit Research Institute, Washington, D.C., telephone conversation with Kinder, Lydenberg, Domini & Co., June 23, 1992.

3. *Giving USA 1991* (New York: American Association of Fund Raising Counsel, 1991), p. 64. Figure is for 1990.

4. Data drawn from *Standard & Poor's Corporate Stock Guide,* December 1991, p. 244, and "Barron's/Lipper Fund Listings," *Barron's,* November 11, 1991, p. M41.

5. Ibid.

6. All numbers in this section are drawn from "Barron's/Lipper Fund Listings," pp. M23ff.

7. For this definition and the other Lipper definitions discussed below, see "How to Read Our Listings," *Barron's,* November 11, 1991, p. M22.

8. "Economic and Financial Indicators," *The Economist*, November 2, 1991, p. 99.

9. E. Giltenham, "Follow-through: Torray! Torray!," *Forbes*, January 20, 1992, p. 12.

10. P. Hemp, "Mutual Fund Managers Finally Beat the Market," *Boston Globe*, January 5, 1992, pp. 63, 67; F. Williams, "Active Managers Finally Top Market," *Pensions & Investments*, January 20, 1992, pp. 2, 84. Pension-fund managers have not done any better. See "Pension Fund Robbers," *The Economist*, June 20, 1992, p. 84, summarizing J. Lakonishok et al., "The Structure and Performance of the Money Management Industry" (Washington, D.C.: Brookings Institute, 1992).

11. For a more complete description of the Domini Social Index, see the authors' *The Social Investment Almanac* (New York: Henry Holt & Co., 1992), chap. 25.

12. L. Litvak, "Do Social Screens Harm Performance?," *Values* (U.S. Trust Co. of Boston), June 1992, pp. 1, 5.

13. R. Lowry, *Good Money* (New York: W. W. Norton & Co., 1991), pp. 42–48.

14. Fax, Joe Klein, *Good Money*, to Peter Kinder, January 22, 1992, pp. 2, 3.

15. P. L. Bernstein, *Capital Ideas* (New York: Free Press, 1992), pp. 36–38.

16. S. G. Harvey and S. J. Levine, "Another Benchmark Portfolio for Social Investors— Ex Defense Contractors," *Prudential Securities Strategy Weekly*, April 17, 1991, pp. 13ff; idem, "What Is the Cost of Good Intentions? A New Prudential Securities Service," ibid., April 3, 1991, pp. 12ff; idem, "Social Investors Draw a Bead on Weapons Makers," ibid., May 15, 1991, pp. 10ff; idem, "Social Investors and Organized Labor Join Hands in the United States and Mexico," ibid., June 19, 1991, pp. 12ff; idem, "It Paid to Be Environment Friendly in the First Half," ibid., July 17, 1991, pp. 17ff; idem, "Avoid Toxic Polluters and Make Money Too," ibid., August 21, 1991, pp. 14ff.

17. Harvey and Levine, "Another Benchmark Portfolio," p. 16.

18. S. G. Harvey, S. J. Levine, and C. E. Mott, "Social Investors Breathe Easier as Polluters Come Clean," *Prudential Securities Strategy Weekly*, September 16, 1992, pp. 16–18.

19. S. G. Harvey, et al., "The Social Investor Through the Mid-Cap Looking Glass," *Prudential Securities Social Investing Service Update*, March 25, 1992.

20. EIRIS, "The Financial Performance of Ethical Investments" (London, 1988), p. 1. "[In] 1986 Ann Woodall at the City of London Polytechnic found that when applying a broad range of ethical criteria investors could expect no more than a 0.08% loss in return." Ibid.

21. K. Wood, "Ethical Investments in the U.K.—The BARRA/EIRIS Study," *BARRA Newsletter*, March/April 1992, pp. 5–8.

22. World Markets Company, *1989 Annual Review: Charity Fund Service* (London, 1990), p. 4.

23. Harvard College v. Amory, 26 MASS. (9 Pick.) 446, 461 (1830).

24. J. Peebles, "Legal Principles Applicable to Socially Responsible Investment and the Private Trust," paper given at the American Bar Association Section of Real Property, Probate, and Trust Law, Atlanta, Ga., August 13, 1991.

25. ERISA § 404(a)(1)(A); 29 U.S.C. 1104 (a)(1)(A).

26. J. H. Langbein and R. A. Posner, "Social Investing and the Law of Trusts," 79 MICH. L. REV. 72, 73 (1980). It bears noting that then-Professor Posner's field was not trusts or retirement plans in any of their varieties.

27. Ibid., p. 96.

28. Ibid., p. 76.

29. Ibid., p. 99. The following is a listing of the important articles on the subject, most of which were not available to then-Professor Posner. "Note: Environmental In-

vesting: A Suggestion for State Action," *Columbia Journal of Environmental Law* (forthcoming). (It also appears in Kinder, Lydenberg, and Domini, *Social Investment Almanac.*) R. H. Jerry II and O. M. Joy, "Social Investing and the Lessons of South Africa Divestment," 66 ORE. L. REV. 685 (1987); J. C. Dobris, "Arguments in Favor of Fiduciary Divestment of 'South African' Securities," 65 NEB. L. REV. 209 (1986); E. A. Zelinsky, "The Dilemma of the Local Social Investment," 6 CARDOZO L. REV. 111 (1984) (a ground-breaking article in its study of fiduciary responsibilities on alternative investment); and R. B. Ravikoff and M. P. Curzan, "Social Responsibility in Investment Policy and the Prudent Man," 68 CALIF. L. REV. 518 (1980).

30. A. Scott, *The Law of Trusts,* 4th ed. (Fratcher) § 227.17.

31. *Restatement (Third) of Trusts,* § 227 cmt. c (1991).

32. 317 Md. 72, 562 A.2d 720 (1989).

33. At 562 A.2d 737, quoting Dobris, "Arguments in Favor of Fiduciary Divestment," *op. cit.,* p. 232.

34. Ibid.

35. Ibid.

36. Ibid., p. 727.

37. Internal Revenue Service General Counsel Memorandum 39870 (April 7, 1992), *Pension Coordinator,* pp. 94, 358–63 (April 27, 1992).

38. Joan Shapiro, speech, Midwest Bridges Conference, Chicago, June 14, 1990.

CHAPTER 3

1. "Socially Responsible Investing," "NBC Nightly News," March 1, 1992.

2. This screen is loosely adapted from the environmental screen of the Calvert World Values Global Equity Fund.

3. Bishop of Oxford v. Church Commissioners (Queen's Bench), as reported in *The Independent* (U.K.), October 25, 1991.

4. Revised Model Business Corporation Act (1984), § 16.20(a). State law controls the organization and governance of corporations domiciled in that state. The Model Act and the Delaware and the New York codes are the most influential.

5. E. I. du Pont de Nemours and Co., *Annual Report (1990),* p. 8.

6. Ibid., p. 17.

7. J. L. Garcia, M. L. Mayer, and D. C. Silver, *E. I. du Pont de Nemours and Company,* pamphlet (New York: Wertheim Schroeder & Co., Inc., 1991).

8. S. Hemmerick, "Schroeder Goof Costs $662,974," *Pensions & Investments,* June 8, 1992, p. 1.

9. D. Spittles, "Cashing In on Guilt-Free Gains," *London Evening Standard,* May 6, 1992. For more detail on the U.K. situation, see EIRIS, "Alcohol, Tobacco and Gambling: A Briefing for the Ethical Investor," London, 1992.

10. "The Delight of Digital Maps," *The Economist,* March 21, 1992, p. 69.

11. P. Camejo, "Year One: The Proenvironmental Funds Outperform Wall Street," in P. D. Kinder, S. D. Lydenberg, and A. L. Domini, eds., *The Social Investment Almanac* (New York: Henry Holt & Co., 1992), pp. 479–88.

12. See generally R. B. Sobol, *Bending the Law* (University of Chicago Press, 1991). Anyone tempted to believe the stories about massive abuses by the plaintiffs' bar in product-liability cases should study A. H. Robins's defense of the Dalkon Shield and the asbestos manufacturers' decades-long struggle to avoid liability.

CHAPTER 4

1. B. Burrough and J. Helyar, *Barbarians at the Gate* (New York: Harper & Row, 1990), p. 218.
2. Rudolf "Minnesota Fats" Wanderone, as quoted in "Ask the Globe," *Boston Globe,* October 2, 1991, p. 36.
3. "Discussing the Constitutional Right to Booze," *The Economist,* December 21, 1991, pp. 29–30.
4. Interfaith Center on Corporate Responsibility, *Church Proxy Resolutions 1992* (New York, 1992), p. 10.
5. Ibid., pp. 1–4.
6. Ibid., pp. 7, 8.
7. Ibid., p. 9; ICCR, *Church Proxy Resolutions 1991* (New York, 1991), p. 53.
8. Ibid., p. 12.
9. Ibid., p. 50.
10. *"Rien ne va plus,"* *The Economist,* December 15, 1990, p. 23.
11. R. Cohen, "A Las Vegas for the Orlando Crowd," *New York Times,* October 2, 1991, pp. D1, D5. See also J. R. Nash, *Bloodletters and Badmen* (New York: M. Evans & Co., 1973), pp. 500–504.
12. Department of Defense, Directorate for Information, Operations & Reports, *100 Companies Receiving the Largest Dollar Volume of Prime Contract Awards Fiscal Year 1990* (Washington, D.C., 1990), p. 7. This publication is cited hereafter as *DOD FY90.*
13. Ibid.
14. Nuclear Free America, *Defense Contractors FY 1989* (CD-ROM data base).
15. *DOD FY90,* p. 7.
16. Ibid.
17. Ibid.
18. Ibid., p. 22.

CHAPTER 5

1. "The Ethical Way to Invest," *Financial Times* (London), April 14, 1990, p. 6.
2. L. Thompson, *A History of South Africa* (New Haven: Yale University Press, 1990), p. 92.
3. C. P. Thunberg, *Travels at the Cape of Good Hope* [1773], ed. V. S. Forbes (Cape Town, 1986), p. 153, as quoted in ibid., p. 43.
4. T. R. H. Davenport, *South Africa,* 4th ed. (Toronto: University of Toronto Press, 1991), pp. 105–106.
5. Ibid., p. 336ff.
6. Thompson, *History of South Africa,* p. 217.
7. D. Vogel, *Lobbying the Corporation* (New York: Basic Books, 1978), p. 85.
8. Ibid., pp. 175–76.
9. Ibid., p. 179.
10. Ibid., pp. 179–80.
11. See W. Somplatsky-Jarman, "South Africa Shareholder Resolutions," in P. D. Kinder, S. D. Lydenberg, and A. L. Domini, eds., *The Social Investment Almanac* (New York: Henry Holt & Co., 1992).
12. Vogel, *Lobbying,* p. 177.

13. "1992 Proxy Season Update—23 March 1992," *The Corporate Examiner,* vol. 20, no. 10, 1991, pp. 3–4.

14. See generally K. Paul and D. Aquila, "Trade Sanctions, Ethical Investing, and Social Change in South Africa," in Kinder, Lydenberg, and Domini, *Social Investment Almanac.*

15. "Mobil's Board Clears Sale of Operations in South Africa, Citing Onerous U.S. Laws," *New York Times,* May 1, 1989, p. B14.

16. T. Furlong, "J. Robert Fluor Dies of Cancer," *Los Angeles Times,* September 10, 1984, pp. 1, 3.

17. C. Lazzareschi, "Fluor Sells Unit in South Africa," *Los Angeles Times,* December 6, 1986.

18. "South Africa," *The Corporate Examiner,* vol. 20, no. 4 (1991), p. 6.

19. Ibid.

20. G. M. Fredrickson, "No Going Back for Either Side," *New York Times Book Review,* April 5, 1992, p. 3, citing the Investor Responsibility Research Center.

21. Ibid., p. 234.

22. Cited in "Colleges Wary of Easing Curbs on South Africa," *New York Times,* December 22, 1991.

23. J. Authers, "Not Just a Black and White Choice," *Financial Times,* June 27/28, 1992, p. v.

24. As quoted in V. Blackburn, "First Among Equals," *Investors Chronicle* (U.K.), November 1, 1991, p. 17.

25. Tim Smith, executive director, ICCR, conversation with the authors, June 17, 1992.

26. "Businessman's Burden," *The Economist,* November 3, 1990, p. 14.

CHAPTER 6

1. M. Lubber, communication with the authors, July 7, 1992.

2. "The Greening of McDonald's, *Restaurant and Institutions,* December 26, 1990, p. 28.

3. See S. Hume and P. Strand, "Consumers Go Green," *Advertising Age,* September 25, 1989. The article cites a Gallup survey in which U.S. adults responded between 87 percent and 96 percent in favor of better environmental packaging, even at higher prices and a loss of convenience.

4. "McDonald's and the Environment," Case N9-391-108, Publishing Division, Harvard Business School, 1990, pp. 14–15; "Management Brief: Food for Thought," *The Economist,* August 29, 1992, pp. 64, 66.

5. James M. Schoessler, Esq., interview with the authors, May 13, 1992. In the words of a lawyer deeply involved in the case, Reserve was "the case that wouldn't die." It took years of litigation and negotiation to reach this stage. And, the path was strewn with mines—land mines.

6. Joan Bavaria, presentation at the Social Investment Forum panel on Codes of Conduct, June 15, 1992.

7. "CERES' Impact on Corporate Environmental Performance," *On Principle,* Summer 1992, pp. 4–5.

8. The Global Tomorrow Coalition, W. H. Corson, ed., *The Global Ecology Handbook* (Boston: Beacon Press, 1990), p. 246.

9. Ibid. The most complete guide to toxic substances is J. Harte et al., *Toxics A to Z* (Berkeley: University of California Press, 1991).

10. Global Tomorrow Coalition, *Global Ecology Handbook,* p. 246.

11. S. Postel, *Defusing the Toxic Threat,* Worldwatch Paper 79 (Washington, D.C.: Worldwatch Institute, September 1987), p. 8.

12. Ibid.

13. Ibid.

14. See, e.g., "The Toxic Mess Called Superfund," *Business Week,* May 11, 1992, p. 32.

15. E. T. Smith, "Why AT&T Is Dialing 1 800 GO GREEN," *Business Week,* Quality 1991 issue, April 25, 1991, p. 49.

16. "Toxic Terrorism Invades Third World Nations," *Black Enterprise,* November 1988, p. 31.

17. Food and Drug Administration, *Residues in Food,* 1987, as cited in World Resources Institute, *1992 Information Please Environmental Almanac* (Boston: Houghton Mifflin, 1992), p. 46.

18. J. Harte, et al., *Toxics A to Z,* pp. 268–70.

19. *1992 Information Please Environmental Almanac,* pp. 43, 49–51.

20. J. Keehn, "Mean Green," *Buzzworm,* January/February 1992, p. 33.

21. *1992 Information Please Environmental Almanac,* pp. 155–56.

22. Derived from data of British Petroleum, *BP Statistical Review of World Energy, 1989* (London, 1989), p. 34.

23. S. D. Lydenberg, "Clearing the Air: Franklin's Insight Study of Natural Gas and the Environment" (Boston: Franklin Research and Development Corp., 1989), p. 5–6.

24. Global Tomorrow Coalition *Global Ecology Handbook,* p. 194.

25. "Big Stink on the Farm," *Business Week,* July 20, 1992, p. 31.

26. S. Budiansky, *The Covenant of the Wild* (New York: William Morrow & Co., 1992), p. 159.

27. A. Jack, "Bank Bans Blood Sport Accounts over Ethics," *Financial Times,* April 24, 1992, p. 9; "Co-op Takes a Stand," *Financial Times,* May 2/3, 1992, p. iv. See also *The Co-operative Bank: What We Are and What We Stand for,* an undated pamphlet that expands on the screens.

28. *Covenant of the Wild,* pp. 10–11.

29. P. Singer, *Animal Liberation* (New York: Avon Books, 1977), pp. x–xiii.

30. Ibid., p. 7.

31. "Animal Rights: Man's Mirror," *The Economist,* November 16, 1991, pp. 21–24.

32. P. Camejo, "Year One: The Proenvironmental Funds Outperform Wall Street," in P. D. Kinder, S. D. Lydenberg, and A. L. Domini, eds., *The Social Investment Almanac* (New York: Henry Holt & Co., 1992), p. 481.

33. W. Rathje and C. Murphy, *Rubbish!* (New York: HarperCollins, 1992), pp. 161–62. To say the least, it is infuriating that this important book lacks an index, footnotes, and a bibliography.

34. Ibid., pp. 188ff.

35. D. L. Dadd and A. Carothers, "Greenlabeling," *Greenpeace,* May/June 1990, as quoted in *Is It Really Green?,* pamphlet (Colchester, Vt.: Seventh Generation Publications, 1990), pp. 4–5.

36. Isaiah 2:4.

37. J. Mooney, "The Ghost Dance Religion and the Sioux Outbreak of 1890," *Annual Report of the Bureau of Ethnology to the Smithsonian Institution,* 1892–1893, XIV, pt. 2, 72, as quoted in A. W. Crosby, *Ecological Imperialism* (Cambridge: Cambridge University Press, 1986), p. 291.

CHAPTER 7

1. M. Waldholz, "B-M-Squibb Co. to Give Away Its Heart Drugs to Those Who Can't Pay," *Wall Street Journal,* January 24, 1992, no p.n.
2. Cited in "Philanthropy Is Not Marketing," *Responsive Philanthropy,* Summer 1991, p. 9.
3. "Doing More with Less: Corporations Donate Volunteers," *New York Times,* October 29, 1989, p. F13.
4. "On Company Time: The New Volunteerism," *Business Ethics,* March/April 1992, p. 33.
5. See generally "Room for Improvement," *Franklin's Insight,* January 1988.
6. D. Cordtz, "Corporate America's New Mission: Housing the Poor," *Financial World,* November 29, 1988, p. 26. The article lists two dozen companies participating in these ventures. See also the sources cited in the balance of this section.
7. LISC, 1991 Annual Report, per phone conversation.
8. The National Equity Fund, *1991 Limited Partnership: Executive Summary,* (Chicago, 1990).
9. P. Kruger, "A Game Plan for the Future," *Working Woman,* January 1990, p. 74.
10. "Why We Should Invest in Human Capital," *Business Week,* December 17, 1990, p. 89.
11. See *Workforce 2000* (Indianapolis: The Hudson Institute, 1987).
12. R. B. Reich, "Metamorphosis of the American Worker," *Business Month,* November 1990, pp. 58–66.
13. Ibid., p. 59.
14. C. Strickland, "A Risk Worth Taking," *Foundation News,* September/October 1989, p. 21.
15. E. Branch, "Can Business Save Our Schools?," *Black Enterprise,* March 1991, p. 49.
16. Ibid., p. 50.
17. A. Atkins, "Big Business and Education," *Better Homes and Gardens,* March 1991, p. 32.
18. J. Novack, "Earning and Learning," *Forbes,* May 11, 1992, p. 150.
19. Kruger, "Game Plan," p. 75.
20. Ibid., pp. 74–75.
21. "City Joins Local's Fight to Retain Jobs," *AFL-CIO News,* March 19, 1988.
22. J. B. White, "Worker's Revenge," *Wall Street Journal,* March 8, 1988, p. 1.
23. Ibid.
24. As quoted in Investors Responsibility Research Center (IRRC), "Proxy Issues Report: Plant Closings," *IRRC Social Issues Service* (Washington, DC: Investor Responsibility Research Center Inc., March 15, 1989), p. O-4. This report provides excellent coverage of the important economic studies of plant closings and their effects on workers and communities.
25. L. C. Thurow, *The Zero Sum Society* (New York: Penguin, 1981), p. 77.
26. B. Bluestone and B. Harrison, *The Deindustrialization of America* (New York: Basic Books, 1988).
27. IRRC, "Plant Closings," p. O-6.
28. Ibid., p. O-4.
29. A. Mariano, "Blacks Having Difficult Time Buying Homes," *Washington Post,* August 11, 1990, p. E1.
30. C. N. Rosenthal, "Community Development Credit Unions," in P. D. Kinder, S. D.

Lydenberg & A. L. Domini, eds., *The Social Investment Almanac* (Henry Holt & Co., 1992), pp. 575–76.

CHAPTER 8

1. R. P. Phalon, "Miscalculated Risk?," *Forbes,* June 12, 1989, p. 41; "Labor Ruling Finds Coal Company Guilty in Strike," *New York Times,* July 12, 1989, p. A10.
2. F. Norris, "Unusual Proxy Fight at Pittston," *New York Times,* May 5, 1989, p. D1; "The Mine Workers Must Win This Fight to Survive," *Business Week,* October 9, 1989, p. 144.
3. "Pittston Should Stand By Its Promises," *Business Week,* October 9, 1989, p. 182.
4. Cited in "Labor Ruling Finds Coal Company Guilty in Strike," *New York Times,* July 12, 1989, p. A10.
5. M. A. Versepej, "Labor Will Be the Partner, Not the Enemy," *Industry Week,* April 18, 1988, p. 31.
6. "Phelps Dodge Workers Vote Against Union," *Dun's Business Month,* March 1985, p. 21.
7. J. Rosenblum, "The Dismal Precedent That Gave Us Caterpillar," *Wall Street Journal,* April 16, 1992, p. A25. *See also* P. T. Kilborn, "Caterpillar's Trump Card," *New York Times,* April 16, 1992, p. A1.
8. L. Silk, "Worrying Over Weakened Unions," *New York Times,* December 13, 1991, p. D2.
9. G. N. Smith, "Stronger Unions?," *Financial World,* January 21, 1992, p. 8.
10. As this book was being written, a hearing officer for the National Labor Relations Board issued an opinion that would, if upheld by the Board itself, effectively end the use of the team approach on factory floors. "Putting a Damper on That Old Team Spirit," *Business Week,* May 4, 1992, p. 40; J. Novack, "Make Them All Form Unions," *Forbes,* May 11, 1992, p. 174.
11. Estimate made by National Safe Workplace Institute, Chicago.
12. S. Cohen, "Danger at Work," *Los Angeles Times,* October 29, 1989.
13. R. D. Hershey, Jr., "Meatpacker Fined a Record Amount on Plant Injuries," *New York Times,* October 29, 1988.
14. "Repetitive Stress: The Pain Has Just Begun," *Business Week,* July 13, 1992, p. 142.
15. D. Kirkpatrick, "How Safe Are Video Terminals?" *Fortune,* August 29, 1988, p. 66.
16. As quoted in P. Keepnews, "Read His Lips," *New York Times Book Review,* May 24, 1992, p. 6, quoting J. Bines, A. Sullivan, and J. Weisberg, eds., *Bushisms* (New York: Workman, 1992).
17. J. Cohen, E. Zinbarg, and A. Zeikel, *Investment Analysis and Portfolio Management,* 5th ed. (Homewood, Ill.: Irwin, 1987), p. 230.
18. K. Springen, "Can No-Layoff Policies Survive the Recession?," *Business Ethics,* November/December 1991, p. 15.
19. Ibid., p. 15.
20. N. J. Perry, "Here Come Richer, Riskier Pay Plans," *Fortune,* December 19, 1988, p. 51.
21. Ibid., p. 51.
22. "Improving 401(k)s," *Pensions & Investments,* April 13, 1992, p. 14.
23. "Gainsharing for Fun and Profit," *The Employee Ownership Report,* vol. VIII, no. 6, November/December 1988, p. 7.
24. *Employee Ownership Report,* vol. XI, no. 1, January/February 1991, p. 11.

25. See "New Research Shows More Positive Results from Employee Ownership," *Employee Ownership Report,* vol. X, no. 6, November/December 1990, pp. 1, 4–5.

26. "ESOPs: Are They Good for You?," *Business Week,* May 15, 1989, p. 117.

27. "Willing and Able," *Business Week,* October 28, 1991, p. 15.

28. Allstate Insurance Company, *AIDS: Corporate America Responds,* n.d., n.p.

29. J. J. Koch, "Wells Fargo's and IBM's HIV Policies Help Protect Employees' Rights," *Personnel Journal,* April 1990, pp. 40–51.

30. "Lack of Health Insurance Puts Many on the Edge," *Boston Sunday Globe/North Weekly,* April 5, 1992, p. 8.

31. G. Milkovich and J. Newman, *Compensation,* 3rd ed. (Homewood, Ill.: BPI/Irwin, 1990), p. 415.

32. Ibid., pp. 369–70.

33. G. B. Trudeau, *But the Pension Fund Was Just Sitting There* (New York: Holt, Rinehart & Winston, 1979), n.p.

34. This pattern, albeit much reduced, continues today. See, e.g., R. L. Stern and R. Abelson, "The Imperial Agees," *Forbes,* June 8, 1992, pp. 88, 91–92.

35. A. Sloan, "GM Returns to Basics, Sells Stock," *Boston Globe,* May 3, 1992, p. 82.

36. R. Zolkos, "Cash-hungry States Scare Public Funds," *Pensions & Investments,* June 8, 1992, p. 33.

37. "Improving 401(k)s," p. 14.

38. For an excellent, if critical, overview (on which we have drawn significantly), see S. Sasso, "Public Pension Dos and Don'ts," *Regional Review* (Federal Reserve Bank of Boston), Spring 1992, pp. 21–24.

39. C. B. Knoll, presentation to Investment Management Institute Tenth Annual Portfolio Management Conference, May 30, 1991.

40. "Funds Put Assets in Social Investment," *Pensions & Investments,* July 6, 1992, p. 33.

41. Sasso, "Public Pension Dos and Don'ts," pp. 23–24.

CHAPTER 9

1. D. Levine, "The Quality Movement," *Dollars & Sense,* September 1992, p. 20.

2. "At Rubbermaid, Little Things Mean a Lot," *Business Week,* November 11, 1991, p. 126.

3. For an excellent discussion of Deming's contribution to quality control in Japan and the United States, see A. Gabor, *The Man Who Invented Quality* (New York: Times Books, 1990).

4. S. Caudron, "How Xerox Won the Baldrige," *Personnel Journal,* April 1991, p. 98.

5. Ibid.

6. "1992 Award Criteria, Malcolm Baldrige National Quality Award" (Gaithersburg, Md.: U.S. Department of Commerce, Technology Administration, National Institute of Standards and Technology, 1991), p. 30. It takes the Department of Commerce 36 mind-numbing, double-columned 8½-by-11-inch pages to describe the award process. But we are informed on page i, "If you plan to apply for the Award in 1992, you will also need to obtain a second document entitled '1992 Application Forms and Instructions,' as soon as possible." (Italics and emphasis omitted.)

7. W. Glaberson, "Listening to the Consumer Again," *New York Times,* April 6, 1988.

8. "Future Perfect," *The Economist,* January 4, 1992, p. 61.

9. K. B. Clarz, *Product Development Superiority* (Boston, Harvard Business School Press, 1991).

10. "Where Did They Go Wrong?" *Business Week,* October 25, 1991, p. 34.
11. "Quality Programs May Be Shoddy Stuff," *Wall Street Journal,* October 4, 1990.
12. F. Rose, "Now Quality Means Service Too," *Fortune,* April 22, 1991, p. 102.
13. D. I. Levine, *op. cit.,* pp. 20–22.
14. "Where Did They Go Wrong?," p. 34.
15. Ibid., pp. 34–35.
16. J. Main, "Is the Baldrige Overblown?," *Fortune,* July 1991, p. 62.
17. John Hancock Financial Services, Louis Harris Associates, as cited in *Boston Globe,* November 19, 1990, p. 47.
18. P. Sellers, "How to Handle Customers' Gripes," *Fortune,* October 24, 1988, p. 92.
19. Dow-Corning announced in March 1992 that it would no longer manufacture or sell silicon breast implants.
20. "The Gillette Company: Liquid Paper (A)," Case 9-389-070, Publishing Division, Harvard Business School, 1988, pp. 1–5.
21. F. Rice, "Leaders of the Most Admired," *Fortune,* January 29, 1990, p. 40.
22. Ibid.
23. R. A. G. Monks and N. Minow, *Power and Accountability* (New York: Harper-Business, 1991), pp. 126–29.

CHAPTER 10

1. As quoted in "Fighting to Break the Chain," *New York Times Book Review,* February 2, 1992, p. 31.
2. P. Keepnews, "Read His Lips," *New York Times Book Review,* May 24, 1992, p. 6, quoting J. Bines, A. Sullivan, and J. Weisberg, eds., *Bushisms* (New York: Workman, 1992).
3. D. Vogel, *Lobbying the Corporation* (New York: Basic Books, 1978), pp. 71ff.
4. J. Fierman, "Why Women Still Don't Hit the Top," *Fortune,* July 30, 1990.
5. Based on 1990 median earnings for full-time workers. U.S. Bureau of the Census, as quoted in K. Pennar, "Women Are Still Paid the Wages of Discrimination," *Business Week,* October 28, 1991, p. 35.
6. Equal Employment Opportunities Commission, 1990.
7. "Race and Money," *Money,* December 1989.
8. W. B. Johnston and A. H. Packer, *Workforce 2000: Work and Workers for the 21st Century* (Indianapolis: Hudson Institute, 1987), p. 95.
9. F. N. Schwartz, *Breaking with Tradition* (New York: Warner Books, 1992).
10. E. Galinsky, D. E. Friedman, and C. A. Hernandez, *Corporate Reference Guide to Work-Family Programs* (New York: Families and Work Institute, 1991).
11. M. Moskowitz and C. Townsend, "The 85 Best Companies for Working Mothers," *Working Mother,* October 1991, pp. 29ff.
12. Ibid., pp. 29, 54.
13. E.g., "The Mommy Track," *Business Week,* March 20, 1989, pp. 126–27.
14. Adapted from a shareholder resolution submitted for the 1992 proxy season to Dayton-Hudson, K Mart, May Department Stores, and Wal-Mart, as quoted in *Church Proxy Resolutions,* Interfaith Center on Corporate Responsibility, January 1992, p. 33.
15. As quoted in Monks and Minow, *Power and Accountability,* p. 77.
16. S. H. Tucker and K. D. Thompson, "Will Diversity = Opportunity + Advancement for Blacks?," *Black Enterprise,* November 1990, pp. 52–53.
17. "25 Best Places for Blacks to Work," *Black Enterprise,* February 1992, pp. 72–96.

18. Ibid., p. 94.
19. C. Coy, "Let's Make a Deal," *Hispanic,* December 1990, pp. 20–23.
20. Ibid., p. 23.
21. L. L. Castro, "More Firms 'Gender Train' to Bridge the Chasms That Still Divide the Sexes," *Wall Street Journal,* January 2, 1992, pp. B11, 14. Also see "Women at Work," *Business Week,* August 6, 1990, p. 53.
22. C. Hymowitz, "One Firm's Bid to Keep Blacks, Women," *Wall Street Journal,* February 16, 1989, p. B1.
23. "25 Best Places for Blacks," p. 96.
24. *Board of Directors Seventeenth Annual Study, 1990,* Korn Ferry International, New York, 1990.
25. J. Eckhouse, "High Pay, Few Hours for Members of Boards," *San Francisco Chronicle,* December 8, 1990.
26. Moskowitz and Townsend, "85 Best Companies," p. 34.

CHAPTER 11

1. A. Bierce, *The Devil's Dictionary* [1906], as reprinted in *The Collected Writings of Ambrose Bierce* (New York: Citadel Books, 1946), p. 216.
2. J. Schwartz, "Sears Shareholders Strike Discordant Note," *New York Times,* May 15, 1992, p. D1.
3. The Apprentices' Fund Case (Franklin's Adm'x v. Philadelphia), 13 Pa. C. 241, 247 (C.P. 1893).
4. A. Smith, *The Wealth of Nations* [5th ed., 1789] (Chicago: University of Chicago Press, 1976), vol. 1, pp. 138–39, 144–45.
5. W. Werner and S. Smith, *Wall Street* (New York: Columbia University Press, 1991), p. 244, n. 2.
6. Smith, *Wealth of Nations,* vol. 2, p. 265; D. L. Ratner, "The Government of Business Corporations," 56 CORNELL L. REV. 1, 3–5 (1970).
7. Ibid. We have substituted modern American terms in brackets for Smith's archaic terms. They do not alter his meaning.
8. Ibid., pp. 264–65.
9. J. S. Davis, *Essays in the Earlier History of American Corporations* (Cambridge, Mass.: Harvard University Press, 1917), vol. 2, p. 24, as cited in L. M. Friedman, *A History of American Law,* 2nd ed. (New York: Simon and Schuster, 1985), p. 189.
10. A. D. Chandler, *The Visible Hand* (Cambridge, Mass.: Belknap Press, 1977), pp. 36ff.
11. Smith, *Wealth of Nations,* vol. 2, p. 264.
12. Werner and Smith, *Wall Street,* pp. 158–59.
13. L. Hartz, *Economic Policy and Democratic Thought* (1948), p. 38, as discussed in Friedman, *American Law,* p. 189.
14. W. F. Swindler, *Court and Constitution in the Twentieth Century* (Indianapolis: Bobbs-Merrill Co., 1969), vol. 1, p. 36.
15. Ibid., p. 37. Swindler is summarizing the views of Judge Thomas M. Cooley, perhaps the most influential writer on constitutional law in this bleak period.
16. Ibid., p. 36. See in particular Santa Clara County v. Southern Pacific R.R. Co., 118 U.S. 394 (1886).
17. The cases referred to here restricted the application of the ancient writ of quo warranto. This writ, whose Latin name is translated "by what authority," was used

by the crown to enforce the terms of its charters to both corporations and officials it had appointed. (The application of a common remedy here should answer those who argue that historically chartered entities did not have a quasipublic role.) Quo warranto was the device used in the first successful antimonopoly case, by Ohio against the Standard Oil Company in 1891. By 1940 the writ was, for all practical purposes, not available in Ohio or elsewhere, to enforce corporate obligations to society.

18. A. A. Berle and G. Means, *The Modern Corporation and Private Property,* rev. ed. [1968] (New Brunswick, N.J.: Transaction Publishers, 1991), p. 251.

19. Ibid., pp. 3–9.

20. Ibid., p. 4.

21. See generally Werner and Smith, *Wall Street.* The late Professor Werner's law journal articles, cited in *Wall Street*'s bibliography (p. 296), bear close reading.

22. P. L. Bernstein, *Capital Ideas* (New York: Free Press, 1992); pp. 4, 91.

23. R. A. G. Monks and N. Minow, *Power and Accountability* (New York: Harper-Business, 1991), pp. 3–19.

24. See, for example, "Sears Shareholder Revolt Is Cooling," *Pensions & Investments,* May 11, 1992, pp. 1, 26.

25. Monks and Minow, *Power and Accountability,* p. 4.

26. Ibid., p. 181.

27. Ibid.

28. Ibid., pp. 84ff.

29. B. Burr, "Appalling Compliance of Directors," *Pensions & Investments,* April 27, 1992, p. 8.

30. Ratner, "Government of Business Corporations," pp. 25–26.

31. E. J. Waitzer, "Are Institutional Investors Really Impacting Corporate Governance?," *Canadian Investment Review,* Fall 1991, pp. 9, 10.

32. M. T. Jacobs, *Short Term America: The Causes and Cures of Our Business Myopia* (Boston: Harvard Business School Press, 1991), p. 73.

33. Ibid., p. 70.

34. Monks and Minow, *Power and Accountability,* p. 181. See generally Bernstein, *Capital Ideas,* which explores in detail the theorists underpinning Monks and Minow's argument.

35. T. Cedraschi as quoted in "Corporations and Institutional Investors: Five Key Players Look Ahead," *Canadian Investment Review,* Fall 1991, pp. 17, 23.

36. Ibid. For a contrasting view, *see* Waitzer, *Institutional Investors Impacting,* pp. 9, 10.

37. J. A. Maunder, as quoted in "Corporations and Institutional Investors," pp. 17, 20.

38. See, e.g., S. B. Graves and S. A. Waddock, "Institutional Ownership and Control: Implications for Long-Term Corporate Strategy," *Academy of Management Executives,* vol. 4, no. 1 (1990), p. 75.

39. N. Cohen, "Institutions Tackle 'Short-Termism,' " *Financial Times,* April 30, 1992, p. 8.

40. Ratner, "Government of Business Corporations," p. 18.

41. J. Chernoff, "Funds Pull No Punches with Champion CEO," *Pensions & Investments,* April 27, 1992, p. 30.

42. M. Moskowitz, R. Levering, and M. Katz, eds., *Everybody's Business* (New York: Doubleday, 1990), p. 501.

43. Chernoff, *Fords Pull No Punches.* Astoundingly, the article does not give a date for

the Council's annual meeting. For another, much more positive view of Mr. Sigler, see S. Oliver, "The Day They Booed Andy Sigler," *Forbes,* May 11, 1992, p. 46.

44. C. Cox and S. Power, "Executive Pay: How Much Is Too Much?" *Business Ethics,* September/October 1991, p. 18.

45. G. S. Crystal, *In Search of Excess* (New York: Norton, 1992).

46. "How CEO Paychecks Got So Unreal," *Business Week,* November 18, 1991, p. 20.

47. J. Lorsch, *Pawn and Potentates: The Reality of America's Corporate Boards* (Boston: Harvard Business School Press, 1989), p. 12.

48. See Jacobs, *Short Term America,* pp. 79–80.

49. M. G. Star, "Avon CEO Tackles Compensation Issue," *Pensions & Investments,* November 11, 1991.

50. N. M. Better, "A Hidden Upside in All the Downsizing," *New York Times,* October 24, 1991.

51. Cox and Power, "Executive Pay," p. 19.

52. Ibid., p. 22.

53. K. G. Salwen, "The People's Proxy," *Wall Street Journal,* February 13, 1992.

CHAPTER 12

1. N. Tait, "Chink in the Armour of US Regulation," *Financial Times,* June 14, 1992, p. 23.

2. T. Watterson, "Investment Options Going International," *Boston Globe,* October 10, 1991, pp. 77, 83.

3. Securities and Exchange Commission, "American Depositary Receipts," Securities Act Release No. 6894, Exchange Act Release no. 29226, International Series Release no. 274, May 23, 1991; N. Tait, "SEC May Relax Rules for Foreign Fund Sales in US," *Financial Times,* May 22, 1992, p. 1; D. B. Henriques, "S.E.C. Asks for Sweeping Changes in Rules Governing Mutual Funds," *New York Times,* May 22, 1992, p. A1.

4. C. Makin, "The Rise of the Superleague," *Institutional Investor,* October 1991, pp. 190, 193.

5. Ibid.

6. F. Norris, "At the S.E.C., Another Move for Secrecy," *New York Times,* October 13, 1991, p. F1.

7. A. Lewis, "Mr. Maxwell's Lesson," *New York Times,* December 12, 1991, p. A18; F. Norris, "Maxwell Saga: Bad Accounting Aided Fraud," *New York Times,* December 3, 1991, p. F1; Taki, "When Libeling in Britain, It's Best to Stick with Dead Men," *New York Observer,* May 4, 1992, p. 15.

8. "Capitalism's Creative Destruction," *The Economist,* April 4, 1992, p. 15.

9. R. Reich, "Who Is Us?," *Harvard Business Review,* January-February 1990, p. 55.

10. *Catalyst,* vol. VIII, nos. 3 and 4, p. 13.

11. E. Mattlin, "Money Management Notes: The Currency Conundrum," *Institutional Investor,* September 1991, p. 177. *II* should have noted that tax laws in the United Kingdom and the United States make it prohibitively complicated to invest in mutual funds across national borders. To this extent, the comparison is an unjust one, since British investors do not have the option of buying U.S. mutual funds.

12. As quoted in E. Foner, "She Didn't Know Her Place," *New York Times Book Review,* January 26, 1992, pp. 13–14, reviewing D. Sterling, *Ahead of Her Time: Abby Kelley and the Politics of Antislavery* (New York: W. W. Norton & Co., 1991).

13. As quoted in J. S. Nye, Jr., "The Company We Keep," *New York Times Book Review,*

December 15, 1991, pp. 16–17, reviewing D. Pipes and A. Garfinkle, eds., *Friendly Tyrants* (New York: St. Martin's Press, 1991).

14. "Oppressive Regimes," *The Ethical Consumer,* February/March/April 1992, pp. 16, 21. See also R. Sivard, *World Military and Social Expenditures 1991,* 14th ed. (World Priorities, 1991) and "Oppressive Regimes" (London: Ethical Investment Research Services, 1992). The latter formed the basis for *Ethical Consumer*'s work, but it is singularly un–user friendly.

15. "Myanmar Investments Raise Ire of U.S. Churches," *Responsive Investing News,* May 25, 1992, pp. 4–5.

16. "Petro-Canada to Review Myanmar, Social Responsibility Policies," *Responsive Investing News,* May 11, 1992, pp. 1, 4.

17. A. Schwimmer, "Social Issues Won't Be Swept Out," *Pensions & Investments,* March 30, 1992, p. 16.

18. "Will California's Anti-China Syndrome Spread?," *Business Week,* July 24, 1989, p. 33.

19. J. Barnathan, "It's Time to Put the Screws to China's Gulag Economy," *Business Week,* December 30, 1991, p. 52.

20. Ibid.

Glossary*

affirmative action program A description, prepared in compliance with federal civil rights laws, of an entity's plans to hire, train, and promote minority workers and women.

agricultural chemicals Artificial substances manufactured by the chemical or petrochemical industries that are used in farming. Fertilizers, herbicides, insecticides, and pesticides are the most important types.

air pollution The contaminants or pollutants in the air that do not disperse properly and that interfere with human health or produce other harmful environmental effects.

alternative investment A catch-all term used to describe any social investment that does not fit into the category of a publicly traded security or mutual fund. See **community-development investment.**

animal rights A philosophy based on the assumption that nonhuman species are sentient beings due the same consideration humans extend to other humans.

asset Anything one owns that has commercial or exchange value.

back end of the fuel cycle The disposal of spent nuclear fuel and contaminated water used to cool a nuclear reactor.

backtesting The use of computer modeling to analyze how a portfolio might have performed in the past.

benchmark A standard against which something is measured; a reference point.

beneficiary A person for whose benefit funds are managed.

benefit A service or noncash compensation an employee receives that

*Adapted from *The KLD Social Investment Lexicon*. Copyright © 1992 by Kinder, Lydenberg, Domini & Co., Inc. All rights reserved. Adapted by permission.

the employer pays for or facilitates, such as insurance, pension, and vacation time.

beta A measurement of the fluctuation in portfolios and securities due to marketwide events; a measurement of a portfolio's sensitivity to changes in an underlying index.

big cap Of or relating to a company whose market capitalization places it among the largest publicly traded companies.

buy list The investments that an investment adviser has researched and recommends.

CEO Chief executive officer.

closed-loop recycling Reclaiming or reusing in an enclosed process; the remanufacturing of a material to its original use, such as a glass or aluminum container into another container.

cogeneration A process that produces simultaneously heat and electrical or another form of energy from a single source.

community-development bank A financial institution regulated by either a state or federal agency whose business is the permanent, long-term economic development of low- and moderate-income communities and which targets loan resources to residents of its primary service area.

community-development investment A grant made primarily to support or encourage community development that is paid back and may produce income. Such grants are sometimes called "community investments," or "direct" or "economically targeted" or "high social impact" investments. They may take the form of loans or deposits in financial institutions often at below-market rates of return.

Comprehensive Environmental Response, Compensation and Liability Act (CERCLA) This federal law, as amended by the Superfund and Reauthorization Act (SARA), established the **Superfund** program to clean up hazardous-waste sites.

control The power of a shareholder or a group of shareholders has to run a corporation.

corporate governance The manner in which a corporation is operated from the top; the structure defining the ultimate management of a corporation, stated in articles of incorporation and bylaws; the relationships between and among the shareholders, senior management, and the board of directors.

corporation A form of business that comes into existence when the secretary of state of a state issues a certificate of incorporation and whose owners' liability for its debts ordinarily is limited to the amount of their investment.

damages A monetary valuation made by a court of the effects of a party's injury; money paid to an injured party that compensates for an injury.

debt Corporate borrowings in the form of bonds, debentures, or commercial paper.

defense A reason why the plaintiff should not recover from the defendant. An excuse or justification available to someone who has committed a criminal act.

defined-benefit plan A pension plan that specifies the size of the pension the beneficiary will receive or a rule for determining it. Contributions to the plan are determined by estimates of what is necessary to produce the contracted for return.

defined-contribution plan A pension plan that provides a separate account for each person covered and pays benefits on amounts allocated to each account.

deregulation The stripping away of regulations restricting competition in entire industries, particularly railroads, airlines, and trucking; nonregulation; the elimination or avoidance of regulations, particularly in the environmental, health, and safety areas that cannot be justified on a strict cost-benefit basis.

development bank An insured depository facility whose corporate mission establishes community development as its key organizational goal. Development banks are proactive lenders that use subsidiaries and affiliates to provide technical assistance for borrowers, advocate for new resources, and develop housing and small business.

disinvestment The withdrawal of corporations from South Africa by not investing new capital or by selling or closing existing operations.

diversification An investment strategy that spreads risk across a portfolio by owning several types of assets whose returns are not related to one another.

divestiture Selling securities out of repugnance for their issuers' actions.

divestment The elimination of securities from a portfolio for moral reasons.

domicile As applied to corporations, the country or state of incorporation. The term does not necessarily refer to the location of a company's headquarters.

duty of loyalty A fiduciary's duty to act in the best interest of another, even when the action is contrary to the fiduciary's interests.

ecology The relationship of living things to one another and their environment.

ecosystem The totality of a biological community and its environment.

emission Pollution discharged into the atmosphere.

employee benefits Services or noncash compensation to an employee that the employer either pays for or facilitates.

Employee Retirement Income Security Act of 1974 (ERISA) The federal law governing the operation of most private pension and benefit plans.

employee stock-ownership plan (ESOP) A mechanism by which employees receive shares of the company for which they work. To create an ESOP, a company sets up a trust fund that borrows money to buy company stock. The company makes tax-deductible contributions to the trust, which uses the money to repay the loan. As the loan is repaid, the trust releases shares and allocates them to accounts for individual employees, who receive their shares when they leave the company.

environment All the physical, social, and cultural factors and conditions influencing the existence or development of a biological community.

equity Ownership; the value of the owners' investment in a firm; a security that represents an ownership interest in a corporation; common stock.

ethical investor The term used for a **socially responsible investor** in the United Kingdom and Canada.

ethics Standards of conduct or moral judgment; moral obligations; the study of such obligations.

exclusionary social screen An ethical criterion that, if not satisfied, eliminates companies from consideration for an investment universe. See **screen.**

ex-index The Standard & Poor 500 or another major market index stripped of an industry or a category of companies.

factor Something that contributes to the performance behavior of a portfolio.

fiduciary A person who has undertaken to act for another person's benefit in a circumstance in which the law imposes a duty of trust; a person having the character or nature of a trustee as to a particular undertaking.

fiduciary duties The legal responsibilities of anyone entrusted with property—including money or investments—for another's benefit.

financial statement A report that state laws require every corporation to supply its shareholders that includes a balance sheet as of the end of the fiscal year, an income statement for that year, and a statement of changes in shareholders' equity for the year.

fossil fuels Fuels used in the production of heat or electricity—primarily coal, oil, and natural gas—that were formed by decaying plants and animals millions of years ago.

401(k) plan A thrift plan that allows workers to put aside a portion of their annual pay (within specific limits) and to have taxes deferred on their contributions and on the interest and profits they earn. Employers sometimes match employee contributions up to a certain dollar amount or a percentage of annual income.

genetic engineering The modification of the information content of a cell to alter its characteristics. Genes instruct the cell to assemble particular specific protein molecules. By altering the instructions coded in the DNA in the genes, cells can be "engineered" to produce proteins such as hormones, enzymes, and antibodies.

glass ceiling The invisible barrier of subtle discrimination that separates women and minorities from senior management positions and corporate directorships.

governance See **corporate governance.**

guideline portfolio investor A socially responsible investor who manages holdings of publicly traded securities within social guidelines or screens.

hazardous substances This term includes any matter—including **toxic pollutants**—that poses a threat to human health or the environment.

hazardous waste A waste that because of its quantity, concentration, or physical, chemical, or infectious characteristics causes or significantly contributes to an increase in mortality or serious illness, or poses a present or potential hazard to human health and the environment when improperly managed.

index A means of measuring the performance a sector of or an entire financial market through the combined prices of some or all of that market's constituents.

institution An amorphous category of corporate entities that gather funds from many sources and invest them. In economic and legal terms, they are financial intermediaries and fiduciaries. As a class, institutions include: mutual funds, banks, insurance companies, pension funds, brokerages, endowments (as for colleges), foundations, and charitable trusts.

institutional investor An **institution** that holds money or other assets that it manages on behalf of someone to whom it owes a duty as a fiduciary.

investment adviser A person in the business of advising others on how to allocate their assets, and particularly whether to buy, sell, or hold securities. An adviser may deal directly with clients or indirectly with the public through a newsletter.

investment universe See **universe.**

issuer An entity for whose benefit securities are issued.

keiretsu In Japan, a large industrial group of independent companies (albeit with interlocking ownership) formed for the purpose of cooperative ventures and directing long-term investment.

liability A debt; an obligation enforceable in a legal action.

line manager A management-level employee involved in actually producing or distributing what a firm sells.

management style The technique a manager applies to implement an investment objective.

market See **securities markets.**

market capitalization The market price of a common stock multiplied by the number of shares of common stock outstanding.

market cycle The recurring pattern in the securities markets of expansion (bull market) followed by contraction (bear market).

market rate of return The return similar investments are earning.

military Of or relating to responsibilities of the Department of Defense (DoD) or defense-related activities of the Department of Energy (DoE) or the Central Intelligence Agency (CIA).

minority An ethnic group in the United States that is not considered, by law, to have participated in the benefits of being a part of the Western European majority; an African-American, Hispanic, Asian, or Native American person.

mommy track A career path designed by corporations to take into account the unique needs of women as nurturers. It may include flexible scheduling of work hours, job sharing, and pregnancy leaves.

money manager Portfolio manager.

multinational corporation A large firm whose domicile is in one country but which operates wholly or partially owned subsidiaries in several other countries.

National Priority List (NPL) The U.S. Environmental Protection Agency's catalogue of the nation's worst toxic-waste sites. Required by **CERCLA,** placement of a site on the list means it has entered the **Superfund** Toxic-Waste Cleanup Program and that the EPA can order a cleanup and sue the parties who disposed of waste at the site for the costs of the cleanup. A site must be on the NPL to receive money from the Trust Fund for remedial action.

nuclear power Electricity generated by turbines driven by steam produced in a reactor through heat from the fissioning of nuclear fuel.

oppressive regime An **exclusionary social screen** applied to companies doing business in a country whose government has shown a disregard for fundamental human rights of its people.

ozone depletion The elimination of some part of the layer of protective ozone that surrounds the earth in the upper atmosphere.

partnership A voluntary association of two or more persons to carry on a business for profit as co-owners.

PCBs A group of toxic, persistent chemicals (polychlorinated biphenyls) used in transformers and capacitators for insulating purposes and in gas pipeline systems as a lubricant. Their sale or new use was banned in 1979.

pension plan A legal arrangement for holding investments that allows the income and profits to accumulate tax-free until withdrawn from the plan.

performance The change in the value of a portfolio over time.

portfolio The group term for assets owned by an entity.

potentially responsible party (PRP) Anyone who might have contributed to a **Superfund** site and who may be liable for some or all of its cleanup.

prime contractor One who sells directly to a customer.

productivity A relative measure of the output of goods and services achieved by an organization.

prudent investor rule A duty to the beneficiary of a trust to make such investments and only such investments as a prudent investor would make of his own property having in view the preservation of the estate and the amount and regularity of the income to be derived.

public documents A publicly traded corporation's annual report, its Securities and Exchange Commission Annual Report on Form 10-K, its proxy statement, and its quarterly reports to shareholders.

publicly traded company A corporation whose securities may change hands on an exchange and are therefore registered with the Securities and Exchange Commission (SEC).

public/private partnerships Arrangements in which corporations, unions, universities, and government institutions form alliances to attack community problems. They take the form of a nonprofit organization to which a private corporation contributes and whose mission a government body facilitates with tax benefits, zoning variances, and the like.

qualitative screen A social screen based on complex ethical criteria that takes into account both positive and negative factors relating to a corporation's responses to the demands of today's society, such as environmental quality and employee benefits.

recycling The recovery and reuse of materials from wastes. See also **closed-loop recycling.**

redlining A discriminatory lending practice by a bank in which the bank does not make mortgage loans in an area because of its racial or socioeconomic composition. The practice is generally forbidden by law.

remediation The cleaning up of contaminated soil or water and the prevention of further pollution.

research and development (R&D) The process of creating and bringing out new products or of improving existing products.

return Profit, usually expressed as a percentage, on an investment in securities or other assets.

screen *v.* To look for securities or issuers that meet certain defined criteria. *n.* A criterion or a group of criteria used to select securities or issuers.

sector A group of companies in one industry or related industries.

securities markets The markets for stocks, bonds, and the like.

security An instrument that is of a type commonly bought and sold on securities exchanges or markets, or as a medium for investment. It evidences a share, participation, or other interest in property or in an enterprise or evidences an obligation of the issuer. An investment in a security requires: an investment of money; a common enterprise; and an expectation of profit solely from the efforts of others.

share A unit of ownership in a corporation, mutual fund, or money market mutual fund; **stock.**

shareholder activists Holders of a company's stock who apply direct pressure to a corporation to improve its performance in specific areas.

social investment An investment that combines an investor's financial objectives with his or her commitment to social concerns, such as peace, social justice, economic development, or a healthy environment; an investment, which may or may not have economic return as its principal goal, made with an intent to take into account the impact of the investment on the society in which the investment is made.

socially responsible investor An investor who applies ethical or moral criteria in the investment decision-making process.

social responsibility The obligation to consider the consequences of a decision for society as a whole, for various groups within society, and for particular individuals.

social screen A nonfinancial criterion or set of criteria applied to companies whose stock is being considered in the investment decision-making process. See **screen.**

source reduction A change in production processes to eliminate the use of hazardous substances in the course of normal operations.

standard of care The basis of judging whether a fiduciary acted prudently.

stock An ownership share in a corporation.

stock buyback A corporation's repurchase of its outstanding stock, often for the purpose of maintaining the stock's market price.

subcontractor A company that sells to another business, which incorporates its goods or services into a product sold to the ultimate customer.

Superfund The program operated under the legislative authority of **CERCLA** that funds and carries out the EPA solid-waste emergency and long-term removal remedial activities. These activities include establishing the **National Priorities List,** investigating sites for inclusion on the list, determining their priority level on the list, and conducting or supervising remedial actions. See **Comprehensive Environmental Response, Compensation and Liability Act.**

sustainable development Economic development that meets current needs without jeopardizing—through environmental degradation and social disharmony—the ability of future generations to meet their needs.

tender offer An offer to acquire stock for a certain period at a stated price that is made either to an issuer or its shareholders, who may accept by delivering the stock to the offeror.

toxic pollutants Materials contaminating the environment that cause death, disease, and/or birth defects in organisms that ingest or absorb them. The quantities and length of exposure necessary to cause these effects vary widely.

training Learning activities, usually paid for by an employer, that are designed to improve current or future job performance.

trust A fiduciary relationship created by one person (the creator) in which a second person (the trustee or **fiduciary**) holds title for the benefit of a third (the **beneficiary**).

universe The range of investments, including securities, from which an investment adviser draws recommendations.

volunteerism Direct involvement in charitable activities without pay or compulsion.

war-related Of or relating to any goods or services that could sustain or be used in an armed conflict between nations or peoples.

weapons-related Of or relating to any goods that are designed to inflict physical harm in a conflict between nations or peoples.

Directory

A. Information Providers

UNITED STATES

NETWORKS

Interfaith Center on Corporate Responsibility
475 Riverside Drive, Room 566
New York, NY 10115
(212) 870-2936
    Primarily a network for shareholder activism. Also a good clearinghouse for information about alternative investments and for sources of information on screened investments.

National Federation of Community Development Credit Unions (NFCDCU)
59 John Street, 8th floor
New York, NY 10038
(212) 513-7191
(800) 437-8711
    The network for credit unions meeting the needs of low-income people.

National Association of Community Development Loan Funds
924 Cherry Street, 3rd floor
Philadelphia, PA 19107-2405
(215) 923-4754
    The network for community-development loan funds. Members tend to focus on immediate human needs and job creation.

Social Investment Forum
430 First Avenue North, Suite 290
Minneapolis, MN 55401
(612) 333-8338
    National network of professionals in the field of social investing.

Minority Bank Monitor
Creative Investment Advisers
1321 Rittenhouse Street, N.W.
Washington, DC 20011-1105
(202) 722-5134
  Monitors CRA and county information for women- and minority-owned banks.

PUBLICATIONS/SOURCES OF SOCIAL RESEARCH

The Social Investment Almanac
Peter D. Kinder, Steven D. Lydenberg, and Amy L. Domini, eds.
New York: Henry Holt & Company, Inc., 1992
Reference Books Division
$50.00
  A comprehensive reference book for social investors, the almanac covers screened portfolios, shareholder activism, grass-roots or alternative investments, and international social investing.

Amnesty Action
Amnesty International
322 Eighth Avenue
New York, NY 10001
(212) 807-8400
  Follows human rights abuses abroad.

BankWatch
215 Pennsylvania Avenue, S.E.
Washington, DC 20003
(202) 546-4996

Building Economic Alternatives
Co-op America Quarterly
2100 M Street, N.W., Suite 310
Washington, DC 20036
(800) 424-2667
(202) 872-5307
  Network and resource listings for products and investment services; boycott news.

Business and Society Review
Management Reports Inc.
25-13 Old Kings Highway North, Suite 107
Darien, CT 06820
  General interest stories.

Business Ethics Magazine
1107 Hazeltine Boulevard, Suite 530
Chaska, MN 55318
(612) 448-8864

Catalyst
64 Main Street, 2nd floor
Montpelier, VT 05602
 Information on social change and appropriate technology projects.

Clean Yield
Clean Yield Publications, Ltd.
Box 1880
Greenboro Bend, VT 05842
(802) 533-7178
 General social-investor interest, offers stock picks.

Conscious Consumer
New Consumer Institute
P.O. Box 51
Wauconda, IL 60084
(708) 526-0522
 Newsletter watching safety and environmental impact of consumer products.

Corporate Crime Reporter
P.O. Box 18384
Washington, DC 20036
 Expensive, but good source for OSHA and environmental crimes.

Corporate Examiner
Interfaith Center on Corporate Responsibility
475 Riverside Drive, Room 566
New York, NY 10115
(212) 870-2293
 Shareholder actions networking.

Corporate Giving Watch
The Taft Group
1300 Twinbrook Parkway, Suite 450
Rockville, MD 20852
(301) 816-0210
 Updates on corporate giving programs.

Corporate Philanthropy
2727 Fairview Avenue, East, Suite D
Seattle, WA 98102
(206) 329-0422

Corporate Responsibility Monitor
DataCenter
464 19th Street
Oakland, CA 94612
(415) 835-4692
 Clipping service on social investing.

Council on Economic Priorities
30 Irving Place
New York, NY 10003
(212) 420-1133
    Various social research publications.

Defense Monitor
Center for Defense Information
1500 Massachusetts Avenue, N.W.
Washington, DC 20005
    Defense-spending information.

Domini Social Index 400 Monthly Update
KLD Corporate Profiles
Kinder, Lydenberg, Domini & Co.
7 Dana Street
Cambridge, MA 02138
(617) 547-7479
    Monthly listings and social rankings of the DSI 400. In-depth corporate profiles on S&P 500 companies and on companies in the Domini Social Index. KLD also provides consulting services for institutional investors working with social constraints.

EDF Letter
Environmental Defense Fund
257 Park Avenue
New York, NY 10010
    Monitors environmental spills, actions.

Employee Ownership Report
National Center for Employee Ownership
2201 Broadway, Suite 807
Oakland, CA 94612
    Tracks and reports on ESOPs.

Everyone's Backyard
Citizens Clearinghouse for Hazardous Waste
P.O. Box 6806
Falls Church, VA 22040
(703) 237-2249
    Newsletter on hazardous-waste fines, legislation, and actions.

Franklin's Insight
Franklin's Investing for a Better World
Franklin Research & Development Corporation
711 Atlantic Avenue
Boston, MA 02111
(617) 423-6655
    Newsletter giving stock purchase recommendations for social investors, industry studies, hot-line, and general interest stories.

Green Consumer Letter
Tilden Press Inc.
1526 Connecticut Avenue, N.W.
Washington, DC 20036
    Updates on environmental impact of consumer goods.

Health Letter
Public Citizen Health Research Group
2000 P Street, N.W.
Washington, DC 20036
    Information on public-health threats.

Investor Responsibility Research Center
1755 Massachusetts Avenue, N.W.
Washington, DC 20036
(202) 939-6500
    Research services on issues concerning social investors, South Africa, corporate governance, and the environment.

Left Business Observer
250 West 85th Street
New York, NY 10024
(212) 874-4020
    A different look at business.

Minority Supplier News
National Minority Supplier Council
15 West 39th Street, 9th floor
New York, NY 10018
    Newsletter on minority contracting.

Multinational Monitor
P.O. Box 19405
Washington, DC 20036
(202) 387-8030
    General interest with focus on corporate activity in the Third World.

Nuclear Free America
2521 Guilford Avenue
Baltimore, MD 21218
(301) 633-8478
    Maintains the data base of Prime Contractors with the DoD, DoE, and CIA.

Racheal's Hazardous Waste News
Environmental Research Foundation
P.O. Box 73700
Washington, DC
(202) 328-1119
    Hazardous-waste monitoring.

Toxic Times
National Toxic Campaign
1168 Commonwealth Avenue
Boston, MA 02134
(617) 232-0327
  Survey of environmental infractions, current issues.

Woodstock Institute
407 South Dearborn, Suite 550
Chicago, IL 60605
(312) 427-8070
  Monitors bank/community relationships.

AUSTRALIA

Network
Social Investment Forum Australia
Money Matters Corporation Ltd.
P.O. Box R
1466 Royal Exchange
Sydney 2000
Australia
Contact Mr. Robert Rosen

AUSTRIA

Network
Verband osterreichischer Investmentklubs
Prominade 11–13
A 4041 Linz
Austria
(43) 732 2391/DW 2571
Association of Austrian Investment Clubs

Sources of Social Research
Forschunginstitut für ethisch-ökologische Geldanlagen (FIFEGA)
A-1070 Vienna
Austria
(43) 1 52 62 55

CANADA

Network
Social Investment Organisation
447-336 Adelaide Street East
Toronto, Ontario M5A 3X9
Canada
(416) 360-6047
Contact Mr. Marc de Sousa-Shields

Sources of Social Research
Canadian Social Investment Study Group
858 Bank Street, Suite 100
Ottowa, Ontario K1S 3W3
Canada
(613) 230-5221
Contact Mr. Ted Jackson

EthicScan Canada
P.O. Box 165
Postal Station S
Toronto, Ontario M5M 4L7
Canada
(416) 783-6776
Contact Mr. David Nitkin

New North Finance
50 Emerald Street N.
Hamilton, Ontario L8L 5K3
Canada
(416) 522-6739
Contact Mr. Jim Adams

Taskforce on the Churches and Corporate Responsibility
129 St. Clair Avenue W.
Toronto, Ontario M4V 1N5
Canada

DENMARK

Sources of Social Research
Center for Alternative Social Analysis (CASA)
Linnesgade 14
DK-1361 Copenhagen K
Denmark
45 33 32 05 55

FRANCE

Sources of Social Research
L'Institut de Development de l'Economie Sociale (IDES)
24 Avenue Hoche
75008 Paris
France
33 4359 9494
Contact Mr. Jean Jacques Samuel

SWEDEN

Sources of Social Research
Research on Business and Society Inc.
Urvadersgrand 6B
116 46 Stockholm
Sweden
46 8 44 8463
Contact Mr. Soren Bergstrom

UNITED KINGDOM

Networks
International Association of Investors in the Social Economy (INAISE)
Vassali House
20 Central Road
Leeds LS1 6DE
United Kingdom
44 532 429600
Contact Mr. Malcolm Lynch, Secretary

U.K. Social Investment Forum
Vassali House
20 Central Road
Leeds LS1 6DE
United Kingdom
Contact Mr. Alan Miller, President

Sources of Social Research
The General Synod of the Church of England
Board for Social Responsibility
Church House
Great Smith Street
London SW1P 3NZ
United Kingdom
44 71 222 9011

EIRIS
504 Bondway Business Centre
71 Bondway
London SW8 1SQ
United Kingdom
44 71 735 1351
Contact Mr. Peter Webster, Executive Secretary

End Loans to South Africa
56 Camberwell Road
London SE5 0EN
United Kingdom
44 71 708 4702

Ethical Consumer
ECRA Publishing Ltd.
100 Gretney Walk
Manchester M15 5ND
United Kingdom
44 61 226 6683

Financial Platforms
Keeley House
23/39 Keeley Road
Croydon, Surrey GR0 1TE
United Kingdom
44 81 686 7171
Contact Mr. Alan Miller

The Green Alliance
60 Chandos Place
London WC2N 4HG
United Kingdom
44 71 836 0341

Industrial Common Ownership Finance Ltd. (ICOF)
12–14 Gold Street
Northampton NN1 1RS
United Kingdom
44 604 375563
Contact Mr. David Ralley

Methodist Church
Division of Social Responsibility
Central Hall
Westminster
London SW1H 9NH
United Kingdom
44 71 222 8010
Contact Mr. John Kennedy

New Consumer
52 Elswick Road
Newcastle upon Tyne NE4 6JH
United Kingdom
44 91 272 1148

Pensions & Investment Research Consultants Ltd.
40 Bowling Green Lane
London EC1R 0NE
United Kingdom
44 71 833 4432
Contact Mr. Alan MacDougall, Managing Director
Ms. Anne Simpson, Director

The Religious Society of Friends
Communication Services Department
Friends House
Euston Road
London NW1 2BJ
United Kingdom
44 71 387 3601

Scottish Churches Action for World Development Investments Association
(Ecumenical Development Cooperative Society)
41 George IV Bridge
Edinburgh, Scotland EH1 1EL
United Kingdom
44 31 225 1772

Traidcraft Exchange
Kingsway
Gateshead NE11 0NE
United Kingdom
44 91 491 0591

The WM Company
World Markets House
Crewe Toll
Edinburgh EH4 2PY
Scotland
44 31 315-2000
(212) 593-4747 (U.S.)

B. Mutual Funds and Similar Vehicles

UNITED STATES

Amana Mutual Funds Trust Income Fund
520 Herald Building
1155 North State Street
Bellingham, WA 98225
(800) 728-8762
(207) 734-9900
    Screened for Islamic standards.

Calvert Group
—Calvert SIF, Bond Portfolio
—Calvert SIF, Equity Portfolio
—Calvert SIF, Managed Growth Portfolio
—Calvert SIF, Money Market Fund
—Calvert SIF, World Values Global Equity Fund
—Calvert-Ariel Appreciation Fund
—Calvert-Ariel Growth Fund
4550 Montgomery Avenue
Bethesda, MD 20814
(800) 368-2748
(301) 951-4820
　　Varying social screens, Managed Growth and Equity most comprehensive.

Christian Brothers Investment Services, Inc.
—Catholic United Investment Trust Balanced Fund
—Catholic United Investment Trust Growth Fund
—Religious Communities Trust Certificates of Deposit Fund
—Religious Communities Trust College Fund
—Religious Communities Trust Intermediate Bond Fund
—Religious Communities Trust Money Market Fund
—Partners for the Common Good Loan Fund
675 Third Avenue, Suite 3100
New York, NY 10017-5704
(800) 592-8890
(212) 490-0800
　　Few social screens, but in first rank of shareholder activists; Common Good
is an alternative investment portfolio. Open only to entities listed in the *Official
Catholic Directory*.

Covenant Investment Management
309 West Washington Street, Suite 1300
Chicago, IL 60606
(312) 443-8472
　　Social screens weighted by decision makers' opinions as gathered in a poll.
New fund.

Domini Social Index^{sm} Trust
6 Saint James Street
Boston, MA 02116
(800) 762-6814
　　Multiple social screens, both positive and negative.

Dreyfus Third Century Fund
144 Glenn Curtiss Boulevard
Uniondale, NY 11556-0144
(800) 782-6620
　　Multiple social screens. No screen on military.

Global Environmental Fund, LP
412 North Coast Highway
Laguna Beach, CA 92651
(714) 494-8392
    Environmental screens. Some venture capital investments.

Green Century Capital Management, Inc.
—Green Century Money Market
—Green Century Balanced
28 Temple Place, Suite 200
Boston, MA 02111-1305
(617) 482-0800
    Multiple social screens. New funds.

Green Earth Liquid Assets
New World Advisors
1661 Lincoln Boulevard, Suite 400
Santa Monica, CA 90404
(800) 874-4287
    Environmental money market fund.

Lincoln National Social Awareness Fund
1300 South Clinton Street
P.O. Box 2340
Fort Wayne, IN 46801
(219) 427-2000

Muir California Tax Free Fund
1 Sansone Street, Suite 810
San Francisco, CA 94104
(415) 616-8500
(800) 648-3448
    California municipal bonds.

New Alternatives Fund, Inc.
295 Northern Boulevard
Great Neck, NY 11021
(516) 466-0808
    Multiple social screens.

The Parnassus Fund
—Equity Portfolio
—Balanced Portfolio
—Fixed Income Portfolio
—California Tax Free Portfolio
244 California Street, Suite 210
San Francisco, CA 94111
(800) 999-3505
(415) 362-3505
    Multiple social screens.

Pax World Fund
224 State Street
Portsmouth, NH 03801
(603) 431-8022
(800) 767-1729
   Multiple social screens. Less emphasis on environmental.

The Pioneer Group
—Pioneer Fund
—Pioneer Fund II
—Pioneer Fund III
60 State Street
Boston, MA 02109
(800) 225-6292
(617) 742-7825
   Screened for alcohol and tobacco.

Rightime Social Awareness Fund
The Forst Pavillion, Suite 1500
Wyncote, PA 19095-1596
(800) 242-1421
   Multiple social screens.

Shield Progressive Environmental Fund
P.O. Box 1608
Pacifica, CA 94044
(415) 952-8853
   Environmental screens.

Socially Responsive Equity Fund
Bank of Boston
The Private Bank
100 Federal Street
Boston, MA 02110
(617) 434-6732
   Available only to trust clients of the Bank of Boston.

State Street Bank & Trust Co.
Asset Management Division
225 Franklin Street, 3rd floor
Boston, MA 02101
(617) 786-3000
   Institutional clients, screened index products.

TIAA/CREF
—Social Choice Account
730 Third Avenue
New York, NY 10017
(212) 490-9000
    Available only to TIAA/CREF participants. Multiple social screens.

Working Assets Capital Management
—Working Assets Money Fund
—Citizens Income Portfolio
—Citizens Growth Portfolio
—Citizens Balanced Portfolio
111 Pine Street
San Francisco, CA 94111-4516
(800) 533-3863
    Multiple social screens.

AUSTRALIA

Directed Financial Management Limited
Suite 66
Canberra Business Centre
Bradfield Street
Canberra ACT 2602
Australia
62 42 1988

Friends' Provident Life Office
80 Alfred Street
Milsons Point, NSW 20
Australia
61 2 925-9255
Contact Ms. Susan Gavan

Occidental Life Insurance Company of Australia
—Environmental Opportunities Fund
Occidental Centre
601 Pacific Highway
St. Leonards, NSW 2065
Australia
61 2 957-0957

Purvis, van Eyk & Company Ltd.
—The Earthrise Investment Pool
—Mercator Master Superannuation Plan
43 Phillips Street
Sydney NSW 2000
Australia
61 2 247-6000

AUSTRIA

OKO-INVEST
—Ethische-okologisher Investmentklub
Lindengrasse 43/17
A-1070 Vienna
Austria
43 22 5262 555

Raiffeisen-Umweltfonds
Raiffeisen-Kapitalanlage Gesellschaft m.b.H.
Am Stadtpark 9
A-1030 Vienna
Austria
43 222 71707
Contact Dr. Mathew Bauer

Z-Umweltfonds
—Z-INVEST Gesellschaft
Invalidenstrasse 3
A-1030 Vienna
Austria
43 222 71 25 454
Contact Mrs. Gale

CANADA

CEDAR Investment Services
—CEDAR Balanced Fund
902, Kapilano 100, Park Royal
West Vancouver, BC V7T 1A2
Canada
(604) 926-7355

Crown Life Insurance Co.
—Crown Commitment Fund
120 Bloor Street East
Toronto, Ontario M4W 1B8
Canada
(416) 928-5722

Desjardins Trust
—Fonds Desjardins Environment
1 Complex Desjardins
P.O. Box 34
Montreal, Quebec H5B 1E4
Canada
(418) 835-4403

EIF Fund Management Ltd.
—Environmental Investment Canada Fund
—Environmental Investment International Fund
225 Brunswick Avenue
Toronto, Ontario M5S 2M6
Canada
(416) 978-7014

Investors Group
—Investors Summa Fund Ltd.
447 Portage Avenue
Winnipeg, Manitoba R3C 3B6
Canada
(204) 956-8536
Contact Mr. Patrick W. Ireland

Vancouver City Savings Credit Union
—Ethical Growth Fund
515 West 10th Avenue
Vancouver, BC V5Z 4A8
Canada
(604) 877-7613

FRANCE

Biosphere
—Cyril Finance Gestion (CFG)
20, rue de la Ville l'Eveque
F-75008 Paris
France
33 14 266 6888
Contact Mr. Didier Jened
Mr. Xavier D'ornellas

GERMANY

Artus Ethische Renten GbR
Artus Ethische Vermogensverwaltung GmbH
von-Werth-Strasse 20-22
D-5000 Köln 1
Germany
49 221 135056
Contact Mr. Jurgen Conrads

Concorde International
Concorde KGaA iG, Germany
Weidenauer Strasse 179
D-5900 Siegen
Germany
49 271 403721
Fax: 49 271 403733
Contact Ms. Alison MacDonald

Credit Suisse
—CS Oeko Protec
Kaiserstrasse 30
6000 Frankfurt
Germany
49 69 26912625
Contact Mr. Gundermann

DG Capital Management GmbH
—DG Capital Oko 2000
Platz der Republik
D-6000 Frankfurt 1, Germany
49 69 744701
Contact Mr. Hartmut Korn

EthiK (Erster Ethischer Investmentclub Koln)
Maria-Hilf-Strasse 6
D-5000 Köln 1
Germany
49 221 325272
Contact Mr. Hans Berner

Focus Umwelttechnologie
—Focus
Gunther Strasse 21
8000 Munich 19
Germany
49 89 1784010
Contact Mr. Carl Fischer

LUXEMBOURG

Hypo Capital Management
—HCM Eco Tech
27 Boulevard du Prince Henri
L-1724 Luxembourg
352 474 979
Contact Mr. Dieter Wimmer

Secura-Rent Lux
BFG Luxinvest Management S.A.
2 Rue Jean Bertholet
1-1233 Luxembourg
352 4522551
Contact Mr. Claus Pyter

NORWAY

MiljoInvest Environment Fund
5020 Bergen
Norway
47 5 17 20 50
Contact Mr. Carlos Jolly

SWEDEN

Fria Kulturfonden
Robyggehuset
153 00 Jarna
Sweden
46 7 55 50450

Svenska Kyrkansfond AB
St Eriksgatan 63
112 34 Stockholm
Sweden
46 8 7377000

UNITED KINGDOM

Abbey Unit Trust Managers
—Ethical Trust
80 Holdenhurst Road
Bournemouth, BH8 8AL
United Kingdom
44 20 229 2373
Contact Mr. Trevor Forbes

Acorn Unit Trust Managers Ltd.
—Acorn Ethical Unit Trust
1 White Hart Yard
London Bridge
London SE1 1NX
United Kingdom
44 71 407 5966
Contact Mr. Roger Noddings

Allchurches Investment Management Services
—Amity Fund
19/21 Billiter Street
London EC3M 2RY
United Kingdom
44 71 528 7364
Contact Mr. G. A. Prescott

Allied Provincial
—Allied Provincial Green PEP
Town Centre House
Merrion Centre
Leeds LS2 8LA
United Kingdom
44 532 420303

D. J. Bromige & Partners, Ltd.
—Ethical Investment Fund
10 Queen Street
Mayfair, London W1X 7PD
United Kingdom
44 71 491 0558
Contact Mr. David Bromige

Clerical Medical Unit Trust Managers
—Evergreen Trust
Narrow Plain
Bristol BS2 0JH
United Kingdom
44 27 226 9050
Contact Mr. Peter Hill

Commercial Union Asset Management
—Environmental Exempt Pension Fund
St. Helens
1 Undershaft
London EC2P 3DQ
United Kingdom
44 71 283-7500
Contact Mr. Ian Williams

Cooperative Insurance Society
—Environ Trust
CIS Unit Managers
Miller Street
Manchester M60 0AL
United Kingdom
44 61 832 8686
Contact Mr. Philip Deverel Smith

Credit Suisse Buckmaster & Moore
—Fellowship Trust
Beaufort House
15 St. Botolph Street
London EC3A 7JJ
United Kingdom
44 71 247 7474
Contact Mr. Tony Franks

Eagle Star Unit Trust Managers
—Environmental Opportunities Trust
Eagle Star House
Bath Road
Cheltenham
Gloucestershire GL53 7RN
United Kingdom
44 24 222 1311
Contact Ms. Fiona Cutting

Fidelity Investment Services Ltd.
—Fidelity Famous Names Trust
Oakhill House
130 Tonbridge Road
Hildenborough, Tonbridge
Kent TN11 9DZ
United Kingdom
44 73 236 1144
Contact Mr. Peter Holland

First Charter Investment Management Ltd.
—First Charter Ethical PEP
Graylands
High Street
Chipping Ongar
Essex CM5 9LD
United Kingdom
44 277 364949

Friends Provident Unit Trust Managers
—North American Stewardship Trust
—Stewardship Income Trust
—Stewardship Unit Trust
—Stewardship Pension Fund
72/122 Castle Street
Salisbury SP1 3SH
United Kingdom
44 72 241 1622
Contact Mr. Richard Lowman

Henderson Financial Management Ltd.
—Henderson Green PEP
3 Finsbury Avenue
London EC2M 2PA
United Kingdom
44 71 638 5757

Homeowners Friendly Society
—Green Chip Investment Fund
P.O. Box 94
Homeowners House
Springfield Avenue
Harrogate
North Yorkshire HG1 2HN
United Kingdom
44 42 352 2070

Medical Investments Ltd.
—Health Fund
1 White Hart Yard
London Bridge
London SE1 1NX
United Kingdom
44 71 407 5966
Contact Mr. Roger Noddings

Merlin Jupiter Unit Trust Management Ltd.
—Merlin Ecology Fund
—Merlin International Green Investment Trust
197 Knightsbridge
London SW7 1RB
United Kingdom
44 71 581 3857
Contact Ms. Tessa Tennant

NM Financial Management Ltd.
Enterprise House
Isambard Brunel Road
Portsmouth PO1 2AW
United Kingdom
44 705 827733
Contact Mr. Peter Hunt, Investment Marketing Consultant

Scottish Equitable Fund Managers
—Ethical Pension Fund
—Ethical Unit Trust
28 St. Andrew Square
Edinburgh EH2 1YF
United Kingdom
31 556 9101
Contact Mr. Tom Copeland

Sovereign Unit Trust Managers, Ltd.
—Sovereign Ethical Fund
12 Christchurch Road
Bournemouth BH1 3LW
United Kingdom
44 20 229 1111
Contact Mr. Ron Spack

Target Trust Managers
—Target Global Opportunities Trust
Alton House
174/177 High Holborn
London WC1V 7AA
United Kingdom
44 71 836 8040
Contact Mr. Quentin Toalster

Touche Remnant
—TR Ecotec Environmental Fund
Mermaid House
2 Puddle Dock
London EC4V 3AT
United Kingdom
44 71 236 6565
Contact Mr. Peter Wolf

TSB Unit Trusts
—Environmental Investor Fund
Charlton Place
Andover
Hants SP10 1RE
United Kingdom
44 26 456 789
Contact Ms. Julie Lineham

Appendix: Social Screens

In preparing its 1991–1992 cycle of KLD Company Reviews[sm], Kinder, Lydenberg, Domini & Co., Inc. (7 Dana Street, Cambridge, MA 02138-5401), applied the social screens described here. Except as otherwise noted, KLD also applies these social screens to companies considered for the Domini Social Index[sm].

Each screen is assigned a letter. These letters correspond to similarly coded screens in the KLD Social Investment Database[sm]. The letters were assigned chronologically, and they do not indicate parallel screens or that the screens are balanced.

COMMUNITY

Areas of Strength	*Areas of Concern*
A. The company in recent years has consistently given over 1.5 percent of pretax earnings to charity.	A. The company has paid fines or civil penalties, or is involved in major controversies, relating to a community in which it operates.
B. The company gives substantial amounts to innovative programs, *e.g.,* affordable housing, job training, AIDS support, etc.	B. The company's relations with a community in which it operates have become strained due to recent plant closings or to a general breach of covenants with the community.
C. The company is a leader in participating in public/private partnerships directed toward the economically disadvantaged, *e.g.,* the National Equity Fund.	C. The company has been the subject of a recent, substantive Community Reinvestment Act challenge or of a controversy relating to community lending practices.
Z. Other.	Z. Other.

EMPLOYEE RELATIONS

Areas of Strength	*Areas of Concern*
A. The company has good relations with its unions relative to others in its industry.	A. The company has poor relations with its unions relative to others in its industry.
B. The company has maintained a consistent no-layoff policy.	B. The company has recently paid fines or civil penalties or been involved in a major controversy relating to employee safety.
C. The company has maintained a long-term policy of cash profit sharing.	
D. The company encourages a substantial sense of worker ownership through either gainsharing, a substantial employee stock-ownership plan (ESOP) with pass-through voting rights, or a sharing of financial information to encourage employee participation in management decision making.	C. The company has recently laid off more than 15 percent of its employees in a twelve-month period.
	D. The company has a substantially underfunded pension plan or a significantly inadequate benefits plan.
	Z. Other.
E. The company has taken exceptional initiatives to hire, retain, and promote the disabled, persons with AIDS, or other disadvantaged groups.	
F. The company offers its employees exceptional benefits relative to its industry.	
Z. Other.	

Note: Affirmative action issues are covered in the Diversity Screen, below.

ENVIRONMENT

Areas of Strength	*Areas of Concern*
A. The company derives more than 4 percent of revenues from products or services used in cleaning up the environment. Or, it has developed innovative products with environmental benefits.	A. The company's liabilities for hazardous-waste disposal sites exceed $20 million or extend to more than twenty Superfund sites. Or the company has Superfund sites at its facilities.
B. The company as a whole has made changes in production processes to minimize or eliminate the use of toxic or hazardous chemicals.	B. The company has recently paid significant fines or civil penalties, or it has been involved in major controversies involving some form of environmental degradation.
C. The company is a substantial user of recycled materials as raw materials in its manufacturing processes. Or it is a major factor in the recycling industry.	C. The company is among the top producers or legal emitters of chlorofluorocarbons (CFCs), hydrochlorofluorocarbons (HCFCs), methyl chloroform, or other ozone-depleting chemicals.
D. The company derives more than 4 percent of revenues from developing, using, or marketing fuels with environmental advantages. Or it is a major factor in the cogeneration market.	D. The company is among the top legal emitters of toxic chemicals. Or its emissions play a substantial role in the formation of acid rain.
E. The company maintains its property, plant, and equipment with above average environmental performance for its industry.	E. The company is among the major producers of agricultural chemicals.
Z. Other.	Z. Other.

PRODUCT

Areas of Strength	Areas of Concern

Areas of Strength

A. The company has a reputation for high-quality products or services relative to others in its industry.

B. The company is consistently among the leaders in its industry in research and development (R&D) expenditures as a percentage of sales. The company has a reputation for exceptional inventiveness in new product development.

C. The company has committed itself to serve the economically disadvantaged.

Z. Other.

Areas of Concern

A. Several major recent lawsuits allege that one of the company's products caused life-threatening injuries.

B. Several major recent lawsuits allege that one of the company's products caused non–life-threatening injuries.

C. The company derives more than 4 percent of its revenues from the manufacture of alcohol or tobacco products, or firearms, or from goods or services relating to gambling.

D. The company has paid recent fines or civil penalties as a result of questionable advertising, marketing, or production practices. Or these practices have led to a major public controversy.

E. The company has paid recent fines or civil penalties relating to price fixing, antitrust violations, or consumer frauds.

F. The company has recently been involved in a major controversy over exploitation of the economically disadvantaged.

Z. Other.

DIVERSITY

Areas of Strength	*Areas of Concern*
A. The company's chief executive officer is a woman or a member of a minority group.	A. The company has paid fines or civil penalties or been involved in major controversies relating to its affirmative action record.
B. The company has made notable progress in promoting women and minorities, particularly to line and operating positions. The company has received recognition for its progress in hiring women and minorities from groups advocating fair hiring policies.	Z. Other.
C. Women, minorities, and the physically challenged hold four board seats in aggregate or one-third of the board seats if the board numbers fewer than twelve (with no allowance for double counting).	
D. The company has outstanding employee-benefits programs or programs addressing work/family concerns, *e.g.,* child care, elder care, and flextime. Groups advocating such programs have recognized the company's efforts.	
E. The company has a long, consistent, and exceptional record of support for women- and minority-owned businesses.	
Z. Other.	

OTHER

KLD tracks these issues because significant numbers of social investors do so. However, they are not screens applied by the Domini Social Index.

Areas of Strength	Areas of Concern
A. The company has exceptional policies on limiting the compensation of board members or senior managers.	A. The company has operations in Northern Ireland.
B. The company's initiatives in pursuing alternatives to animal testing are exceptional.	B. The company has a record of compensating excessively its board members and top management.
C. The company owns more than 20 percent of another company cited by KLD as having areas of social strength.	C. [Reserved.]
	D. The company is involved in major controversies relating to animal testing.
D. [Reserved.]	E. The company is involved in major disputes over nonpayment of federal, state, or local taxes.
Z. Other.	F. The company is more than 20 percent owned by a company cited by KLD as having an area of social concern.
	Z. Other.

EXCLUSIONARY SCREENS

KLD's three exclusionary screens—military, nuclear power, and South Africa—are different from KLD's other screens in that a company cannot do "well" under them. A company either passes them or it does not.

Military Weapons	Nuclear Power

Military Weapons

A. The company's substantial involvement in weapons-related contracting is evidenced either by the company's receipt of over 2 percent of its revenues from such sales, its ranking among the top fifty defense contractors, or its receipt of more than $10 million in nuclear weapons–related prime contracts.

B. The company's minor involvement in weapons-related contracting is evidenced by either the company's receipt of less than 2 percent of its revenues from such sales, its receipt of less than $10 million from nuclear weapons-related prime contracts, or its receipt through subcontracting relationships of less than 10 percent of revenues from the sale of off-the-shelf components used in weapons systems.

C. During the last fiscal year, the company received from the Department of Defense more than $50 million for fuel or other commodities related to weapons.

Z. Other.

Nuclear Power

A. The company is an electric utility that derives more than 2 percent of its electricity from nuclear fuels or owns more than 20 percent of a nuclear power plant under construction.

B. The company is an electric utility that derives less than 2 percent of its electricity from nuclear fuels or owns less than 20 percent of a nuclear plant under construction.

C. The company derives more than 2 percent of its sales from the construction or management of nuclear power plants.

D. The company mines, processes, or enriches uranium, or is otherwise involved in the nuclear fuel cycle.

E. The company derives more than 4 percent of sales from the sale of specialized parts or equipment for generating power through the use of nuclear fuels.

Z. Other.

South Africa

A. The company currently has an equity interest in a company doing business in South Africa.

B. The company appears to have, or to have had recently, a substantial nonequity involvement in South Africa in areas of strategic importance to the government.

C. The company appears to have, or to have had recently, nonequity interests in South Africa in nonstrategic industries.

Note. A company that has a licensing or sales agreement in South Africa in nonstrategic industries will not be cited unless such an agreement appears, in substance, to be the equivalent of one of the areas of concern.

Index

Permissions

The authors gratefully acknowledge the following permissions granted to reprint or adapt copyrighted material:

"25 Best Places for Blacks to Work," *Black Enterprise,* February 1992. Copyright © 1992 by The Earl G. Graves Publishing Co., Inc., 130 Fifth Avenue, New York, NY 10011.

J. Moore, "Corporate Giving Still Stalled," *The Chronicle of Philanthropy,* October 22, 1991. Reprinted by permission of *The Chronicle of Philanthropy.*

"The Weed of Liberation," *The Economist,* December 21, 1991. Copyright © 1991 by The Economist Newspaper Group, Inc. Reprinted by permission.

Michigan Center for Employee Ownership and Gainsharing, "Increased Participation with Employee Ownership," as discussed in *Employee Ownership Report,* volume X, no. 6, November/December 1990, pp. 1, 4.

"The Good Money Averages," courtesy of Good Money Publications, Inc., P.O. Box 363, Worcester, Vermont, 05682. Telephone: (800) 535-3551.

"The Ethical Way to Invest," *Financial Times,* April 14, 1990.

J. Helyar and B. Burrough, *Barbarians at the Gate.* New York: HarperCollins Publishers, 1991.

KLD Social Screens, Copyright © 1992 by Kinder, Lydenberg, Domini & Co., Inc., 7 Dana Street, Cambridge, MA 02138-5401.

"Statement of Principles for South Africa (Abridged)," *Fourteenth Report of the Signatory Companies to the Statement of Principles for South Africa,* Arthur D. Little, Inc., 1990.

C. Cotts, "Condoning the Legal Stuff?: Hard Sell in the Drug War," *The Nation,* March 9, 1992. Copyright © 1992 by The Nation Company, Inc.

R. B. Reich, "Metamorphosis of the American Worker," *Business Month,* November 1990. Copyright © 1990 by Robert B. Reich.

"Philanthropy Is Not Marketing," *Responsive Philanthropy,* Summer 1991.

The World Markets Co., *1989 Annual Review: Charity Fund Service,* courtesy of the World Markets Company PLC, World Markets House, Crewe Toll, Edinburgh EH4 2PY. Telephone: (44) (31) 315-2000 (U.K.); (212) 593-4747 (U.S.).